THE GOURMET GARDEN

The Fruits of the Garden transported to the Table

GERALDENE HOLT

Photographs by Hugh Palmer

A BULFINCH PRESS BOOK

LITTLE, BROWN AND COMPANY

BOSTON TORONTO LONDON

DEDICATION

for Marie-Pierre Moine, who first suggested that I write about growing
good food

Text copyright © 1990 by Geraldene Holt
Photographs copyright © 1990 by Hugh Palmer
Plant illustration copyright © 1990 by Fiona Bell Currie

First United States Edition

First published in Great Britain by Pavilion Books Limited

Designed by David Fordham

ISBN 0-8212-1815-8

Library of Congress Catalog Card Number 90-61407

Library of Congress Cataloging-in-Publication information is
available.

Bulfinch Press is an imprint and trademark of Little, Brown and
Company (Inc.)

PRINTED IN ITALY

PUBLISHER'S NOTE

1. In the recipes, measures are given in the following order: Metric/
Imperial/American cups and spoons (where required). All three measures
have been calculated separately, and they are not exact equivalents.
Therefore, when preparing a recipe, use just one set of measures.

2. All spoon measures are level and are based on the following metric
equivalents:

  1 teaspoon = 5 ml
  1 tablespoon = 15 ml

These correspond very closely to standard American spoon measures.
However, Australian readers should note that their tablespoon contains
20 ml.

3. American equivalents for ingredients and both cooking and gardening
terminology are given in parentheses in the recipes. For American
readers, the term 'growbag' or 'growing-bag' denotes a rectangular plastic
bag containing about 40 litres of compost. It can be replaced by two/three
ten-litre pots of compost.

Contents

Above: A mixed border beside one of the glasshouses at Hunstrete House, Somerset. Left: Fine old tools, still used today, at Sharrow Bay, Cumbria.

DURING THE LAST DECADE IN BRITAIN, WE HAVE SEEN A HUGE revival of interest in good food. Indeed, it has almost amounted to a palate revolution. Not only have the number of serious food books and good restaurants increased, but there has been a resurgence of interest in real food and the quality of what we eat. So it is, perhaps, only to be expected that our new-found enthusiasm for the skills of the kitchen is spreading out into the kitchen garden itself.

As a gardening cook, I see no break in the thread that links how we grow food to how we eat it. I grow food for the sheer sensual pleasure and deep satisfaction of producing the freshest, most beautiful vegetables, fruit and herbs; and I garden because I feel happier when my life is in tune with the seasons, the weather and the forces of nature. To me, the activities of growing and eating are interdependent – each amplifies and enhances the other. For it is when we disregard this vital relationship that problems arise, as recent food scares testify.

Small wonder, then, that the interest in kitchen gardening has been boosted by concern over the purity of our food supplies. The result is the re-greening of

our country. 'Marmande' tomatoes and unusual lettuces sprout from allotments (community gardens) and gardens and a million grow-bags. And the backyard and the windowsill sport pots of basil, thyme and bay. One possible effect of global warming is that our gardens may soon burst forth with a cornucopia of Mediterranean fruits and vegetables – and all gardening cooks would welcome the prospect.

Yet even in today's climate, white peaches and walnuts, asparagus and globe artichokes, scarlet radicchio and cherry tomatoes, yellow raspberries, golden zucchini, nineteenth-century potatoes, and physalis in their paper cases (Chinese lanterns) can be grown quite easily in many gardens. My decades of gardening have taught me the importance of growing the food that you most like to eat. I have forsaken the attitude to kitchen gardening that ensures all the hard work of small-scale agriculture with its attendant gluts of produce.

I hope that my approach to the new kitchen garden will encourage even the part-time or leisure gardener as well as the serious and experienced grower to take a fresh look at what they grow and how they prepare their produce for the table. In the new kitchen garden, all the plants qualify solely on account of their outstanding taste and fine flavour. For, to my mind, the wholesome produce of the gourmet's garden should grace equally well the gourmet's table.

Each chapter is devoted to a notable garden where the influence of the cook and the exacting demands of the kitchen are paramount. But these are no ordinary cooks. Each is a highly-rated chef recognized for the excellence of a cuisine which draws heavily upon home-grown produce. The garden is the starting point for many of their dishes and the inspiration for their cooking. Vegetables like the Florence fennel grown at Le Manoir aux Quat' Saisons are harvested when their flavour is at its peak.

For the perfect freshness of garden vegetables is a unique virtue unobtainable in produce that has to travel. Furthermore, produce not normally available in shops is at the kitchen door. The tender young leaves of seedling radishes or golden beetroot can be plucked for adding to a green salad, with the petals of marigolds and blue sage flowers strewn over it in a revival of an Elizabethan conceit. Not only is the choice of home-grown produce wider than any shop could provide, but one discovers that how things are grown organically and when they are harvested matters more with regard to their flavour than their named variety.

In endeavouring to illustrate the proper purpose of the kitchen garden, one cannot remain unaware of our fine tradition of cook-gardeners, from John Evelyn in the seventeenth century to Constance Spry of a generation ago. The anonymous authors of the volume entitled *Adam's Luxury and Eve's Cookery* exemplify what Alan Davidson, author of *The*

Oxford Companion to Food, has described as 'An eighteenth-century marriage – the gardener and the cook'. Some of the finest kitchen gardens of today represent the progeny of that marriage. For we have inherited a world enriched by both the adventurous gardeners of the past and the imaginative gardeners of the present. We are fortunate, indeed, to step into that world.

This book is also about the pleasure of the kitchen garden. Every true gardener knows the primitive thrill of watching seeds germinate and grow. Every true cook knows the pleasure of preparing garden-fresh food. And every true gourmet appreciates the beauty in both activities. Some people understand these related pleasures from an early age, almost instinctively, others come to them later in life. Nevertheless, all agree that such growing, caring, eating pleasures enrich our experience of life and our environment in a deep and worthwhile way.

CHAPTER ONE

CABBAGE, CAULIFLOWER, KOHLRABI, SWEDE *and* RUTABAGA, BEETROOT *and* BEET, RADICCHIO, LEMON BALM, LIME FLOWER, PEPPERS, CHERRIES, GRAPE, CURRANTS, HYBRID BERRIES, MINT, GREEN GAGE PLUM, SAVORY

A SCOTTISH KITCHEN GARDEN IN THE BORDERS
CRINGLETIE HOUSE

'GARDENING IS MUCH MORE NECESSARY AMONGST YOU THAN WITH us,' said Dr Samuel Johnson, the eighteenth-century lexicographer and critic, to his Scottish friend and biographer, James Boswell. 'Which makes people learn it. It is all gardening with you. Things, which grow wild here (in England), must be cultivated with great care in Scotland.'

Few things, anywhere, are cultivated with such great care as within the historic walled garden of Cringletie House, close to the town of Peebles and just fifteen miles south of Edinburgh. Here, protected by the Moorfoot Hills, is a jewel of a garden.

A view of part of the restored seventeenth-century kitchen garden to the side of the house at Cringletie. Close to the town of Peebles, the garden is protected by the Moorfoot Hills.

The first Cringletie House, a long low building with battlements, was built in 1660, and the kitchen garden dates from that time. The massive double yew hedge which forms the central spine of the garden was probably planted towards the end of the seventeenth century so that today the hedges are 1.5 m/5 ft thick and have taken on the shape of a railway tunnel, curved and closely clipped.

You enter the garden at the south end of the yew walk through a wrought iron gate, planted on either side with honeysuckle and pineapple mint. On a hot summer's day the scent of these plants blends with the

aromatic oils of the yew, and you know that you are in an ancient place. The peace and tranquillity of an old garden is, for me, an important element in its appeal. And I find myself thinking of earlier gardeners and visitors who have trodden here before me – all of them people who cared about growing things.

Halfway along the yew walk, a stone sundial stands sentinel over the other grass path that disects this 0.8-hectare/2-acre garden to create its simple cruciform shape. This wide, grassed path, bordered by beds of herbaceous flowers, herbs and fruit trees, stretches north-south to meet the gravelled walk that surrounds the garden at the foot of the 3 m/10 ft high

walls. From the sundial in the centre, the yew path continues in a straight line, across the garden, to bring you to the peach and vine houses that are built against the warm south-facing wall.

Scotland has been famous for its fruit for centuries. As early as the thirteenth century, the abbey at Haddington was renowned for its orchards. Up until the nineteenth century, the extensive orchards of the Carse of Gowrie, the Clyde valley, Stirlingshire and the Borders provided most of Scotland's apples and pears, cherries and plums. And for a time during the eighteenth century, the county of Angus produced so many gooseberries that they were turned into gooseberry vinegar. Even today,

Right: The blooms of a fuschia pink ivy-leaved geranium trained against the rear wall of a glasshouse. Left: Bright pink cornflowers provide contrasting colour to a bed of salad lettuces.

the soft fruit of Fife, Perth and Lothian makes Scotland the largest exporter of raspberries in the European Community.

However, fruit-growing did not end with these hardy outdoor varieties, for there has long been a spirit of adventure in Scottish gardening. At Cringletie, as elsewhere, eighteenth-century gardeners heeded the advice of James Justice, who, in *The Scots Gardiner's Director* (1754) made the rather astounding claim that by cultivating exotic fruit, like pineapples, on a hot-bed of straw and manure, they could be grown 'as freely as in their own native land'. And the Father of Scottish Agriculture, John Cockburn of Ormiston, wrote regularly from London to his Scottish gardener to encourage him to grow new plants: 'I'm not sure that Mulberries won't do. If in any place in our climate I believe it will be at the bottom of your father's Garden.'

Growing such tender plants in this challenging climate, where frosts can occur as late as June, requires considerable dedication and zeal, qualities that Cringletie has found in their young gardener, Nick Cross. From a background in agriculture, Nick arrived at Cringletie only two years ago and yet is already bringing the garden to an enviable condition. In the row of glasshouses, he grows nectarines and green gage plums, a bay tree and a grape vine, a camellia for winter blooms and a most spectacular climbing, ivy-leaved geranium whose bright pink flowers bedeck the dining tables in the hotel all summer long.

The rear wall of this row of glasshouses is hollow with internal flues to conduct the hot gases from a fire lit at the base of the wall. Small chimneys were constructed – sometimes they were cunningly disguised as garden statues – at intervals along the top of the wall for the fumes to escape. The temperature of each glasshouse was carefully controlled by a system of wire-mesh dampers and sliding shutters operated by metal struts at the entrance.

This form of heated wall, which dates from the middle of the eighteenth century, is still to be found in many of the walled kitchen gardens of Scotland and the North of England. The heated wall was a later refinement of the hot wall which was warmed by open fires lit at its base every 9 m/30 ft or so on its northern side. A heated wall meant that tender wall fruits like apricots and peaches could, with care, be grown in areas of the country normally considered too cold.

Lady Castlehill, who lived at Camnethan House on the north bank of the Clyde, gives recipes for fresh apricots and figs in her manuscript book of 1712. And Sydney Smith, the eighteenth-century cleric and gourmet, recalls eating local peaches in Scotland, although he commented that he thought the fruit would have tasted better pickled.

Later, when glass became affordable, it was logical to build either a glass canopy or a complete enclosure against the wall to contain the heat and allow yet more tender subjects such as table grapes, nectarines and even pineapples to be grown in these northern gardens. During the nineteenth century, it became a matter of social status for a land-owner to display the produce of his well-equipped kitchen garden on his dinner table.

Almost every outdoor wall at Cringletie is used for growing fruit. Espalier-trained apples and pears spread their branches in pleasing patterns. Red currants are trained 2.4 m/8 ft high so that the trusses of ripe, glistening berries look like a scarlet waterfall. And gooseberries, both the cooking and the succulent dessert varieties, are trained against the north- and east-facing walls. Even the outside walls of this kitchen garden are used for growing the magnificent bitter-sweet cherry, the Morello.

Lady Castlehill gives a recipe for black cherry wine which starts, 'Take the ripest full black cherries, and pick them from their stalks, being early in the morning, for it is best to make this wine in the coole of the day.' Another lover of cherries once planted an avenue of the trees beyond the south wall of the garden at Cringletie. Close by the cherries stands a

Left: A spray of creamy-white lime (linden) flowers with their pale green 'keys' ready for drying. Right: Baskets of freshly-picked Scottish strawberries waiting to be carried to the kitchen.

The four large beds in the garden are devoted to an inspiring range of vegetables. There are six kinds of potato, for Scottish potatoes are world-renowned for their fine flavour and healthy stock: 'Maris Piper' grows next to 'Sharpe's Express', 'Epicure', 'Golden Wonder', 'King Edward' and 'Estima'. Then towers the taller top growth of two kinds of Jerusalem artichokes, 'Fuseau' with its long slim tuber and another variety, of unknown name, but with the familiar nobbly round roots.

The second vegetable bed contains serried rows of the parsnip, 'Tender and True', with its attractive celery-like leaves, and three varieties of carrots, their feathery foliage swaying in the light breeze. Then come the stiff-stemmed onions, shallots and leeks, growing in regimented rows and destined for Mrs Maguire's repertoire of mouth-watering broths and winter soups.

The brassicas congregate in the third bed: untouchable red cabbage, filmy with an eerie grey bloom, beside the heavy footballs of 'White Drumhead'. Creamy heads of cauliflower nestle under their strap-shaped leaves next to a sea of fern-like curly kale. And three varieties of the turnip-rooted cabbage, kohlrabi, startle you with their subterranean looks and pale green or purple skins, for we are accustomed to bulging roots growing beneath the soil.

All the exotic Italian vegetables familiar to Castelvetro in seventeenth-century Modena gather in the fourth quarter of the garden. The sculptural globe artichoke, 'Violetta di Chioggia', which Nick Cross grows from seed each spring, and four varieties of courgette (zucchini) are separated by rows of Florence fennel and mangetout peas (edible pod peas) now grown in preference to shelling peas. There is every shade of lettuce – green and russet and red – with every style of leaf – smooth or frilled or puckered. Broad beans and celeriac, sweet peppers and beetroot, herbs and marigolds, elderflower and strawberries, raspberries and blackcurrants – everywhere there is an astonishing scene of plenitude.

Even though Nick Cross inherited a garden in good condition, his achievement is considerable. The cornucopia of vegetables, fruits and herbs that he produces for the kitchen is a true celebration of the kitchen garden. The potting shed is crammed with seed packets, antique gardening tools and a library of gardening books that he consults almost everyday. Like all the best gardeners, he says he still has much to learn. Such an enterprising and enthusiastic attitude to the kitchen garden puts one in mind of seventeenth-century gardener John Reid who, in 1683, at the age of twenty-seven, published Scotland's first gardening book, *The Scots Gard'ner*. This fine book follows in the tradition of John Evelyn, whom Reid openly admired, by making the essential connection between

majestic row of lime (linden) trees which, in July, are covered with the delicate scented flowers loved by the Cringletie bees. The same lime (linden) flowers, when dried, make the kind of lime tea that, when served with a *Madeleine*, so jolted the memory of Marcel Proust that he was inspired to write his masterpiece, *La Récherche du Temps Perdu*.

These lime trees must have been saplings in 1861, when the owner of Cringletie decided to pull down the seventeenth-century mansion to build a fine turreted house in pink sandstone, designed by a fashionable local architect, David Bryce. The new kitchen was built on the kitchen garden side of the house and it has now been extended at first floor level by the present owner and cook at Cringletie, Mrs Aileen Maguire.

'When we arrived here nearly twenty years ago the hotel served tinned and frozen vegetables. The kitchen garden was devoted to strawberries which were sold by the gardener as part of his wages,' remembers Mrs Maguire. 'Well, although I might be new to cooking for a living, at least I know how to grow and cook fresh vegetables.' And so she and her husband Stanley set about restoring the kitchen garden in order to provide a good supply of fresh vegetables, herbs and fruit throughout the year for use in the kitchen.

The double wrought-iron gates that lead into the kitchen garden at Cringletie House.

the kitchen garden and the kitchen, for the final chapter contains recipes and recommendations for the cook.

It is fascinating to see that the garden at Cringletie, which was established during John Reid's lifetime, still displays many of the horticultural ideas current during the seventeenth century and advocated in the book.

On the shape and size of the garden with its pattern of paths, Reid writes, 'Its also ordinary to divide the garden into four plots, by two walkes crossing from side to side.' He would approve of the high Cringletie walls: 'As there is no Countrey can have more need of planting than this, so non more needfull of Inclosing: for we well know how vain it is to plant unless we inclose', because the Scottish kitchen garden is created of 'cold, chilled, barren Rugged-natur'd-ground' which the gardener attempts to 'soften and tender'. He sings the praises of generous manuring, and Nick Cross continues this sound practice of forking plenty of farmyard muck into the Cringletie soil that, after centuries of tilling, is a fine, workable tilth.

I visited the garden during a heat-wave, and after a ten-week period of drought when no watering had been carried out. To investigate the nature of this fertile ground we dug a hole in the middle of some fallow space so that we could see a profile of the soil. It was satisfying to note that only 5 cm/2 in below the surface, the soil was dark, moist and rich with humus. Little wonder that none of the surrounding plants were flagging in the heat.

The resourceful John Reid grew his garden produce because, at the time, it was almost impossible to buy a supply of fine vegetables, fruits and herbs. And certainly not the amazingly wide range of plants from asparagus to scorzonera that he grew. Curiously it is for almost the same reason that, three hundred years later, the Cringletie garden of today is developed to such a high degree. 'You just can't buy vegetables as fine as those we grow here,' according to Aileen Maguire. 'In the past, gardeners only ever brought large vegetables to the kitchen door, but for twenty years we have always had the produce we want, and moreover it is pure, grown organically and with no harmful sprays. Growing your own food makes a great deal of sense, because it brings not only good health but also peace of mind.' No one who cares about the quality of what we eat could disagree with the words of John Reid: 'The Kitchen Garden is the best of all Gardens.'

BORDERS' BEETROOT (BEET) SOUP

1 medium onion, chopped

30 g/1 oz/2 tbsp butter

1.2 litres/2 pints/5 cups beef stock

225 g/8 oz cooked beetroot (beet), skinned and roughly chopped

sea salt and freshly milled black pepper

GARNISH:

150 ml/¼ pint/⅔ cup soured cream or plain yoghurt

1 tbsp snipped chives

Sauté the onion in the butter over medium heat for 4 minutes. Add the stock and bring to the boil. Simmer for 8-10 minutes until the onion is tender.

Pour the liquid into a blender or food processor with the beetroot and whizz until reduced to a smooth purée. Season with salt and pepper and return to the pan.

Reheat when required, but do not boil for more than a few minutes or the bright red colour will be spoilt. Pour into hot soup bowls and garnish with a spoonful of soured cream or yogurt and a few chives. *Serves 4-6*

SPINACH AND GRUYÈRE ROULADE FILLED WITH *AYRSHIRE* CHEESE

GRUYÈRE CHEESE LAYER:

175 g/6 oz/1¹/₂ cups Gruyère cheese, grated

60 g/2 oz/1¹/₃ cups soft white breadcrumbs

4 eggs, separated

150 ml/¹/₄ pint/²/₃ cup single (light) cream

2 tbsp warm water

¹/₄ tsp Dijon mustard

salt and freshly milled black pepper

SPINACH LAYER:

1 medium onion, chopped

30 g/1 oz/2 tbsp butter

450 g/1 lb/2 cups cooked puréed spinach

¹/₂ tsp freshly grated nutmeg

4 eggs, separated

FILLING:

450 g/1 lb Ayrshire cheese or medium-fat curd cheese (part-skim ricotta cheese)

2 tbsp finely chopped chives

GARNISH:

young salad leaves

few slices of cucumber

light vinaigrette dressing

Mix the Gruyère cheese with the breadcrumbs in a bowl and stir in the egg yolks beaten with the cream, warm water and mustard. Season to taste with salt and pepper. Whisk the egg whites until stiff and fold into the mixture.

Pour into a Swiss roll tin (jelly roll pan) (30 × 20 cm/12 × 8 in) lined with non-stick baking paper (parchment) and bake in an oven preheated to 180°C/350°F/Gas Mark 4 for about 15 minutes or until risen and golden. Place a clean tea (dish) towel on a wooden board or the work surface, turn out the cheese layer on to it and allow to cool.

For the spinach layer, soften the onion in the butter over medium heat. Add to the spinach and mix in the nutmeg, egg yolks and salt and pepper to taste. Whisk the egg whites until stiff and fold into the spinach mixture. Pour into a Swiss roll tin (jelly roll pan) lined with non-stick baking paper (parchment) and bake in the same pre-heated oven as above for 15-20 minutes or until risen and springy in the centre. Turn out on to a towel and allow to cool.

To assemble the dish, cut both cheese and spinach layers lengthways to make four pieces. Make the filling by creaming the cheese with the chives and some salt and pepper. Set aside one of the spinach layers for the top, and spread the other three layers with the filling. Place alternately one on top of the other and trim the edges to form a rectangle. Chill for 1 hour.

To serve, cut into slices and garnish with salad leaves and cucumber lightly dressed with vinaigrette. *Serves 10-12*

SUMMER FRUIT TARTLETS

PÂTE SUCRÉE:

150 g/5 oz/1 cup plain (all-purpose) flour

30 g/1 oz/2 tbsp vanilla-flavoured caster (superfine) sugar (see below)

90 g/3 oz/6 tbsp unsalted butter, softened

2 egg yolks

FILLING:

225 g/8 oz/¼ cup cream cheese

60 g/2 oz/¼ cup vanilla-flavoured caster (superfine) sugar

60 ml/2 fl oz double (heavy) cream

ripe summer fruits: strawberries, raspberries, red and black currants, peaches, nectarines, blueberries, figs

4 tbsp red currant or apple jelly, warmed

few sprigs of mint, to decorate

Sift the flour and sugar into a wide shallow bowl or on to a cold work surface. Add the butter and egg yolks and work together with your finger-tips until the dough can be rolled into a ball. Wrap the dough and chill for 30 minutes.

Roll out the pastry dough on a floured board and use to line eight greased tartlet tins (10 cm/4 in in diameter). Prick the bottom of each pastry case and place the tins on a baking sheet. Bake in an oven prehe-ated to 200°C/400°F/Gas Mark 6 for 12-15 minutes or until the pastry is crisp and golden. Cool in the tins, then transfer to a wire rack. If made ahead, store the pastry cases in an air-tight container until needed. These pastry cases freeze well; thaw at room temperature for 1 hour before filling.

Blend the cheese with the sugar and cream and spread a layer in the bottom of each pastry case. Arrange the fresh fruits attractively on top and spoon over the warmed jelly to glaze them. Set aside for 1 hour to set, then decorate with the sprigs of mint and serve the same day. *Serves 8*

Note: for vanilla-flavoured sugar see page 55.

Right: A sea of grey-blue leaved red cabbage with green drumhead cabbage and cauliflower beyond. Left: The kitchen garden at Cringletie House with its protective backdrop of mature trees and rolling hills.

CABBAGE

Brassica oleracea var *capitata, B. o.* var. *sabauda, B. o.* var *rubra*

HAS OVER-FAMILIARITY WITH CABBAGE BRED A LOW-STATUS VEGETABLE? OR IS IT our ways of cooking it? The value that we attribute to different foods is founded upon a rich diversity of reasons, and none of us is free from the influence of childhood, memory and the pressure of the market place. As a result, there has been a massacre of the innocents where the brassica family is concerned. I've seen Italian, French and German families licking their lips in anticipation of a beautifully succulent slow-cooked cabbage dish, though we persist in denying ourselves the charms of this vegetable that has provided the basis of many classic dishes of European cooking – the *garbure* and *potée* of France, German sauerkraut, and Tuscan red cabbage.

Perhaps only the kitchen gardener truly knows how good a cabbage can taste. The puckered leaves of a bronzed 'January King' Savoy, the pointed head of a grey-green 'Greyhound' and the fresh crisp squeakiness of Cornish Greens are satisfying to grow, cook and eat. But their freshness is essential to their flavour.

The cultivated cabbage was probably introduced to Britain by the Romans, who were totally convinced of its virtues. Columella was inspired to write:

'That herb, which o'er the whole terrestial globe
Doth flourish, and in great abundance yields
To low plebian and the haughty king,
In winter Cabbage, and green Sprouts in spring.

Yet, no mention of the vegetable appears until Gerard in the sixteenth century. Evelyn writes in 1699: 'Tis scarce a hundred Years since we first had Cabbages out of Holland. Sir Anth. Ashley of Wiburg St Giles in Dorsetshire, being (as I am told) the first who planted them in England.'

Today's seed catalogues carry a wide choice of cabbages for every season with far more varieties than you ever see for sale in the greengrocers. I believe that gardeners must eat more interesting cabbages than anyone else. And look at how healthy they are. One is reminded that Caton the Censor said that because of the sulphur-rich cabbages in their diet, the Romans were able to do without doctors for ten centuries.

Cabbages are fierce feeders. They need a rich, fertile soil with plenty of moisture-retaining humus. I usually sow seed of several varieties in a small seed-bed during the spring, and transplant 15-30 cm/6-12 in apart on a damp day during the summer. Alternatively – in good gardening areas – cabbage plants are often on sale from mid-summer onwards. All cabbage seedlings need to be watered well when they are planted, and again in dry weather.

Keep them weed-free and hoe the soil to a light tilth to discourage slugs. Harvest cabbages whenever their size suits you – the younger the leaves, the more tender the dish. I recommend quick-maturing varieties that do not take up garden space for too long: 'Hispi' F1, 'Minicole' F1, 'Red Ruby Ball', FI, Savoy 'Dwarf Green Curled', and 'Earliest of All'.

CAULIFLOWER

Brassica oleracea Botrytis group

THIS VEGETABLE IS GROWN FOR ITS SINGLE, CREAMY-WHITE, UNDEVELOPED flowerhead known as a curd. The cauliflower probably originated in Egypt. The vegetable was eaten by the Romans, and Cyprus has grown magnificent examples for centuries. The cauliflower arrived in Britain from Italy, and John Evelyn wrote that the best seed came from Aleppo.

Cauliflower is delicious eaten raw, blanched or cooked – it can be boiled, steamed or stir-fried and eaten hot or cold. The vegetable also makes a very fine creamy soup such as the French classic, Crème DuBarry.

Cauliflowers take up quite a bit of space in the garden. Because local farmers grow the cauliflower as a field crop for market, I rarely grow them now. However, enthusiasts can produce cauliflower during the whole year by growing a range of varieties. Depending on the variety, sow seed from early spring to midsummer, and plant out 60 cm/2 ft apart in fertile, well-drained soil. Keep the plants free of weeds and well watered – if necessary mulch to retain moisture – and firm the soil around the stems. Cut the cauliflower when large enough to eat and discard the stump – break it up or shred it, otherwise it will take some time to rot on the compost heap. Winter

cauliflowers need to have their strap-like leaves curved over the curd to prevent damage from frost or rain.

Recommended varieties are 'Alpha-Polaris', 'All The Year Round', the Australian variety 'Wallaby', the US variety 'Violet Queen' F1 and a very hardy variety, 'Ashmer Pinnacle'.

KOHLRABI
Brassica oleracea var. gongylodes

IN HIS SPLENDID BOOK, *FOOD*, WAVERLY ROOT TAKES THE *ENCYLOPAEDIA Brittanica* to task on the subject of kohlrabi. He is critical of the *Britannica*'s phrase 'of recent European origin' in its description of the vegetable. Mr Root informs us that 'Charlemagne ordered that kohlrabi be grown in his domains twelve centuries ago' and, true to style, proceeds to tell us more fascinating facts about the kohlrabi than any other writer I know. How I should like to have met Mr Root. He died in 1982, and his legacy is several elegant and absorbing volumes about food and eating and life.

Arthur Young, the English agriculturist who travelled widely in Europe during the eighteenth century, described the kohlrabi as a cattle-feeding plant, so it is not quite certain when the vegetable began to appear in the English garden. It was grown

in the nineteenth century, but there are few contemporary English recipes for it. The vegetable is still not widely grown.

The kohlrabi is also known as the turnip-rooted cabbage, which is an apt description since it belongs to the brassica family and the stem swells, just above the ground, into a turnip-like shape with a pale green or a purple skin. The flavour is more like turnip than cabbage. And young specimens have a pleasing crispness that makes them better than turnips for eating raw or blanched in salads. In Germany and Switzerland, where the vegetable is popular, the root is peeled and added to slowly-cooked meat dishes.

Although I like the taste of kohlrabi, I grow it only occasionally – not every year. Sow seed thinly in fertile soil during the spring. Thin to 20 cm/8 in apart and keep weed-free. Harvest the roots when no larger than a tennis ball. The varieties 'Purple Vienna' and 'White Vienna' mature in ten to twelve weeks from sowing. Kohlrabi tastes particularly nice par-boiled and roasted around a joint of meat. Or peel the root thinly and cook in the same way as for turnips.

SWEDE (RUTABAGA)
Brassica napus var. napobrassica

MY 1920 EDITION OF *VEGETABLES AND THEIR CULTIVATION,* BY T W SANDERS, lists swedes (rutabagas) in the Uncommon Vegetables section and says, 'These are better known as a farm, rather than a garden crop.' This is still true in Devon where string-net sacks of swedes are on sale at farm gates during the autumn and winter. But it is in Scotland that the swede is truly appreciated. A dish of buttered neeps (turnips) is the traditional accompaniment to the Scots haggis and whisky of a Burns' Night Supper. My own preference for serving this root vegetable is influenced by this alliance of swede and whisky. I combine the two flavours in one dish by mashing the cooked vegetable with butter and black pepper and adding Scotch whisky to taste. Serve as a purée, or beat in a couple of eggs, some thick cream and some finely chopped parsley or thyme and bake the mixture in a hot oven for twenty to thirty minutes. Serve this baked swede custard with grilled or roasted lamb or mutton.

The swede probably originated in Bohemia during the seventeenth century. Its talent for surviving the harsh winters of northern Europe made this yellow-fleshed winter root highly attractive to the farmers of Scandinavia. When the vegetable arrived in Scotland it was known as the Swedish turnip or rutabaga, from a dialect word meaning ram's foot. Scottish farmers began to grow swedes not just for their animals but for themselves, retaining the name 'neeps', until then reserved for the white-fleshed turnip.

Swedes like a light, well-drained soil, manured during the previous season. Sow from late spring in rows 37.5 cm/15 in apart, or broadcast the seed if you prefer. Thin to 15 cm/6 in apart at an early stage. Keep the soil moist to avoid woody roots. Start to harvest the swedes when tennis-ball size. In mild, dry areas, swedes can be left in the

ground until required, otherwise dig and store as for potatoes. Recommended varieties include 'Purple Top Yellow' and the globe-shaped 'Marian'.

BEETROOT (BEET)
Beta vulgaris subsp. *vulgaris*

THE HEYDAY OF THE BEETROOT (BEET) MUST HAVE BEEN 2000 YEARS AGO WHEN IT is claimed that the Greeks so valued the vegetable that its prize roots were offered on a silver platter to Apollo. At that time beetroot leaves were used in preference to lettuce, and one horticultural source says that the Greeks 'placed a weight on the plant to convert the foliage into a cabbage'. I find myself trying to picture this unusual gardening experiment.

Both the sleek, glossy leaves and the sweet-tasting root of the beetroot have long been appreciated for their medicinal properties. Cooks have been less inspired by the vegetable. The cuisines of Eastern Europe and Russia have contributed the best beetroot recipes. Russian bortsch is a very fine dish with endless variations. It might be a huge sustaining broth, rich with sausages or pork or duck, or a refined and delicate dish of beetroot bouillon. I sometimes serve this latter version as a light and pretty start to a Christmas meal, with a handful of small puff pastry stars floating on its surface.

The cultivated beetroot is related to the wild subspecies, *Beta vulgaris* subsp. *maritima*, found growing on the shores of Europe, North Africa and Asia. Garden beetroot likes a deep, rich soil. A poor, dry soil can result in pale, wiry roots that are not pleasant to eat. Sow a quick-maturing variety like 'Boltardy' or 'Early Wonder' in rows or patches during the spring. Thin to 7.5 cm/3 in apart and take the thinnings to the kitchen (in French country markets, bundles of the thinnings are sold as a green vegetable). Harvest the beetroot when still small and tender. Simply wash well in cold water. Cut off the leaves and cook them like spinach. Cover the roots with cold water, salt lightly and simmer until cooked. Peel and serve, hot or cold, with soured cream and chives. Small golfball-size beetroot are sweet and delicious, and far better for never coming near vinegar. If the sweet flavour needs correcting, use the finely grated zest (rind) and juice of an orange, lemon or lime. And if you prefer to pickle beetroot for winter eating, prepare a less acidic blend, and spice it and sweeten with honey – this enhances the natural taste of the vegetable.

I normally sow 'Boltardy' in succession throughout the summer since it does well in my garden, but some gardeners prefer beetroot with tapering roots which need a deep, rich soil. I also recommend 'Burpee's Golden' and the Italian variety 'Barbatietola di Chioggia'. In areas with harsh winters, late autumn beetroot are best lifted, trimmed and stored in moist peat in a cool, dry place. Recommended beetroot varieties are 'Detroit', 'Little Ball', 'Globe', 'Cheltenham Green Top' and 'Cylindra'.

RADICCHIO
Cichorium intybus

RADICCHIO IS SIMPLY THE ITALIAN NAME FOR CHICORY although in America, only the red-heading chicories are called Radicchio. The red-leaved varieties of this vegetable are relatively recent introductions into Britain. And in our chilly, sunless climate we have welcomed this colourful vegetable from the south.

The taste of red-leaved radicchio is little different from the green and white sugar-loaf type grown in open ground in the garden. I have been growing red-leaf chicory for a decade with seed brought back from France; but now several varieties are available from most seedsmen. Radicchio is quite easy to grow although, naturally, it does better in a warm, sunny summer.

The variety 'Rossa di Treviso' (Red Treviso) produces long, strap-like green leaves that turn red in September. When blanched the green fades to cream, but the red colour remains. The more well-known variety is the round-leaved 'Rossa di Verona' (Red Verona), whose leaves redden slightly earlier in the season. Both these varieties can be eaten unblanched, although blanching makes their leaf colour more dramatic and their bitter flavour more mild. Other recommended varieties are 'Giulio', 'Cesare', 'Variegata di Castelfranco' and 'Variegata di Chioggia'.

I have found that radicchio plants are quite hardy, and those that survive the winter and continue growing the following year produce particularly fetching edible blue flowers that look marvellous strewn over a green salad.

Sow seed thinly in fertile soil from early summer and thin to 15 cm/6 in apart. Give a liquid organic feed in midsummer, and keep the ground moist but not wet. Blanch a few plants at a time by excluding all light and cut when each plant has developed a heart.

The leaves of red radicchio are usually added to a salad of mixed leaves. Dress with a vinaigrette made with a Tuscan olive oil or a nice fresh nut oil. Italian cooks prefer to cook with the Treviso long-leaf radicchio rather than the round-leaf variety. One of the tastiest dishes is very simple and quick to prepare: Cut a head of Treviso radicchio in half or quarters with a sharp knife, shallow-fry in butter or olive oil and place in an oven-dish. Sprinkle with grated Parmesan or diced Gorgonzola cheese and place under a very hot grill until the cheese is melting. Serve straight away.

LEMON BALM
Melissa officinalis

Culinary use: chopped leaves in sauces for vegetables and fish; whole leaves in syrups for fruit, and in tisanes.

Cultivation: hardy herbaceous perennial, white flowers, height 90 cm/ 36 in; grow in well-drained soil in full sun or light shade.

LIME FLOWERS (LINDEN FLOWERS)
Tilia cordata

Culinary use: the creamy-yellow flowers are used fresh or dried for making a digestive and calming tisane or herbal tea.

Cultivation: hardy perennial, deciduous tree, height up to 10.5 m/ 35 ft; grow in well-drained soil in full sun.

SWEET PEPPER, CHILLI PEPPER
Capsicum annuum

THE CAPSICUM WAS INTRODUCED INTO EUROPE FROM SOUTH America by the Spanish. The name of the plant is derived from the Greek word 'to bite', which presumably indicates that those early capsicums were of the chilli variety with their fiery flavour. Chilli peppers are characteristic of the cooking of Mexico and Latin America where the choice of varieties is bewildering and their names reflect the different degrees of hot, peppery flavour.

During the early nineteenth century, London market gardeners grew chilli peppers as a crop to be sold at Covent Garden. Then they appear to have fallen from favour until about ten years ago. The chilli pepper, with its small tapering pods which start green and gradually ripen to yellow and red, is an easy plant to grow. But due to their South American home, they like plenty of sun. Even so, this plant often grows remarkably well on a sunny windowsill all over the British Isles. And since the chilli pepper is still seen as an exotic vegetable, it can be most convenient to have your own kitchen supply. Even if you don't like their hot spicy taste, a chilli pepper plant makes a highly decorative pot plant.

Sow seed, two or three to a pot, under glass or on a windowsill, during the spring. Remove the weaker seedlings and leave one plant per pot. Transfer to a larger pot when necessary, but bear in mind that capsicums have small roots and fruit better when slightly pot-bound. Give a liquid organic feed once the flowers have set and feed again one month later. Don't let the plant dry out. Pick the pods as soon as large enough to use, to encourage further production.

Handle chilli peppers with care; they contain capsaicin which burns sensitive skin like the mouth or the eyes. When preparing the vegetable, work near the sink and plenty of cold water, so that you can wash your hands quickly if you are getting an unpleasant reaction. The seeds and white membrane are the hottest part of a chilli pepper, so cut in half lengthways and remove them with a knife then run cold water inside the chilli to remove every trace. Cut the chilli into small pieces for adding to a dish. Some recipes call for a whole chilli pepper, in which case simply add the whole pod and don't disturb the seeds.

The bulbous sweet pepper is a more recent arrival in Britain. This vegetable now has green-, yellow-, red-, orange- or black-skinned varieties. These juicy and delicious peppers go well, diced or slivered, in salads. They taste marvellous cooked, either left whole and stuffed or grilled and skinned. This healthy vegetable, so rich in Vitamin C, with its distinctive flavour, has now become a popular food in our sun-starved island.

The sweet pepper does need the sun to grow well, but if you can provide a south-facing sheltered corner outside or, even better, a cold-frame or a greenhouse, then the newer F1 hybrids should grow successfully. In Mediterranean markets, small plants of sweet peppers are sold from May onwards. Sometimes the plants are available here. These will give you a flying start. Plant them in a pot of rich compost and grow in the same way as the chilli pepper. Alternatively, sow seed during the spring and pot on.

Most seed companies now have an excellent choice of varieties of sweet pepper. The variety 'New Ace' F1 is popular but not fleshy enough for my taste. However 'Early Prolific' F1, 'Gypsy', the compact 'Triton', and the yellow-fleshed 'Luteum' F1 are excellent. Good chilli pepper varieties include 'Serrano' and the yellow-skinned 'Karlo'. Good US varieties are 'Marconi' and 'Violetta'.

CHERRY
Prunus avium, Prunus cerasus

IN ONE OF THE GALLERIES OF THE GULBENKIAN MUSEUM IN LISBON HANGS A LARGE tapestry of a cherry harvest. It is a jolly scene full of enjoyment, and I can still see the chubby, laughing children climbing among the branches of the cherry tree while the adults carry away baskets of the fruit.

Ripe cherries have to be picked and eaten, or sold, quite quickly. The fruit will store fresh for only a few days. Hence the street cry, 'Cherry Ripe, Cherry Ripe' of the cherry seller in eighteenth-century London, and of the folksong that is now rarely heard. I remember we often sang it at my primary school, but then today's children are also denied the sight of hundreds of cherry trees in blossom and the excitement of picking the tempting fruit. This is because most of the famous orchards in Kent, along with the Tamar Valley cherry trees, have disappeared. Now the bulk of the crop in Britain is imported from France.

The sweet cherry is one of our oldest fruits. The tree arrived with the Romans and they planted the first cherries in Kent, transporting the fruit up the Thames to London. After the Romans left, no records of cherries appear until the fourteenth century. Two hundred years later, named varieties of the sweet cherry, *Prunus avium*, and the sour cherry, *Prunus cerasus*, were developed.

Most of the modern cultivated cherries were introduced by the famous Victorian hybridizer, Thomas Andrew Knight, and the distinguished fruit nursery of Thomas Rivers in Sawbridgeworth. The Royal Horticultural Society, in 1827, grew 246 named varieties of cherry in its collection at Chiswick. Unfortunately, these cherries made large trees that were better suited to an orchard than the average garden.

The introduction of the Colt rootstock has made the size of a cherry tree more manageable; the overall height of an eight-year-old tree can be kept below 2.7-3.6 m/9-12 ft. The only problem that remains is that many varieties of cherry are self-sterile. However, the John Innes Horticultural Institution, working with the Summerland Experiment Station in British Columbia, has developed some highly successful new varieties of cherry, some of which are self-fertile and of direct interest to the gourmet gardener.

Cherry trees grow best in a good, well-drained soil in a protected position. Sweet cherries prefer to be in full sun; however, the sour cherries like the Morello grow well in shade and even trained against a north-facing wall. The blossom of the self-fertile Morello cherry, or its cultivar, the black-fruited 'Nabella', is just too pretty not to have in your garden. The cherry will even grow in a good-sized tub which makes it suitable for a flat dweller with a balcony. The best self-fertile sweet cherries are the dependable 'Stella', 'Compact Stella', 'Sunburst', 'Lapins' and the American variety, 'Bing', which is ideal for growing in a container.

GRAPE
Vitis vinifera

THERE HAVE BEEN SEVERAL WELL-MEANING ATTEMPTS TO GROW GRAPES IN OUR northern climate. Long before man made wine from grapes, the fruit was a food – grape seeds have been found in early lake dwellings in central Europe.

The vine is native to Asia Minor and still grows wild in Armenia and Azerbaijan. The cultivated varieties were developed for eating and for wine-making well before the Greek civilization. The Romans introduced grapes and wine to Britain and almost certainly the vines. In AD 280, the Emperor Probus reversed the policy that forbade the growing of vines outside Italy and decreed that Roman troops should grow vines wherever they were stationed. It is believed that they must have been planted in Britain thereafter (if not unofficially before). Vineyards did exist by the time of the Norman invasion, however, and their numbers increased with the encouragement of the French gardeners.

It has never been easy to grow productive outdoor grapes in Britain. During the Middle Ages, the monasteries cultivated the vine, and some of these vineyards, like that of the Bishop of Ely, were important for centuries. The Reformation led to the decline of English vine-growing, but English vineyards have been replanted during the last twenty years using German and American varieties, and they are now coming into full production.

The widespread introduction of the glasshouse during the nineteenth century encouraged gardeners to grow dessert grapes. The best-flavoured dessert grapes are still grown under glass. Of the muscat-flavoured varieties, the black grape 'Madresfield Courtand' and the white grape 'Muscat of Alexandria' are highly recommended – they both need a little heat. The varieties 'Black Hamburgh' and 'Buckland Sweetwater' can be grown in an unheated greenhouse, even in pots.

I have grown the outdoor black grape *Vitis* 'Brandt' for some years with great success. Planted against a warm south- or west-facing wall, the black grapes ripen in September when the leaves are a glorious red and orange. Some of the grapes are large and sweet and perfect for dessert. The rest I turn into a claret-coloured jelly for serving with roast game. Some years, the vines produce lots of small, sharp grapes which a friend makes into wine. The following year she delivers the wine in bottles with labels decorated with her drawing of our house.

Vines should be planted in the spring in a deep but not necessarily rich soil. Prune during the winter before the sap rises, and train and tie in the vine against a trellis or wall. Thin the bunches of grapes while still very small. Vines grown under glass often do best when the rootstock is planted outside the greenhouse and the leaders are trained along wires under the glass roof.

BLACK, RED AND WHITE CURRANTS
Ribes nigrum, Ribes rubrum

IN THE SIXTEENTH-CENTURY KITCHEN GARDEN, BUSHES OF RED, WHITE AND black currants were grown around seats and trained over bowers. How pretty the tumbling sprigs of fruit must have looked, peeping through the trellis of leaves. Sadly, we are less imaginative in our kitchen gardens today and flights of fancy are rare.

My currant bushes grow in the former chicken run, now converted into a fruit cage. It amazes me how well that old chicken muck has supported those bushes for almost a decade. Every autumn, after pruning the branches that have fruited, I add a mulch of well-rotted compost, topped up every three to four years – when part of our roof is rethatched – with a thick blanket of rotting reed.

Cultivated currants have been developed from the wild form native to northern Europe. The first major advance for the fruit came in 1611, when John Tradescant Senior introduced the Great Red Currant from Holland. Within a few years English gardeners began to uproot their bushes of the smaller-fruited English Red. The fruit was highly valued for making jellies and preserves and for wine-making. Then, in 1910, the famous fruit firm of Laxton Brothers developed two improved varieties of red

Trusses of ripe red currants glowing against an east-facing wall.

currant, most notably 'Laxton's No. 1'. Ten years later the American variety, 'Red Lake', was launched. Both these varieties are still widely grown. They have recently been joined by the early-ripening variety, 'Jonkheer van Tets', and the mid-season 'Stanza'.

White currants are truly a gourmet fruit and well worth growing for their sweet grape-like flavour. The variety 'White Versailles' is over 150-years-old and still highly recommended.

Black currants contain more Vitamin C, weight for weight, than almost any other fruit. There are at least twenty good varieties to choose from. I grow 'Mendip Cross' and 'Boskoop Giant'. Clearly it is important to plant a late-flowering variety if you live in a cold area and a wind-resistant variety for an exposed garden. A reliable guide to varieties of all fruit is *The Good Fruit Guide* by Lawrence D. Hills. A good US guide is Lewis Hill's *Fruits and Berries for the Home Garden*.

In the past, gardeners devised all manner of ways to extend the season for currants. Some fruit was forced under glass, some was allowed to ripen naturally, and other bushes were planted against east-facing walls and the unripe fruit was covered with straw and matting to delay its ripening even until Christmas. Nowadays, we regard currants as a summer fruit, and preserve the surplus for winter eating.

Plant currant bushes from November to March (in early spring in the US) in deeply dug, fertile soil. Prune back and stake if necessary so that newly planted bushes are not loosened by the wind. Fork in a dressing of phosphate in the spring and give a good mulch in early summer. Prune the fruit-bearing branches after harvesting the fruit.

HYBRID BERRIES

WHEN YOU LOOK AT THE WIDE RANGE OF DELECTABLE HYBRID BERRIES BRED during the last hundred years you realize that in the fruit world – promiscuity pays. It is getting quite difficult to stay up to date with the berry business; new berries arrive every year. Some are launched at the Royal Horticultural Society's Chelsea Show in May, where you can inspect the pink-flowered strawberry or the jostaberry. But rarely can you taste their fruit which is, of course, what really matters. For other introductions, you have to depend on the description in the catalogue of a reputable grower. My advice is to grow what you feel drawn too – even if no one else on the allotments (community gardens) has heard of it – and bring some excitement into your fruit gardening.

LOGANBERRY

JUDGE J. H. LOGAN SAYS IT WAS ALMOST UNINTENTIONAL: HE SOWED SEEDS OF the Californian wild blackberry, *Rubus ursinus*, between a kind of evergreen blackberry, 'Texas Early', and a forty-year-old 'Red Antwerp'-type raspberry. And, in the fullness of time, which was 1883, in his Santa Cruz garden the loganberry was born. Every good cook has thanked him since, for as Jane Grigson says in her *Fruit Book*, 'The cooking berry par excellence is the loganberry.'

The long, fleshy, claret-fruited loganberry (there is now a black-fruited loganberry too) is an easy-to-grow and tolerant plant. It prefers a sheltered south-facing wall, but mine flourishes, trained on a trellis, in an exposed position in full sun. When really ripe and claret-red, the fruit can be eaten raw with a dusting of sugar and some clotted cream. The fruit tastes like a sharp raspberry with a hint of gooseberry. But the loganberry really comes into its own when cooked. Its intense flavour and bright red juice adds a summery depth to lack-lustre cooking apples or pears, most of all, perhaps, in a fruit pie served during the depths of winter – ah . . . English cooking at its best. Loganberries behave like red currants in a mixture of summer fruits: their acidity brings out the flavour of its companions, and in jellies and jams contributes to their setting.

I grow a thornless loganberry, now described in a brave-new-world-style, as LY654, and it is healthy and trouble-free. I try to keep it weeded, give it a mulch of compost in the spring and pick the fruit in July – some of which goes into the freezer. Then I leave it well alone, except for one sunny afternoon every winter when I prune out the old fruiting canes and tie in the new ones, listen to the birdsong and feel glad to be alive. Plant loganberry plants 1.2 m/4 ft apart, in deeply-dug, fertile soil from November to March (in the spring in the US).

SUNBERRY

THIS IS ANOTHER NEW HYBRID BRED FROM A RASPBERRY AND BLACKBERRY. THE loganberry-like fruit ripen from July onwards. Grow in the same way as a loganberry.

KING'S ACRE BERRY

A RASPBERRY/BLACKBERRY CROSS, THIS WAS INTRODUCED BY MR J. WARD OF Shobdon, Herefordshire, and awarded the RHS Award of Merit in 1911. The shiny, red fruit ripen in July and they are about the size of a juicy wild blackberry. Grow and cook in the same way as a loganberry.

BOYSENBERRY

THE BOYSENBERRY IS A DARK RED-BLACK FRUIT RESEMBLING A CULTIVATED blackberry; the 'Himalaya' blackberry was the female parent, pollinated by an unknown male. The fruit is named after Rudolf Boysen of California who introduced the plant in 1935. The boysenberry has long whippy growths; I grow it on a trellis alongside other cultivated blackberries. Grow and cook in the same way as a blackberry.

YOUNGBERRY

THIS BLACKBERRY-LIKE FRUIT IS THE RESULT OF A CROSS BETWEEN THE Phenomenal berry (which had been introduced by Burbank) and the American dewberry, Mayes. The plant was raised about 1905 by B. M. Young of Morgan City, Louisiana. The fruit of the boysenberry and the youngberry are very similar. Grow and cook in the same way as a blackberry.

DEWBERRY

ONE OF THE NATIVE AMERICAN BLACKBERRIES, *RUBUS FLAGELLARIS,* THIS HAS been used as a parent for several hybrid berries. The dewberry can be grown on wires or a trellis like other blackberries. Or the long whippy canes can be laid along the ground and pegged down as a ground-cover plant.

TAYBERRY

THIS CRIMSON BERRY, WHICH WAS INTRODUCED IN 1977, LOOKS VERY LIKE A loganberry which is not surprising since it has the same genetic parentage: a hexaploid raspberry crossed with a blackberry. However, the tayberry usually crops earlier and some claim the flavour is superior. The virus-free 'Medana' tayberry was raised by the Scottish Crop Research Station at Invergowrie. The perennial plant is not temperamental and will grow well in a wide range of climatic conditions. Grow and cook the tayberry in the same way as the loganberry.

TUMMELBERRY

HAVING DEVELOPED THEIR TAYBERRY, THE SCOTTISH CROP RESEARCH STATION crossed the plant with a sister seedling, and have bred the tummelberry. The plant has a more upright growth and appears to be hardier than either the loganberry or the tayberry. The tummelberry is recommended for gardens in exposed areas. Cultivate and cook like the loganberry.

JAPANESE WINEBERRY
Rubus pheonicolasius

THIS IS A VERY DECORATIVE PLANT. I BOUGHT MINE TEN YEARS AGO BY MISTAKE. The label had fallen off and I thought I was buying a loganberry. When I unwrapped the bundle I discovered the beautiful red stems with crimson spines. The maple-leaf shaped leaves are matt mid-green with a paler reverse and the fruit, which grows in pretty clusters, appears during June, first orange then ripening to cherry red. The Japanese wineberry fruits for at least eight weeks in my garden. The fruit are like small, shiny raspberries with a flavour like a sultana (golden) grape. I use the fruit for decorating tartlets, cream cheese and cakes. Grow the wineberry in the same way as a loganberry. Some people train the plants over an archway – but make sure it has a wide span – because the canes are very prickly. The Japanese wineberry looks particularly attractive grown against a wooden fence or cream-painted wall.

MINT
Mentha spicata

Culinary use: the chopped leaves are added to sauces, stuffings and dressings for fish, white meats and vegetables, in tisanes, sorbets and ice creams.

Cultivation: hardy perennial, pale mauve flowers, height 15-80 cm/6-30 in; many varieties with different aromatic leaves e.g. spearmint, peppermint, eau-de-cologne, pineapple and ginger; grow in moist soil in full or light shade.

PLUM, GREEN GAGE
Prunus domestica

ALL PLUMS ARE UNDER VENUS, AND ARE, LIKE WOMEN, SOME BETTER, SOME worse,' wrote the herbalist, Nicholas Culpeper. Today's dessert and cooking plums are descendants of the European wild plum. Britain has three varieties of native wild plum: the bitter-fruited sloe, *Prunus spinosa*, the black or yellow-fruited bullace, *Prunus institia*, known in France as the *mirabelle*, and the cherry plum or myrobalan, *Prunus cerasifera*.

Plum stones have been found in many archaeological sites from Neolithic times to the Roman occupation. Our earliest plums were damsons; this oval, black fruit develops its rich, winey flavour when cooked. The popular variety 'Merryweather' produces a good crop in my Devon garden, although, on the whole, plums prefer the drier continental climate of Eastern Britain.

Cultivated varieties of plum have been grown in Britain from the sixteenth century. Parkinson named sixty-one. He described the German prune or quetsche, a black-skinned plum grown by the Romans. And the green gage, then known by its Italian name, *verdocchia*. In France, the green gage was called the *Reine-Claude*, after the wife of François I. But when a Roman Catholic priest in Paris sent a *Reine-Claude* sapling to his brother, Sir Thomas Gage, at Hengrave Hall near Bury St Edmunds, the label was lost. The tree with green plums took the name of its owner and became the green gage. And a most delicious fruit it is, particularly when allowed to ripen on the tree.

The best of today's plums date from the last century when this fruit was immensely popular. 'Coe's Golden Drop' is an exquisite plum with a juicy, almost clear flesh and yellow skin. The aptly named 'Warwickshire Drooper', with its cascading branches, produces another golden plum that is superb when cooked. A hundred-year-old 'Czar' plum tree grows in the cider orchard next to our farmhouse. Although usually regarded as a purple-skinned cooking plum, the fully ripe fruit is sweetly flavoured and a fine dessert plum. And the 'Victoria' plum, criticized by some writers, can have a honeyed lusciousness when fully ripe and eaten straight from the tree. It's worth remembering Edward Bunyard's advice: 'No fruit more than the Plum depends on its best flavour for judicious thinning.' Most plums are self-fertile. But it's wise to consult a good catalogue before choosing a variety.

The most important advance in the plum world has been the recent introduction of the dwarfing rootstock, 'Pixy' which has brought the plum back into the domestic garden. The most attractive way to restrict its growth is by using the old method known as 'festooning'. The young branches are curved over and tied to the trunk of the tree. This is repeated in the following year, and then the fountain shape of the tree established, the branches can be pruned to a neat shape. To avoid silver-leaf disease, prune plum trees from April to September.

Plum trees should be planted during the late autumn and winter (or in the spring in the US). They fruit best when grown in cultivated ground rather than in grass – so they are ideal subjects for a kitchen garden. Because plum trees blossom early they are best planted in a warm, sheltered position or against a south-facing wall. Dig a good-sized hole, incorporate plenty of compost and plant the tree at the same depth as in the nursery, shown by the muddy line on the stem. Stake securely.

WINTER SAVORY/SUMMER SAVORY
Satureja montana/Satureja hortensis

Culinary use: Winter savory has a strong peppery flavour and is useful for adding to rich or fatty dishes to make them more digestible. Summer savory has a more delicate flavour and therefore wider application in cooking. Chopped leaves in sauces for meat and vegetables, particularly broad (fava) beans, and in pâtés and casseroles.

Cultivation: Winter savory is a hardy evergreen, pale pink flowers, height 28 cm/15 in; grow in well-drained soil in full sun. Summer Savory is a hardy annual, height 25 cm/10 in, pale lilac flowers; grow in fertile loam in full sun.

RUMBLEDETHUMPS

*This curiously-named Scottish dish is traditionally made with
kale. In the past, kale was such a staple part of the Scottish diet
that the evening meal itself was named after the vegetable, and
200 years ago the Clan Grant were so keen to cultivate their
kitchen gardens that they were known as 'the soft, kail-eating
Grants'.*

450 g/1 lb potatoes, thickly sliced

450 g/1 lb kale or spring cabbage, sliced

white part of 2 leeks or 1 onion, sliced

90 g/3 oz/6 tbsp butter or 150 ml/¼
   pint/²/³ cup double (heavy) cream

salt and freshly milled black pepper

Cook the vegetables separately in a
little water, then drain well. Mash
the potatoes roughly.

Melt the butter in a large heavy
pan or heat the cream. Stir in the
leeks or onion for a few minutes until
heated through. Add the potatoes
and cabbage. Season with salt and
pepper and beat the mixture with
a wooden spoon for 1-2 minutes.
Serves 4

Note: In her classic book, *The Scots
Kitchen* (1929), F. Marian McNeill
says that chives are often added to
Rumbledethumps and that the
finished mixture can be put in a
baking dish, covered with grated
cheese and browned in the oven.

STIR-FRIED SPROUTED VEGETABLES WITH *FRESH*
GINGER AND CASHEW NUTS

225 g/8 oz sprouted vegetables including
   bean sprouts, alfalfa and cress

1 tbsp sunflower oil

1 tsp sesame oil

1 clove garlic, cut into shreds

walnut-size piece of fresh root ginger,
   peeled and cut into shreds

60-90 g/2-3 oz/¹/³-²/³ cup shelled cashew
   nuts (unsalted)

2 spring onions (scallions), chopped

soy sauce

Rinse the sprouted vegetables under
cold running water, then drain well.

Heat the sunflower and sesame
oils in a wok or large frying pan and
stir in the garlic and ginger. Do not
allow them to change colour; simply
remove the pan from the heat if it's
getting too hot – the purpose is to
flavour the oil. Then either remove
the garlic and ginger from the pan or
scrape to one side.

Add the cashew nuts and stir-fry
for 1-2 minutes until just starting to
change colour. Finally add the
sprouted vegetables and spring onions (scallions) and stir-fry for 2-3
minutes or until lightly cooked but
still crisp. Season lightly with soy
sauce, toss well and transfer to a hot
serving dish. *Serves 2-4*

Freshly-dug onions drying on the ground before being stored for winter use.

VEGETABLE PÂTÉ

I devised this dish for a vegetarian friend, but I find that meat-eaters tuck in too.

175 g/6 oz/1 cup dried haricot beans (Great Northern, navy or other white beans)

1 bouquet garni

salt

1 small aubergine (eggplant)

90 g/3 oz/6 tbsp butter

1 onion, chopped

1 stalk celery, chopped

1 clove garlic, chopped

juice of 1 lemon

4 tbsp tahina (sesame seed paste)

soy sauce

Tabasco sauce

1-2 tbsp dry sherry

1 carrot, finely diced

1 red sweet pepper, seeded and finely diced

1 green sweet pepper, seeded and finely diced

few black olives, stoned and chopped

finely chopped herbs, to garnish

Soak the beans in cold water for 4-8 hours. Rinse and cover with fresh water in a saucepan. Cook with the bouquet garni for about 40 minutes or until tender. Add a little salt towards the end of the cooking. Discard the bouquet garni, drain the beans and set aside.

Halve the aubergine (eggplant) lengthways and cook, skin-side up, under a hot grill (broiler) for 10-15 minutes or until the flesh is soft. Set aside to cool.

Melt the butter in a pan and soften the onion, celery and garlic, but do not brown. Set aside to cool.

Scoop out the flesh of the aubergine (eggplant) and purée it with the beans and the onion mixture. Mix in the lemon juice and tahina, and season to taste with soy sauce, Tabasco and sherry. Add salt, if desired.

Cook the carrot in salted boiling water. When almost tender, add the sweet peppers and cook until slightly softened. Drain and stir into the bean purée with the olives.

Spoon the pâté into a bowl, smooth level and sprinkle chopped herbs on top. Chill until needed. Serve with crusty bread. *Serves 6-8*

HERB TISANES

For some people adversely affected by the caffeine in coffee, a herb tisane is a delightful alternative. These herbal teas are soothing and comforting. Any herb can be used but some are outstandingly successful, notably lime (linden) flowers, rosemary, mint, lemon balm, lemon verbena, sage, lavender, hyssop, angelica and chamomile.

When I make a tisane, I simply place a sprig of the fresh herb – rosemary is my favourite – in a cup and pour on freshly boiled water. Allow the herb to infuse for 3-4 minutes, then remove and drink the tisane.

To make a tisane for several people simply place the herb – one sprig per person – in a clean china or glass teapot and pour on the boiling water. Leave to infuse for several minutes, then serve.

LESCO WITH EGGS

As a sauce for noodles, pasta and ham, Hungarian lecso is superb. This sauce uses summer's red and green sweet peppers, tomatoes and onions. Any surplus can be bottled and preserved for winter use.

1 tbsp sunflower oil

2 slices smoked streaky (Canadian) bacon, diced

1 large onion, chopped

2 tsp sweet paprika

1 tsp hot paprika

225 g/8 oz/sweet tomatoes, peeled and sliced

3 large green sweet peppers, seeded and sliced

1 large red sweet pepper, seeded and sliced

salt and freshly milled black pepper

4 (or more) eggs

Heat the oil and cook the bacon until the fat runs. Add the onion and cook until golden and translucent.

Stir in the two kinds of paprika, then the tomatoes, sweet peppers and salt to season. Cook gently, uncovered, for 30-40 minutes or until thick like chutney.

Spoon the sauce into a shallow oven dish and make four depressions with the back of a spoon. Break an egg into each and season with salt and pepper.

Cover the dish with buttered paper or foil. Bake in an oven preheated to 190°C/375°F/Gas Mark 5 for 5-6 minutes or until the eggs are set. Serve straight away, with crusty bread. *Serves 4*

PEACH AND HAZELNUT MERINGUE

This dessert cake of crisp hazelnut meringue, soured cream and sliced fruit can be made equally well with nectarines or other summer fruits.

HAZELNUT MERINGUE BASE:

3 egg whites

175 g/6 oz/3/4 cup caster (superfine) sugar

90 g/3 oz/1 cup unblanched hazelnuts, finely ground

FILLING:

4-6 ripe peaches

1 tbsp icing (confectioners') sugar

1 tbsp peach brandy

1 egg white

150 ml/1/4 pint/2/3 cup soured cream

1 tsp caster (superfine) sugar

1/4 tsp ground cinnamon

To make the meringue base, whisk the egg whites until stiff. Gently whisk in half the sugar. Mix the remaining sugar with the ground hazelnuts and fold into the meringue mixture.

Spread two-thirds of the mixture in an even layer inside an 18-20 cm/ 7-8 in circle drawn on a sheet of

Kentish cob nuts, some with their brown papery husks, carefully dried for winter eating.

Four varieties of Autumn pumpkin are stored in a cool place until needed.

non-stick baking paper (parchment) on a baking sheet. Use the rest of the mixture to make twenty-four small blobs on a separate sheet of baking paper.

Bake the meringue in an oven preheated to 100°C/200°F/Gas Mark ¼, allowing 1 hour for the smaller meringues and 2 hours for the larger round. Cool on the baking sheets, then carefully remove the meringue round to a flat serving dish.

Cover the peaches with boiling water for 1 minute, then lift out and peel. Slice the peaches into a dish and discard the stones. Mix the icing (confectioners') sugar with the peach brandy and spoon over the peaches.

Whisk the egg white until stiff, then gently fold in the soured cream mixed with the caster (superfine) sugar and cinnamon. Spoon the cream over the meringue base and arrange the sliced peaches in circles on top.

Place the small meringues around the edge of the cream. Leave the meringue in a cool place for up to 1 hour to soften slightly before serving. *Serves 6-8*

HALLOWE'EN PUMPKIN PIE

175 g/6 oz weight shortcrust pastry (basic pie pastry made with 1 cup flour and ⅓ cup fat)

60 g/2 oz/4 tbs butter

700 g/1½ lb pumpkin, peeled, seeded and diced

100 g/3½ oz/½ cup vanilla-flavoured sugar (see below)

3 eggs, beaten

150 ml/¼ pint/⅔ cup single (light) cream

½ tsp ground cinnamon

¼ tsp ground cloves

¼ tsp freshly grated nutmeg

Roll out the pastry to line a 20 cm/8 in pie dish or flan tin (tart pan) 2.5 cm/1 in deep. Trim and crimp the edges, and chill while you prepare the filling.

Melt the butter in a large pan and add the pumpkin. Cover with a lid and cook over moderate heat, shaking the pan now and again, for 20-30 minutes or until the pumpkin is cooked and can be mashed with a fork. Remove the lid towards the end of the cooking to allow water to evaporate from the pan.

Purée the contents of the pan in a food processor or press through a sieve. Mix in the sugar, eggs, cream and spices. Pour the mixture into the pastry case.

Bake in an oven preheated to 200°C/400°F/Gas Mark 4 for 40 minutes or until the filling is set. Cool, and serve cut in wedges. *Serves 6-8*

Note: for vanilla-flavoured sugar see page 55.

BRUSSELS SPROUT, AUBERGINE *and* EGGPLANT, LEEK, CARROT, CRESS, STRAWBERRY, PEACH *and* NECTARINE, KIWI FRUIT, SWEET CICELY, MULBERRY, LOVAGE, LAVENDER, SORREL, FRENCH TARRAGON

AN HISTORIC WALLED KITCHEN GARDEN ON THE SOUTH DOWNS IN SUSSEX

GRAVETYE MANOR

THE AIM WAS, AS IT ALWAYS SHOULD BE, TO GET AS NEAR THE VISIBLE beauty of things, as it is possible for the artist to go.' So wrote William Robinson, the nineteenth-century gardener, in his book, *The Garden Beautiful*. By then he had spent more than twenty years building his magnificent garden at Gravetye Manor at Sharpethorne, East Grinstead.

William Robinson was forty-seven years of age, and a successful garden writer and publisher with an unrivalled experience of practical gardening, when, in 1885, he achieved his dream. In July he noticed an advertisement in *The Times* for 'a grand old-fashioned

A long flag-stoned path is bordered by the fish ponds at the foot of the woodland garden, and a wide bed of mixed herbaceous plants in the formal garden at Gravetye Manor.

and picturesque Elizabethan mansion' with an estate of 144 hectares/360 acres. On 24 August 1885, he took possession of Gravetye Manor and wrote to his friend Henry de Vilmorin, 'At last, a garden of my own . . .!'

On entering the kitchen garden at Gravetye Manor one is immediately impressed. You have to turn your head both left and right to be able to see the full extent of this handsome garden. The design is remarkable not only for its break with tradition, but moreover, it was 'a major engineering feat', according to garden writer, Graham Stuart Thomas, 'being laid on sloping ground facing south'.

'Commenced to build in early Summer a stone wall round new kitchen garden, chosen after much and long thought as to site', wrote William Robinson in his journal for 1898. 'For various reasons chose the open hill above the house (where the spring that supplies House arises) as the best, and indeed only good, site near the house for the kitchen garden. Got out own stone at the "Beeches" on the estate, said to be the hardest and best of the stone in the district, wall built by men who got out the stone. I prefer stone to brick both for its colour, endurance and the fewer interstices for harbouring insects. An oval plan was followed to suit the ground: as the usual rectangular plan would have led us into awkward angles and levels.'

On the hot July morning that I arrived at Gravetye Manor, the assistant head gardener, Lindsay Davison, was picking soft fruit. Punnets (baskets) of red and white alpine strawberries sat in a box waiting to be carried down to the kitchen. Across the path two assistants picked raspberries – the first of the season's yellow-berried fruit, which was highly popular in the time of William Robinson, and baskets of some of the more familiar red raspberries were already full.

To begin with, William Robinson grew a wide range of vegetables in his oval garden. His knowledge of vegetable-growing was extensive – in the same year he acquired Gravetye, his preface to the first English edition of *The Vegetable Garden* appeared, a book that was to become the Victorian kitchen gardener's bible.

But after a few years he decided to plant the oval garden solely with fruit and grow his vegetables on lower ground nearer the house. Few of his fruit trees still survive although a huge mulberry tree, planted outside the wall, sprawls over it into the garden to provide shade for a stone seat and plaque with the initials WR. An entry in his journal reads, 'Foundation-stone laid July 28, 1898; not completed until middle of July, 1900.' Good gardens take time.

Just two wide paths give the gardener access to the whole garden. One runs from the oak entrance gates straight across the garden to a narrow gateway on to the chicken run. The other follows the curve of the wall and 6 m/20 ft from it. Garden taps (faucets) are well placed, and the spring which William Robinson used for the house is also utilized to provide the running water for the watercress bed that has been constructed in the lowest, shadiest part of the garden.

Today Gravetye's fruit includes 250 alpine strawberry plants of the variety 'Alexandria', which Lindsay Davison says crop over a long season. 'We pick twelve to fifteen of the ¼ lb punnets (strawberry baskets) everyday in July. We keep the plants for 2-3 years then replant with new

stock.' Nearby are new beds of one-year-old 'Elsanta' strawberries which should start to fruit well next year.

The long curved wall, which was built for fruit, is gradually being reclothed with new trees. Five dessert pears, three plums and grape vines are spreading themselves over its grey and yellow stone. Five kiwi fruit vines, which produced 300 fruits last year, blackberries, white currants and the beautiful red-stemmed Japanese wineberry, with its shiny raspberry-like fruit, make a tracery of their branches against the wall.

Ever since his visit to the horticultural stands at the great French Exhibition of 1867, William Robinson had been enthusiastic about fruit trees. From Paris, he told the readers of his *Gardener's Chronicle*, 'I am in love with several peach trees I have seen here.' He had visited M. Lepère, the grower of the famous Napolean peach whose branches were pruned and shaped to form the Emperor's name. So it is no surprise that, in the autumn of 1898, the master of Gravetye, impatient for the garden wall to be built, planted some peach trees against the only section yet finished.

Sadly, the huge peach tree that grew in one of the glasshouses at Gravetye died from lack of water before the present owner Peter Herbert arrived in 1957, twenty-two years after the death of William Robinson.

Peter Herbert has been responsible for the restoration of Gravetye Manor's historic garden. The task has been a great labour of love and every keen gardener is indebted to him. 'The kitchen garden was the last neglected area to be tackled,' says Peter Herbert. 'Today, that garden again produces fruit, flowers and vegetables for the House as it did in Robinson's time.'

Every morning at 11 o'clock the freshly-picked produce from the garden is wheeled down a curved, paved path to the kitchen. Every day, Mark Raffan, the chef at Gravetye Manor, insists on vegetables and fruit that are in peak condition – this morning a box of fifty slim leeks, a basket of yellow courgettes (summer squash) and golden custard-apple squashes, fistsful of sorrel and punnets of strawberries plus a mountain of tiny freshly-dug potatoes will be needed for lunch. Fresh supplies of different produce will arrive from the garden just before dinner.

Once a month Helen Greenwood, Peter Herbert, Lindsay Davison and Mark Raffan tour the garden and discuss the virtues – or lack of them – of the garden crops. Is a cutting lettuce (loose-leaf lettuce) like 'Salad Bowl' ('oak-leaf') more popular with Mark than a cabbage lettuce like 'Continuity'? Lindsay needs to know before she orders the seed for next year. Does the oval-leaved 'Radicchio Rossa di Treviso' have a finer flavour than the round-leaved 'Radicchio Rossa di Verona', and which has brighter crimson leaves? Now that the autumn-fruiting raspberries are starting to crop, the kitchen is over-run with the fruit. Mark is making a good supply of sorbets, ice-creams and jam, but it looks as there still might be a surplus, even given the voracious needs of his huge jars of winter Rumtopf. At what size should the French beans be picked? Is the succession of broad beans assured? And why are the courgettes (zucchini) covered in ants? When should the chicken house be replaced?

These matters and more are weighed upon as the quartet tour the garden and pick and taste, cut and sample some of the best garden produce in the world. This is where the decisions about what is grown and how it is prepared for the table are taken. And it is extremely important. Culinary gardening is not just small-scale farming; it is far more responsive to the needs and interests of both the cook and the gardener. Food is grown in the garden here because it tastes wonderful, not for how well it looks wrapped in plastic on a supermarket shelf. When you have the opportunity to grow your own food, it seems almost perverse not to do it well. Gravetye Manor expertly shows just how superbly kitchen gardening can be done.

It was not until 1881, at the Bath and West Show, that the first

public prize for asparagus was awarded. William Robinson had urged its foundation partly to demonstrate the high standard of English-grown asparagus to the sceptical French. There is just one short row of asparagus at Gravetye Manor. Could it be that William Robinson, although a connoisseur of asparagus – he even wrote a book about it – ran into an insuperable problem? Because, as Graham Stuart Thomas says, Robinson had 'like all of us, to cope with his climate – cool and exposed – and a soil rather heavy and cold'.

Every gardener with heavy, cold ground to till knows the virtues of a glasshouse. William Robinson built his in a warm cleft in the hillside, and it is here that Lindsay Davison cultivates some of the less hardy fruits. She grows the cape gooseberry, *Physalis edulis*, standing the pots on a bed of pea gravel to keep their compost moist and to encourage the humid atmosphere that this South American plant enjoys. In an attempt to produce very early crops of strawberries, she potted up some of the runners from the garden in September and encouraged their fruit in the heat of the glasshouse. She does not consider the experiment a success due to the small amount of fruit produced. So she intends to try again with the new Californian day-neutral strawberries which should produce fruit almost all year round.

New horticultural ideas have always found a home at Gravetye. William Robinson introduced the glass bell cloche that he had discovered at the 1867 Paris Exhibition and which has the advantage of being lighter and easier to move than the leaded lantern light already in use. And he brought to England French secateurs, pruning shears that most of us find

utterly essential in the garden, particularly in the fruit garden. As every French gardener tells you, fruit follows the knife, and even his English equivalent admits that to grow a fruit tree all a man needs is a little knowledge and sharp pruning shears.

Big, generous patches of herbs greet you at the entrance to the oval garden. Tall celery-leaved lovage towers over aniseed-flavoured sweet cicely, its dark brown seed-pods decorative above its flat feathery leaves. Chives are grown in rows, and because this herb is in constant use in the kitchen, the continual clipping of its leaves stimulates plenty of young tender growth with a delicate flavour that is particularly suitable for sauces. Next to the chives grows the prettiest sorrel, buckler-leaved sorrel, with its shield-shaped wavy-edged leaves. Young sorrel leaves are added to green salads and older leaves are cooked to make a sauce to accompany the trout from the lakes on the estate if the guest is sufficiently skilled to catch a brace.

Many more herbs grow in the flower gardens near the house. Here they are cared for by the head gardener, Helen Greenwood. Glaucous-blue rue grows in a low stone pot in the charming paved fountain garden on the south side of the house. In the west garden, William Robinson's flagstone paths define a series of beautifully planted beds, each a canvas of subtle colour and form: a variegated marjoram spreads itself at the base of the canary-yellow feverfew and the silver-grey curry plant; French tarragon grows in a stone urn that can be moved into the shelter of the porch during harsh weather. The star-shaped flowers of borage that fade prettily from blue to pink are contrasted with a lovely mallow with satin wedding-dress flowers of palest pink and the faded lilac blooms of Bowles's mint, and in the background of this group a clump of bronze fennel gives a Mediterranean fragrance to a warm sheltered corner of the garden.

A most spectacular sight in midsummer is the beautiful lavender walk at Gravetye Manor, its waves of purple blooms matched on the other side of the path by a cascade of blue-flowered catmint, *Nepeta gigantea*. The path runs from the azalea bank in the woodland garden to the flight of steps that lead down to the alpine meadow. From early morning until sunset, this perfumed path is a haven for butterflies and bees and any garden visitor that enjoys the heady scents.

One cannot fail to be aware that everywhere in this magical Sussex garden there is a feeling of repose and a vision of beauty. In 1899, Gertrude Jekyll, a good friend of William Robinson and frequent visitor to Gravetye Manor, wrote, 'For I hold that the best purpose of a garden is to give delight and to give refreshment of mind, to soothe, to refine, and to lift-up the heart in a spirit of praise and thankfulness.' Amen.

FRESHWATER PERCH STUFFED WITH CRAB AND FENNEL WITH A TOMATO AND HERB BUTTER

2 freshwater perch, 225-300 g/8-10 oz each, filleted and skinned

6 good leaves of spinach for wrapping the fish

2 flowering courgettes (zucchini), to garnish

FARCE (STUFFING):

225 g/8 oz fresh boneless salmon, minced (ground)

1 egg white

sea salt and freshly milled pepper

600 ml/1 pint/2½ cups whipping cream

1 small bulb Florence fennel, diced

115 g/4 oz button mushrooms, diced

½ glass of dry white wine

½ glass of fish stock

the white meat of 1 small crab, picked over to remove all shell and cartilage

SAUCE:

6 ripe tomatoes, roughly chopped

1 clove garlic, chopped

2 shallots, chopped

60 g/2 oz/4 tbsp butter, softened

1 tbsp finely chopped parsley

Make the farce or stuffing for the fish first. In a food processor, mix the salmon with the egg white and some salt until finely puréed. Pass the mixture through a sieve into a bowl. Surround the bowl with iced water and gradually beat in the cream. Leave in a cold place.

Put the fennel and mushrooms in a pan with the white wine and fish stock. Cook until al dente, then drain and cool. Mix the vegetables into the salmon mixture with the crabmeat. Adjust the seasoning.

Wash the spinach leaves and blanch in boiling water for 5-10 seconds, just to wilt them. Remove and plunge straight into cold water, then drain well on a clean cloth.

Take two fillets of perch. Spread a good layer of salmon farce on one fillet and place the other on top. Carefully wrap the fillets in half the spinach leaves and place on buttered paper. Repeat with the other fish reserving a little farce to fill the courgette (zucchini) flowers. Chill the fish in the refrigerator until needed.

To prepare the sauce, place the tomatoes, garlic and shallots in a food processor and whizz to a purée. Pass the mixture through a fine sieve into a small pan. Blend the butter with the parsley and chill until needed.

To cook and finish the dish, steam the fish for 6-10 minutes or until the fish is cooked and the farce is set. Slice the courgettes (zucchini) thinly lengthways, leaving the flowering end intact. Fill the flowers with the reserved farce and steam for 2 minutes.

Bring the tomato mixture to the boil, then whisk in the parsley butter. Season the sauce and pour some across each plate. Use a very sharp knife to carefully slice the fish, and arrange in a fan on the plates. Garnish with the stuffed courgette (zucchini) flower, fanning out the sliced courgette. Serve straight away.
Serves 2

SALAD OF FOIE GRAS, BEETROOT (BEET) AND GREEN LENTILS GARNISHED WITH *CRISP* CELERIAC CHIPS

Because this salad is served warm, try to assemble it quickly so that the delicious contrast of crisp and soft, warm and chilled ingredients is not lost.

115 g/4 oz/½ cup green lentils, soaked overnight

300 ml/½ pint/1¼ cups chicken stock

1 onion, finely chopped

1 carrot, finely diced

sea salt and freshly milled black pepper

selection of garden salad leaves: 'Oak Leaf', Lamb's lettuce (corn salad), 'Lollo Rosso' and 'Little Gem' lettuce, endive frisée (curly endive)

2 beetroot (beet), cooked and skinned

115 g/4 oz celeriac, cut into very fine 'chips' (French fries)

oil for deep-frying

115 g/4 oz fresh foie gras

DRESSING:

150 ml/¼ pint/⅔ cup grapeseed or other mild oil

30 g/1 oz star anise

2 tsp Dijon mustard

2 tbsp raspberry vinegar

To make the dressing, heat the oil with the star anise to 90°C/180°F, then set aside and allow to cool. Whisk the mustard and vinegar together. Season with salt and pepper, and gradually whisk in the flavoured oil. Taste – the dressing must not be too oily. If it is, add a little more raspberry vinegar.

Drain the soaked lentils and rinse in fresh cold water. Bring the stock to the boil and add the lentils, onion and carrot. Season. Simmer for about 5 minutes, then remove from heat and leave to cool. Drain and mix with some of the dressing. Leave in a warm place.

Wash the salad leaves well, shake off excess water and place in a bowl. Keep in the refrigerator until needed. Just before serving, toss lightly with some of the dressing.

Slice the beetroot thinly, pour on a little of the dressing and leave in a warm place to macerate.

Deep-fry the celeriac 'chips' until crisp. Drain on paper towels, season and keep warm.

Cut the foie gras into four slices and season with salt and pepper. Heat a heavy-based frying pan until very hot and cook the foie gras for about 30 seconds on each side. Keep in a warm place.

To assemble, arrange the beetroot in a circle towards the outside of each plate and spoon some lentils into the middle. Place one slice of foie gras on the lentils and cover with salad leaves. Place another slice of foie gras on top and sprinkle a few more leaves over it. Sprinkle celeriac 'chips' around the plate. Serve straight away. *Serves 2*

SPRING LAMB WITH A CONFIT OF BABY VEGETABLES WITH WILD THYME AND HONEY

1 rack of spring lamb, French trimmed, with 6 bones

selection of baby vegetables to include carrots, turnips, new potatoes, courgette (zucchini) and mangetout (snow peas)

2 cloves garlic

4 small shallots

2 small sprigs of rosemary

600 ml/1 pint/2½ cups light brown lamb stock

115 g/4 oz/1 stick butter

sea salt and freshly milled pepper

½ glass of dry white wine

2 tsp fresh honeycomb honey

1 sprig of freshly-picked wild thyme

350 g/12 oz fresh garden spinach

To prepare the *confit* of vegetables, wash and trim all the vegetables and place in a baking pan or cast-iron casserole with the peeled garlic, shallots and rosemary. Add a little of the lamb stock and about half of the butter. Season lightly, then cover the pan and cook in an oven preheated to 180°C/350°F/Gas Mark 4 for about 45 minutes. Take care not to shake the pan about or the vegetables will not keep their shape.

Roast the rack of lamb in an oven preheated to 200°C/400°F/Gas Mark 6 for about 20 minutes. Remove from the oven and allow to rest in a warm place for 10 minutes. Deglaze the roasting pan with the wine, then add the remaining lamb stock and boil to reduce by half. When ready to serve, add the honey and wild thyme with half of the remaining butter.

Wash and drain the spinach and cook with the rest of the butter. Season well and keep hot.

To finish the dish, place half the spinach in the centre of each plate and make a well in it in which to spoon the *confit* of vegetables, including the cloves of garlic, the shallots and rosemary. Slice the lamb into six cutlets and arrange them around the *confit*. Spoon the sauce around the meat. Serve straight away. *Serves 2*

TIMBALE OF *SUMMER* FRUITS IN AN ALMOND BASKET WITH *LIME* CREAM

ALMOND BASKETS:

60 g/2 oz/4 tbsp unsalted butter

60 g/2 oz/¼ cup caster (US granulated) sugar

60 g/2 oz/3 tbsp glucose (light corn syrup)

60 g/2 oz/6 tbsp plain (all-purpose) flour

60 g/2 oz/½ cup blanched almonds, chopped

JELLY:

60-90 g/2-3 oz/¼-½ cup sugar

60-90 ml/2-3 fl oz cold water

15 g/½ oz/2 envelopes powdered unflavoured gelatine

300 ml/½ pint/1¼ cups black currant juice

115 g/4 oz/¾ cup strawberries

115 g/4 oz/1 cup raspberries

115 g/4 oz/1 cup black currants

115 g/4 oz/1 cup red currants

115 g/4 oz/¾ cup blueberries

LIME CREAM:

2 fresh limes

300 ml/½ pint/1¼ cups whipping cream

a little icing (confectioners') sugar

DECORATION:

4-8 small sprigs of red currants

icing (confectioners') sugar

To prepare the almond baskets, melt the butter with the sugar and glucose, then remove from the heat and whisk in the flour followed by the almonds. Chill the mixture for at least 1 hour. It will set hard.

Roll the mixture into four equal balls. Flatten and press each on to a non-stick baking sheet. Bake in an oven preheated to 170°C/325°F/Gas Mark 3 for about 8 minutes or until the biscuits (cookies) are golden brown. Remove from the oven and have ready four small ramekins. Use a palette knife (narrow spatula) to ease the biscuits (cookies) from the baking sheet and gently press the centre of each one into a ramekin, leaving the edges flaring out to form the basket shape. Leave to cool and set, then gently remove and keep in a dry place or a lidded box until needed.

For the jelly, dissolve the sugar in all the water, bring to the boil and simmer for 4 minutes, then remove from the heat and cool slightly. Soften the gelatine in the remaining water and dissolve over low heat. Mix the sugar syrup with the black currant juice and add the gelatine in a fine trickle, stirring all the time. Chill until almost set. Prepare the fruit by removing the stalks and sprigs and, if necessary, wash and drain on paper towels. Add to the jelly and ladle into four small moulds. Chill until set.

To make the lime cream, wash and dry the limes and grate their zest into the cream. Sweeten to taste with icing (confectioners') sugar.

To finish the dish, place an almond basket in the middle of each small plate. Wrap a hot damp cloth around the outside of the moulds and unmould each jelly upside-down into the centre of each basket. Spoon some lime cream around the basket and garnish with red currants. Put a little icing (confectioners') sugar into a fine sieve and tap gently to dust the whole dish. Serve straight away. *Serves 4*

TRADITIONAL SUMMER PUDDING WITH JERSEY CREAM

350-450 g/12-16 oz/1½-2 pints mixed summer fruits: raspberries, strawberries, blueberries, black currants, red currants, loganberries, tayberries, dessert gooseberries, etc

60-90 g/2-3 oz/¼-½ cup sugar

7 g/¼ oz/1 envelope powdered unflavoured gelatine

1 tbsp cold water

1 loaf of white bread

150 ml/¼ pint/⅔ cup Jersey or other very rich, heavy cream

few extra fruits, to decorate

Prepare the fruits by removing all the stalks, gently wash and drain well.

Place the fruit in a pan with the sugar over a low heat to dissolve the sugar and draw some of the juice from the fruit, but do not let the mixture boil or the fresh flavour will be lost. And don't stir the mixture – the idea is to keep the fruit as whole as possible. Remove from the heat.

Soften the gelatine in the cold water, then dissolve over low heat and add to the fruit.

Cut the crusts from the loaf and cut the bread into 5 mm/¼ in thick slices. Line the sides and bottom of four small moulds or individual pudding basins with the bread. Spoon in the fruit and juice, pressing it well down so that the bread soaks up all the juice. Cover the fruit with a slice of bread and stand the moulds on a flat plate or baking sheet. Place a baking sheet on top of the moulds with a weight on top and leave the puddings in a cold place or the refrigerator for at least 24 hours.

When ready to serve, unmould each pudding on to a small plate. Pour Jersey cream around it and garnish with a few extra summer fruits. Serve straight away. *Serves 4*

BRUSSELS SPROUT
Brassica oleracea Gemmifera group

IT'S CURIOUS THAT ALTHOUGH BRUSSELS SPROUTS HAVE BEEN GROWN IN Belgium since the thirteenth century, they took 500 years to cross the channel to Britain. But since then these miniature cabbages have enjoyed enormous success and are now one of Britain's most popular winter vegetables.

The smallest Brussels sprouts have the best flavour, so one of the advantages of growing your own is being able to pick the vegetable when no larger than a thimble. Although highly delicious, I can do without a glut of this vegetable. So when I grow it I sow just a small amount of seed or I buy a few plants. The varieties 'Peer Gynt' F1 and 'Widgeon' F1 produce uniform dense sprouts on dwarf plants that are useful in windy areas. The red-leaved Brussels sprout, 'Rubine', is interesting but not as productive as green-leaved varieties.

Sow seed in a shallow drill (line) during early spring. Transplant the seedlings during early summer to 37.5 cm/15 in apart. Make sure the soil is well-packed around the stem to prevent wind from loosening the roots and pinch out the top of the plant when the sprouts have formed. The leaves on the top of the plant make an excellent green vegetable.

Brussels sprouts are best lightly cooked in salted boiling water — yellowing, over-cooked Brussels sprouts are a travesty — and served straight away in a simple style such as tossed in butter with freshly grated Parmesan cheese or diced ham. For serving at Christmas, the traditional combination of Brussels sprouts with whole roasted chestnuts has a lot to be said for it. Blanched toasted hazelnuts and almonds also go well with Brussels sprouts — the sweetness of the nuts nicely off-sets the cabbage flavour.

AUBERGINE (EGGPLANT)
Solanum melongena

'BEAUTIFUL TO LOOK AT, THEY ARE MORE OR LESS THE SIZE OF APPLES, BUT OVAL, with a shiny skin like a gourd. Some are all white, some white mottled with pink, and some violet. A little bush no more than a yard high will produce fifteen to twenty aubergines.' Thus Castelvetro tells us about aubergines (eggplants).

Four centuries later, this pregnant-looking fruit still holds a fascination for us. 'Those mad, bad, despised, noxious apples,' wrote Elizabeth David. Nothing else in the garden or the kitchen has the dark, brooding appearance of a purple aubergine. In Spain I've seen small violet and striped aubergines, and my mother grows the oval white aubergines — the only aubergines that could qualify for their alternative name, the eggplant. But the dark-skinned aubergine seems the most popular for British gardeners.

The aubergine is a perennial plant grown as a half-hardy annual. Seed is sown under glass or on a windowsill in spring, and the seedlings are pricked out and transplanted to well-drained, fertile soil when all danger of frost has passed. Aubergines do especially well under glass or in a polytunnel (a plastic tunnel supported by hoops). They can be grown in pots or gro-bags. Pinch out the top of the plant when 25 cm/10 in high. When five to six fruits have set, remove the remaining flowers and

feed with liquid organic fertilizer every seven to ten days. Cut the aubergines when they are the size you like and the skins are shiny. The new F1 varieties, 'Rima' and 'Dusky', crop early and well. The varieties 'Violetta Lunga' and 'Violetta di Firenze' are also good.

There is a splendid repertoire of Middle Eastern recipes for this exotic vegetable, from the famous Iman Bayildi of Persia to the stuffed, fried and braised dishes of Provence and Spain. In Israel I have seen small, purple aubergines pickled in brine with beetroot (beets) so that their flesh becomes as purple as the skin. Recent varieties of aubergines taste less bitter. But, if in doubt, sprinkle the flesh of an aubergine with salt, leave for thirty minutes then rinse in cold water before cooking. My favourite way of cooking this vegetable is halved or sliced and char-grilled or roasted in a hot oven until browned and caramelized on the outside. Serve hot with a bowl of cool, Greek-style yoghurt mixed with zest (rind) of lemon and finely chopped mint — it's superb.

LEEK
Allium porrum

IF YOU ARE IN LONDON DURING THE FIRST WEEK OF OCTOBER, WITH AN HOUR OR so to kill, make your way to Vincent Square to see the Royal Horticultural Society's autumn vegetable show. You are bound to enjoy it. Here you'll find amazing, impressive and sometimes ludicrous specimens of the vegetable kingdom. There are fruits and nuts too. But it is the vegetables that are rivetting — huge statuesque displays of celery and carrots and cauliflowers. But most incredible of all are the Ionic columns of leeks — grown in drain-pipes and cultivated with total dedication by skilled gardeners, who are happy to tell you how they do it. In my garden, I prefer pencil-slim leeks with a delicate flavour.

This ancient vegetable was adopted by the Welsh as their emblem after their victory over the Anglo-Saxons in the sixth century. One thousand years later, Thomas Tusser wrote, 'Now leeks are in season, for pottage ful good.' For the leek is a superb pot herb. Its flavour is highly pervasive and it fills the kitchen (and your wool sweater, unfortunately) with its comforting aroma. The vegetable is not only delicious served on its own, braised in butter or cold with a walnut oil vinaigrette, but its contribution to the flavour of a sauce or stock is invaluable.

Leeks are easy to grow and splendidly hardy because many of the best varieties were bred in Scotland. One of the joys of growing your own leeks is that you can produce a year-round crop of the vegetable, enabling you to prepare a bowl of classic chilled vichysoisse soup in midsummer when leeks are often not available in shops.

In April, sow leek seed as thinly as possible in a box or large pan of seed compost — or, in warm districts, sow in a seed bed outdoors. Plant out 10 cm/4 in apart during May or June, watering in the roots. Some gardeners like to trim the roots and the top growth when they transplant the seedlings, but I find this is only necessary when the seedlings are quite big. Keep the plants weed-free and when large enough for the kitchen, use every other leek to give the others more room. Remember, though, that slim leeks can be planted close together. Leeks like to grow in full sun in ground manured the previous season. The varieties 'Musselburgh', 'St Victor' and 'Kajak' are long-standing and slow to bolt — they often still make excellent leeks a year after sowing. I usually leave some plants to develop their beautiful round heads of lilac flowers, and any seedling leeks that appear I plant out to provide a succession.

Right: Bright green watercress
grows quickly in the running
spring water of the kitchen garden.

CARROT
Daucus carota subsp. *sativus*

I AM PUZZLED BY THE CARROTS IN MY local supermarket. they are a lurid orange colour and, perhaps, because they have been scrubbed, they are wet. Of course, a wet carrot is a heavier carrot, and that age-old deceit is easier to understand than their colour which, I assume, has been developed by some Dutch grower to lure us into buying this humble vegetable. To my mind, such a development has been in totally the wrong direction. The best carrot in the world is young, small and straight out of the ground. It is not grown on a bed of rockwool and fed a non-stop supply of fertilized water. It would strike our grandfathers as extraordinary that a tiny, sweet-tasting garden-fresh carrot, with its plume of feathery leaves, has become a luxurious food available to remarkably few people.

The carrot has been cultivated in Europe for thousands of years. Pliny wrote of the vegetable and Bartholomy, Platinate of Cremona, in his *Grand Cuisinier*, recommends baking carrots moistened with must (the juice pressed from grapes before it is fermented as new wine) and seasoned with spices in the embers of a fire.

Carrots were introduced into Britain during the reign of Queen Elizabeth I, and its sweet flavour made the vegetable an instant success. The pretty green leaves were worn like flowers, on ladies' hats or pinned to a dress with a brooch. The custom continued until Victorian times, when the garden lad on a large estate often tucked a sprig of carrot leaf into his buttonhole to bring him good luck on his evening jaunt.

I was brought up to eat plenty of raw carrots and still enjoy them equally as much as the cooked vegetable. The flavour of a carrot depends on its age, how it is cooked and the temperature at which it is eaten. An appetizing salad of steamed finger carrots dressed with hazelnut oil and tossed with toasted hazelnuts and chopped mint tastes different when served hot, warm or cold. It is odd that the naturally sweet flavour of carrots has led cooks to gild the lily and add even more sugar. So we have carrot cake, a glazed carrot tart and even a carrot jam – known as angel's hair. A pre-Raphaelite angel, perhaps.

But none of of these dishes can compare with a bowl of baby carrots, each with a short handle of stalk, served hot and gleaming with melted butter. Cooked carrots also combine well with citrus flavours like orange and lemon, and spices like coriander and cinnamon. Carrot juice makes a delicious and thirst-quenching drink. In many parts of the middle east, certainly in Tel Aviv, I've seen street vendors selling freshly pressed carrot juice. If you have a juicing attachment to your electric mixer, it is worth making carrot juice at home.

Wherever I've gardened I've been lucky enough to be able to grow this vegetable which the Gauls made their national plant. Small carrots have fresh young leaves which also can be eaten. Tiny carrot leaves can be added to a green salad or used to garnish a dish of vegetables. Slightly larger but still tender carrot leaves make a pretty green purée when cooked and liquidized with cream (creme fraiche) or fromage frais. A simple, yet effective idea is to decorate a bowl of buttery carrot soup with a spoonful of the green carrot-top purée by trailing it across the surface. 'The carrot at its best should be as tender as a Comice pear and no larger than ones' smallest finger,' wrote Edward Bunyard in *The Epicure's Companion*.

Carrots come in all shapes and sizes and most seed catalogues give plenty of choice. For the best flavour I recommend quick-maturing carrots, of the stump- or round-rooted, Nantes or Chantenay type. I also like white carrots whose seed is usually easier to find in France or Italy.

Sow seed thinly in early spring in well-tilled ground manured during the previous season. Use the thinnings in a dish of baby vegetables or add them to the stockpot. Do not allow the ground to get too dry, and plant onions, shallots or French marigolds nearby to discourage carrot-fly. Then, provided that you sow successive crops, you should be able to indulge in one of life's greatest treats – honey-sweet home-grown carrots – nearly every week of the year.

CRESS:

GARDEN CRESS
Lepidium sativum

GREEK CRESS
Lepidium sativum var.,

AMERICAN OR LAND CRESS
Barbarea verna (Synonym *B. praecox*),

WATERCRESS
Nasturtium officinale

I SUPPOSE GARDEN CRESS IS USUALLY THE FIRST SEED WE GROW – AS CHILDREN – mixed with mustard seed, on wet blotting paper. If we were clever and patient, we sowed the cress seed three days ahead of the mustard so that they matured at the same time. And we could snip off their stalks with scissors leaving the seed husks – that, to me, looked suspiciously like tiny snails – embedded in the fine white roots.

Garden cress originated in western Asia and now grows wild in many parts of the northern hemisphere. Small plastic boxes of what are called mustard-and-cress are still a steady seller in British greengrocers, although these are more likely to be rape sprouts. The fresh-tasting mixture is added to egg sandwiches and is used as a garnish for those dismal bridge rolls (soft semi-sweet bread rolls) at parties. Recently though, and despite these fates, the seed of the cress has enjoyed a renewed interest as a sprouting vegetable. Growing sprouted vegetables is a very simple form of windowsill gardening and an ideal way of providing a fresh vegetable during the deepest days of winter when the kitchen garden itself may be hidden under a layer of snow or frost.

Place two tablespoons of garden cress seed in a jar or container and cover the top with a piece of fine terylene netting or cloth (cheese cloth). Tie on the cloth firmly with string or an elastic band. Fill the jar with lukewarm water, shake gently and drain off through the netting. Place the jar on a windowsill in a warm room and repeat the seed-washing twice a day until the seeds have sprouted and are big enough to eat. This takes from five to eight days. The sprouted seed tastes very good when added to a green salad or it can be mixed with other sprouts and stir-fried with fresh ginger and garlic. If you want to sprout mustard and seed together, add the mustard seed two to three days after starting the cress.

Other seeds recommended for growing sprouted vegetables include alfalfa, fenugreek, alphatoco beans, mung beans and packets of mixed seed labelled Salad Sprouts.

Garden cress can also be grown outdoors as a cut-and-come-again crop. An improved variety of garden cress is Greek cress. This is an annual salad plant with peppery, bright green leaves. Sow in shallow drills (lines) or broadcast the seed during the spring in well-tilled soil in half-shade. Cut some of the young leaves when large enough to handle and leave the plants to produce a fresh crop of cress.

American or land cress is an easy-to-grow annual salad plant. The round, dark green leaves taste remarkably like watercress, and the plant replaces watercress perfectly well in recipes. Sow seed thinly in open ground during the spring. Or, for a winter crop, sow in cold frame or under cloches during September. Cut off leaves as required and allow the plants to produce a fresh crop.

Watercress is the most difficult of the cresses to grow in the kitchen garden since the plant grows best in shallow, running water. Its dark green, glossy leaves provide a valuable source of iron and a uniquely delicious, bitter-tasting vegetable.

Rather to my surprise, I have found that watercress can be grown quite easily in my Devon garden even though it unfortunately has no stream burbling through it. Watercress seed is available from seedsmen, but I started growing it with some stalks saved from a bunch of cultivated watercress bought from my greengrocer. Place the stalks in cold water and stand the container on a sunny windowsill. Replace the water every day. After seven to ten days fine white roots should have developed on the stalks.

Plant the watercress in a large clay pot of fertile sandy compost and stand the pot in a deep saucer of cold water which you must refill every day so that the water remains sweet. In warm weather the pot can be kept outdoors. At other times during the year, keep the pot under glass, or on a sunny windowsill or porch. Cut off leaves and stalks of watercress as required.

If you have a part of the garden that has wet soil most of the year, then it is worth trying to grow watercress in the ground, provided that you give it a good soaking with a watering can of fresh cold water every day. Pick the leaves as required.

Watercress is exceptionally delicious fresh, on its own, simply dressed with a vinaigrette. But, equally, cooked watercress makes a fine stuffing for fish or the basis of a sauce or a soup. Try adding some leaves of watercress to other green vegetables like leeks or spinach for the spicy, peppery taste that it contributes.

STRAWBERRY
Fragaria

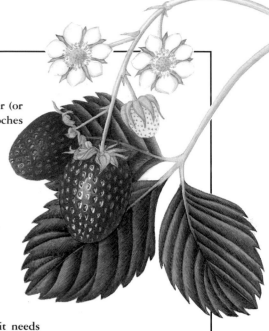

THE STRAWBERRY HAS NEVER BEEN SHORT OF DEVOTEES. 'DOUBT- less God could have made a better berry, but doubtless God never did,' wrote William Butler in the seventeenth century. And doubtless God never needed to, is the response of most of us – man himself was bent on perfecting the fruit. By 1926, over 1362 varieties of strawberry had been developed in North America.

The strawberry is a legendary plant: its name is derived from the Anglo-Saxon 'streabariye' or strayberry, and its leaves and fruit have been a decorative emblem since pre-Christian times. Virgil described 'the ground loving strawberry', and Ovid spoke of 'mountain strawberries'. The strawberries of early mosaics are wild woodland strawberries, *Fragaria vesca*, or fraises des bois, sweet and scented and totally ambrosial. It is worth trying to grow this strawberry in a shady corner from seed that is available in packets from a good seedsman.

The similarly diminutive alpine strawberry, *Fragaria vesca semperflorens*, is rather easier to grow. It will flourish in semi-shade at the foot of other plants and because it does not throw out runners it makes a very good edging plant in a herb garden or mixed border. The bright red fruit, which are larger than woodland strawberries, should be picked fully ripe when their flavour is at its best, sweet and scented. I recommend the varieties 'Baron Solemacher' and 'Alexandria', both easy to grow from seed, or start with plants from a fruit nursery.

A larger-fruited strawberry worth growing from seed, 'Sweetheart' has an excellent flavour, and also has the advantages that when sown under glass in February, it will usually fruit in late summer or early autumn.

It is when you come to the standard varieties that you are spoilt for choice. Many gardeners like the old stand-by 'Royal Sovereign', but I reckon 'Cambridge Vigour' outranks it for taste. If you have plenty of room then it is fun to experiment with several varieties. However, in a small garden I would plant a couple of rows, each with twelve to eighteen plants – one row of 'Cambridge Vigour', which fruits in June/ July, and the other of 'Aromel', an excellent repeat-flowering variety known as a 'perpetual' which fruits from July to October. By using a row of plastic tunnel cloches over the ripening fruit, you should be rewarded with a succession of strawberries from late May until November (or October in the US). The cloches not only extend the growing season; they keep the birds off the ripe berries, too.

Strawberries like a light, fertile soil that is preferably not too chalky. Ideally the soil should warm quickly and drain well. It's worth remembering the advice from *Laxton's Straw- berry Manual* of 1899: 'In the first place the strawberry's chief need is a great deal of water. In the second place, it needs more water. In the third place, I think I would give it a great deal more water.' It is no surprise to learn that a strawberry is ninety per cent water.

Pot-grown virus-free strawberry plants can be bought from late summer onwards. No crop should be picked in the first year, and the flowers should be snipped off so that the roots strengthen instead. The plants should then crop well for up to three to four years. The plants are placed 30 cm/12 in apart in rows or in beds. Plant each one on a small mound of soil, spreading out the roots evenly, making sure that the crown is at soil level. If the weather is warm and dry, water well until you see signs of growth. The runners form in late summer and these can be cut off or grown in the surrounding soil or in pots of cuttings compost. After six weeks, they can be cut from the mother plant and moved to establish a new strawberry bed.

The alternative to starting a fresh row or bed is to allow the runners to root themselves amongst the parent plants. This results in a 'matted bed'. You can still get a good crop as long as you give them some liquid organic fertilizer once the fruit has set. At the same time tuck straw or cork mats under the leaves to keep the fruit clean.

Day-neutral Californian strawberries will fruit at any time of year so long as a minimum temperature of 50°F (10°C) can be maintained. The day-neutral varieties, 'Fern' and 'Selva' are recommended for growing in a warm position in the garden or in pots under glass. When grown in a slightly heated greenhouse, these varieties should enable you to pick strawberries on Christmas Day.

Clusters of kiwi fruits in their brown hairy skins ripen against the Gravetye stone wall.

PEACH *and* NECTARINE
Prunus persica

APERFECTLY-RIPE ENGLISH PEACH IS A FRUIT OF THE GODS — ITS SCENTED WHITE flesh covered with a bloom of pale skin flushed pink on the side nearest the sun. What more could one ask — this is indeed ambrosia. For centuries, gardeners have dreamed of picking such fruit. And many have clearly done so, to judge by the number of peach houses still standing all over the British Isles. But producing the perfect peach calls for skill, patience and good fortune — a trio of virtues for which every gardener prays.

Wild peaches are native to China where gardeners have grown cultivated varieties for 4000 years. To the Chinese, the peach is the symbol of longevity and the blossom is the emblem of the bride. Incidentally, the Italian name for a nectarine, which is simply a smooth-skinned peach, is *pesca noce*.

A century ago, botanists, including Charles Darwin and Thomas Andrew Knight, considered the peach to be a form of almond. Scientists have now disproved this theory, but nevertheless, the plants are markedly similar. Their growing requirements are much the same, and in Italy and the south of France the trees are often grown alongside each other.

In Britain the peach has been cultivated outdoors since the reign of King John — although it's thought that our climate in the thirteenth century was warmer. The fruit has always been highly valued, and in 1676 John Rea listed eleven varieties of nectarine and thirty-five varieties of peach, including the early fruiting 'Nutmeg' peach, often mentioned in gardening and cookery books up until the nineteenth century. During the eighteenth and nineteenth centuries, peaches became an orchard fruit in parts of Kent, where they were grown on heated walls and in open ground. Their commercial value led to the development of dozens of new varieties, and the best have survived until today.

I recommend the peach varieties 'Amsden June', 'Early Rivers' and 'Peregrine', and the nectarines 'Elruge' and 'Lord Napier' for either indoor or outdoor culture. Peaches can be grown quite successfully in containers provided that the top soil is renewed every year. Planted in a congenial position, a peach will crop well for twenty years. They can be fan-trained against a warm wall in the south and east. Further north I've seen some splendid examples grown in an unheated glasshouse in Cumbria — in Scotland you invariably need to provide some heat.

Peaches and nectarines prefer a free-draining, slightly alkaline soil. They object to heavy rainfall — some gardeners even pave over the roots to keep them dry. Peaches and nectarines are self-fertile, but because they flower so early in the year, the gardener usually needs to pollinate the blossom with a fluffy stick — often a rabbit's tail — or camel-hair brush. Trees should be planted when dormant and pruned hard in the first year. Outdoor peaches can be attacked by peach leaf curl which requires spraying. This annoying disease does not attack peach trees grown under glass. Healthy peach leaves can be used to give a delightful almond flavour to custards and creams.

A home-grown peach is such a luxury that I would hesitate to prepare it in any fashion, other than placing it on the table on my most beautiful plate. While one of the attractions of a nectarine is that you can bite into it straight away, a peach needs peeling. Halve and quarter the fruit and gently remove the skin. Slice the fruit and savour it. The flavour of a peach is flattered by a fine sauternes or a muscat dessert wine, or a good champagne. Reserve the final quarter of your peach for the wine: slice it into the glass, leave it to macerate for a short time then eat it slice by slice. Finally, drink the peach-flavoured wine and toast this sumptuous fruit.

CHINESE GOOSEBERRY *or* KIWI FRUIT
Antinidia deliciosa (synonym *A. chinensis*)

THIS BROWN, HAIRY-SKINNED FRUIT WITH ITS JUICY GREEN FLESH CAN BE EASILY grown in Britain, either under glass or in warm areas against a south-facing wall. Getting it to fruit satisfactorily may be a little harder. Gardeners have grown other varieties of actinidia for decades, notably *A. kolomikta*, whose heart-shaped leaves are beautifully shaded in pink, green and white. But the fruiting *A. deliciosa* is a recent arrival. The fruit has been grown in New Zealand since 1906 and is now such a

A young mulberry tree with its branches fan-trained along bamboo canes into a pleasing shape.

SWEET CICELY
Myrrhis odorata

Culinary use: chopped leaves added to tart fruits to reduce acidity; whole leaves in pieces added to vegetable and fruit salads; whole leaves candied for decorating cakes and custards.

Cultivation: hardy, herbaceous perennial, white flowers, height 60-75 cm/24-30 in; grow in moist soil in full sun or light shade.

---

successful commercial crop, with tens of millions exported every year, that it has been given the name of their national bird – the kiwi.

The plant is a native of the Yangtze valley in China. In his book, *On Food and Cooking*, Harold McGee writes, 'It seems never to have been cultivated until about 1900, when a British botanist collected a few plants and brought them to the West.' The varieties of Chinese gooseberry listed by British nurserymen are from New Zealand where the plant's development has been well researched. For growing outdoors, the late-flowering female varieties such as 'Hayward' and 'Bruno' are recommended. The female varieties 'Abbot' and 'Monty' appear to do better under glass. Since the Chinese gooseberry is dioecious, both a male and a female plant need to be planted. The male varieties 'Atlas', 'Matura' and 'Tomuri' are all available in Britain. One male plant will pollinate up to seven female plants.

The Chinese gooseberry is a deciduous perennial climbing plant that quickly spreads across a wall or entwines itself round the posts of a pergola or trellis. Some gardeners in the south-west of England grow the plant with great success, and are able to pick a heavy crop of juicy fruit from September onwards. Others find that the kiwi fruit must be picked before the first frost and stored in a cool place for four to six weeks, to ripen. I planted my kiwi fruit plants in large tubs placed against a warm wall, but they have not done well. I suspect I did not keep the compost damp. So I shall transplant both the male and the female to a site with deep, humus-rich soil in a sheltered position in the garden where I hope they will do better.

Kiwi fruit have a high Vitamin C content and an understated flavour, similar to a honeydew melon. It must be its looks that has led to the phenomenal success of the kiwi fruit: they photograph well, so nouvelle cuisine chefs of the 1980s adopted them. Plant kiwi fruit from November to March in rich soil. Prune back after planting and again the following year. Tie in the twisting growths and ensure the ground around the plants does not dry out. When the fruits have formed, give a liquid feed every month.

MULBERRY
Morus nigra, Morus alba

ABOUT FIVE YEARS AGO I PLANTED A MULBERRY BUSH ON THE LAWN IN FRONT OF our farmhouse. And on a cold and frosty morning we have been known to dance around it, just as in the nursery rhyme. My mulberry is now about 2.7 m/9 ft high, but in time, if I prune away the side growths so that it becomes more of a tree and less of a bush in shape, then it should develop into a stately tree.

The mulberry grows slowly and when mature takes on an attractive gnarled appearance. The Chinese have cultivated the tree for over 5000 years for its leaves, which are fed to silkworms. In 1606, in an attempt to encourage a home-grown silk industry, James I granted a patent to allow one million mulberry trees to be imported. Three years later the king published a monograph on mulberry-growing, and each county town in England received 1000 mulberry trees to be sold at ¾ penny each or 6 shillings per hundred.

Mulberry orchards were established and mulberry gardens in London became popular. Both Samuel Pepys and John Evelyn were regular visitors and the latter wrote, 'My Lady Gerrard treated us at Mulberry Gardens, now the only place of refreshment about for persons of the best quality to be exceedingly cheated at.'

Unfortunately, the royal silk experiment failed, but it is surely possible that some of the huge and picturesque trees to be found in old estate gardens date from the seventeenth century, for the life-span of the tree is measured in centuries.

Ripe mulberries are irresistible. The fruit resembles a stubby loganberry and its flavour is sweet and sharp and scented. (I find that dried white mulberries from Turkey are very good when added to breakfast muesli instead of raisins or sultanas.) The fragile berry, which damages easily and does not travel well, ripens during August and September. Some gardeners leave the grass uncut under the tree so that the ripe fruit makes a soft landing and can be collected unharmed. The deep blood-red fruit juice stains lips and clothing so intensely that, in the past, the juice has been used as a dye for cloth and for adulterating white wine to make it resemble claret.

A good fruit nursery usually sells both black and white mulberry trees. The tree prefers a sheltered, warm and sunny position, and, in exposed areas, the protection of a south-facing wall is advisable. A mulberry tree looks particularly handsome planted in a paved courtyard garden. Prune or trim the branches to maintain an attractive shape, and to encourage fruiting prune the side shoots in late July to four or five leaves. Grown in open ground, the tree is unlikely to fruit until it is eight-years-old; however, a mulberry in a container will often fruit earlier, after only three to four years.

The mulberry is a deciduous tree which is notably cautious about breaking into leaf until all danger of frost is over. For years I've gardened according to John Evelyn's advice for frost-tender subjects and never found it wanting: 'Observe the mulberry tree; when it begins to put forth and open the leaves (be it earlier or later) bring your oranges etc boldly out of the conservatory; 'tis your only season to transplant and remove them.'

SORREL
Rumex acetosa

BUCKLER SORREL
Rumex scutatus

Culinary use: leaves in sauces, soups, omelettes, egg dishes and salads.

Cultivation: hardy perennial, rust red flowers should be removed to ensure a supply of fresh leaves, height 20-60 cm/8-24 in; grow in deep, moist soil in light shade.

LOVAGE
Levisticum officinale

Culinary use: chopped leaves in meat dishes, wholemeal bread, curd (cottage) cheeses, potatoes; young whole leaves in salads, soups and cooked pulses (dried legumes); seeds in cheese pies and biscuits.

Cultivation: hardy herbaceous perennial, greenish-yellow flowers, height 1.8 m/6 ft; grow in well-drained fertile soil in full sun.

LAVENDER
Lavandula

Culinary use: chopped leaves in biscuits, cakes and ice cream; whole leaves used for flavouring oils and vinegars, and for stuffing rabbit and chicken; flowers used for flavouring sugar, ice cream and fruit compotes.

Cultivation: hardy evergreen, mauve, blue, pink or white flowers, height 30-90 cm/12-36 in; grow in well-drained soil in full sun.

FRENCH TARRAGON
Artemisia dracunculus 'Sativa'

Culinary use: chopped leaves in sauces and stuffings for chicken, lamb, fish and vegetables; whole leaves for flavouring oils and vinegars for salads.

Make your own inexpensive Tarragon Vinegar by threading one or two long stems of tarragon into a bottle of white wine or cider vinegar. Or chop some leaves and mix them into softened butter to use as a garnish on grilled beefsteak, lamb cutlets or boiled potatoes.

Cultivation: half-hardy perennial, creamy-green flowers, height 25-45 cm/10-18 in; grow in well-drained loam in sheltered position in full sun.

CREAM OF SORREL SOUP

60 g/2 oz/4 tbsp butter

1 small onion, chopped

1 large potato, roughly diced

900 ml/1½ pints/3¾ cups chicken stock

1 bay leaf

115 g/4 oz young sorrel leaves

2 egg yolks

150 ml/¼ pint/⅔ cup double (heavy) cream

4 tbsp dry white wine

salt and freshly milled pepper

GARNISH:

a little extra cream

6 tiny sorrel leaves

Melt half the butter in a saucepan and stir in the onion and potato for 1 minute. Add the stock and bay leaf and simmer gently for 20 minutes or until the vegetables are cooked. Remove the bay leaf.

Slice the sorrel leaves and place in a food processor. Pour on the contents of the saucepan and whizz until the vegetables are puréed and the sorrel is finely chopped.

Return to the saucepan and reheat. Mix the egg yolks with the cream and add to the pan. Cook until thickened, but do not allow to boil. Add the wine, the rest of the butter and seasoning to taste.

Ladle into soup bowls, and add a swirl of cream and a small leaf of sorrel to each. Serve straight away. *Serves 4*

FRESHLY-PICKED ASPARAGUS WITH PARMA (PROSCIUTTO) HAM AND TARRAGON

24-36 spears fresh asparagus, depending on thickness

salt

60 g/2 oz/4 tbsp butter

1 tsp tarragon leaves

8-12 slices Parma (Prosciutto) ham

60-90 g/2-3 oz/½-¾ cup freshly grated Parmesan or diced Dolcelatte cheese

If necessary, trim the cut ends of the asparagus so that they are more or less the same length. Tie the spears in a bunch and stand the cut ends in 10 cm/4 in of salted boiling water. Cover the tips with a sheet of foil and tuck the edges of the foil down into the pan to make a hood. This way the stems cook in the boiling water and the tips are steamed. Cook for 7-12 minutes, or until the stems are tender (test with the point of a knife).

Meanwhile, melt the butter with the tarragon, then remove from the heat and keep warm. Brush four oval gratin dishes with a little of the butter. Drain the asparagus. Wrap a slice of Parma ham around the middle of three to four spears of asparagus, leaving the tips and stems sticking out. Place on a gratin dish and repeat with the rest of the asparagus.

Sprinkle the cheese over the ham and trickle the remaining tarragon butter on top. Place under a very hot grill (broiler) for a few minutes until the cheese has melted. Serve straight away, with French bread. *Serves 4*

French tarragon with its slim willow-like leaves and delicate aniseed flavour.

The flat edible pods and tiny peas of mangetout peas (snow peas).

LES PRIMEURS À LA DIFFÉRENCE

The French call the first fruits of the vegetable garden les primeurs. All baby vegetables taste very good simply steamed on a bed of herbs and served with melted butter. But here are some delicious alternatives.

BABY SWEETCORN WITH SESAME SEEDS

16-20 cobs (ears) of baby sweetcorn

bundle of lemon thyme or curry plant

1-2 tbsp light sesame oil

2 tbsp toasted sesame seeds

dash of lemon juice

sea salt

Steam the baby sweetcorn on top of the lemon thyme in a steaming basket for 5-7 minutes until cooked to your satisfaction. Heat the oil in a wok or large frying pan. Stir in the sesame seeds. Add the sweetcorn and toss in the oil until well coated with seeds. Spoon into a hot serving dish and sprinkle with sea salt. *Serves 4*

MANGETOUT À LA FRANÇAISE

225 g/8 oz/mangetout peas (snow peas), trimmed

45 g/1 1/2 oz/3 tbsp butter

2 spring onions (scallions), chopped

pinch of sugar

salt

1/2 small cabbage (butterhead) lettuce, shredded

Melt two-thirds of the butter in a pan and stir in the onions. Add the mangetout peas and turn over in the butter. Add the sugar and salt. Cover the pan and cook over a moderate heat for 5 minutes. Add the lettuce and cook briefly, gently tossing the vegetables together until the lettuce has wilted. Stir in the remaining butter and serve straight away. *Serves 3-4*

FINGER CARROTS WITH *LEMON GENEVER BUTTER*

1 bunch of finger or baby carrots with leaves

parsley stalks

60-90 g/2-3 oz/4-6 tbsp butter

finely grated zest of 1/2 lemon

1-2 tbsp gin

1/2 tsp finely chopped parsley

Remove four nice carrot leaves with stalks and set aside. Scrub and trim the carrots. Steam with the parsley stalks for 7-10 minutes or until cooked. Meanwhile, cream the butter with the zest of lemon. Blend in gin to taste with the parsley. Warm the butter until soft. Divide the carrots into four piles and tie loosely with the reserved carrot leaves. Spoon the lemon genever butter over the carrots and serve. *Serves 4*

Flowering clumps of low-growing thyme and marjoram nestle in front of aromatic Lad's Love or southernwood.

BABY BROAD BEANS WITH PANCETTA (CANADIAN BACON)

90 g/3 oz sliced pancetta (Canadian bacon), diced

2 tbsp virgin olive oil

3 spring onions (scallions), chopped

350-450 g/12-16 oz/2½-3 cups shelled baby broad (fava) beans

2-4 tbsp veal stock or water

salt

a little extra olive oil

¼ tsp chopped summer savoy (optional)

Fry the pancetta in the olive oil for 5 minutes. Add the onions and cook, stirring, for 2 minutes. Stir in the broad beans and add the stock or water.

Cook, stirring, for 3-5 minutes or until the beans are just cooked. If necessary, season with salt. Turn the beans into a warmed serving dish and dribble over a little extra olive oil. Sprinkle with the chopped savory and serve. *Serves 3-4*

PARTRIDGE WITH *BABY* ONIONS COOKED IN BEAUJOLAIS

Partridge has a superb flavour and texture and is best cooked fairly simply, either braised or roasted. The season's pickling onions are available at the same time as Beaujolais Nouveau. But if you prefer you can use any of the other primeurs such as Côtes-du-Rhône.

1 young partridge

2-3 sprigs of thyme

60 g/2 oz/4 tbsp butter

salt and freshly milled pepper

3 fresh vine (grape) leaves or a buttered paper

225 g/8 oz baby or pickling onions, peeled

1 tsp plain (all-purpose) flour

150 ml/¼ pint/⅔ cup Beaujolais Nouveau

1 bay leaf

a little brown sugar, depending on the wine

pinch of ground allspice

Place the partridge in a roasting pan and tuck the thyme inside the cavity. Spread half the butter over the breast and season lightly. Place the vine (grape) leaves over the breast and roast in an oven preheated to 200°C/400°F/Gas Mark 6, for 30-40 minutes or until cooked to your satisfaction. When ready, carve the bird in half through the breastbone and place on a hot serving plate.

While the partridge is roasting, melt the remaining butter in a flameproof casserole and cook the onions until golden. Stir in the flour and wine. Season lightly and add the bay leaf. Cover the casserole and place in the oven with the partridge to cook for 30 minutes or until tender but not mushy.

Transfer the casserole to the top of the stove and remove the lid. Add the sugar and allspice and cook for a few minutes until the sauce is syrupy. Spoon the onions and sauce around the partridge and serve. *Serves 2*

ROSEMARY ICE CREAM

Although this luxurious ice cream is delightful at any time of year, it is particularly special at Christmas or during the festive season. Serve with rosemary shortbread.

2 sprigs of fresh rosemary, each about 10 cm/4 in long

4 tbsp white dessert wine such as a Muscat, Sauternes or Monbazillac, slightly warmed

115 g/4 oz/½ cup vanilla- or rosemary-flavoured sugar (see below)

550 ml/18 fl oz double (heavy) cream

2 egg whites

1 tbsp rosemary flowers – fresh or crystallized

few sprigs of flowering rosemary, to decorate

Remove the leaves from the sprigs of rosemary and stir into the wine. Leave in a warm place to infuse for approximately 20 minutes, stirring now and again, until the wine is well flavoured by the rosemary. Strain the wine, mix in the sugar and set aside until cool.

Whip the cream until stiff but still glossy, and gradually mix in the flavoured wine. Whisk the egg white until stiff and fold into the cream. Mix in the rosemary flowers. Spoon the mixture into a sorbetière (ice-cream maker) – or simply freeze in a plastic box for 6-8 hours – until firm. Serve decorated with the sprigs of flowering rosemary. *Serves 6-8*

Rosemary Sugar: place 2-3 sprigs of fresh rosemary in a jar of caster (superfine) sugar. Cover tightly and leave in a warm place for 1-2 weeks, shaking the jar now and again. Use as required in sauces, creams, cakes and biscuits (cookies).

Vanilla Sugar: same process as for rosemary sugar, but substituting the fresh rosemary with 1-2 vanilla pods.

ROSEMARY SHORTBREAD

These biscuits (cookies) make a lovely accompaniment to rosemary ice cream. And they are equally good served on their own. Prettily wrapped with trailing ribbons, they make an attractive present.

115 g/4 oz/1 stick unsalted butter

60 g/2 oz/¼ cup rosemary- or vanilla-flavoured caster (superfine) sugar (see above)

175 g/6 oz/1¼ cups plain (all-purpose) flour

1-2 tbsp finely chopped fresh rosemary leaves

a little extra rosemary sugar

Cream the butter with the sugar until smooth. Work in the flour and the chopped rosemary to make a soft dough, then shape into a ball.

Roll out the dough on a floured board until 5 mm/¼ in thick. Cut out rounds using a 5 cm/2 in fluted cutter.

Bake on a greased baking sheet in an oven preheated to 170°C/325°F/Gas Mark 3 for 15-20 minutes or until the shortbread is just changing colour at the edges.

Cool the shortbread on a wire rack and then dust with rosemary sugar. *Makes about 30*

The delicate grey-green foliage of the highly scented rosemary bush prefers the protection of a wall or hedge.

CHAPTER THREE

GLOBE ARTICHOKE, FLORENCE FENNEL, COURGETTE *and* ZUCCHINI, PEAS, BROCCOLI *and* CALABRESE, TURNIP, WALNUT, PEAR, CHERVIL, BASIL, PARSLEY, THYME

A RESTORED KITCHEN GARDEN IN THE COTSWOLDS

LE MANOIR AUX QUAT' SAISONS

YOUR FIRST GLIMPSE OF THE KITCHEN GARDEN AT LE MANOIR AUX Quat' Saisons is from the south corner of the house. Walking across the lawn, passing close to a majestic blue cedar, you catch sight of some pea sticks and several neat rows of lettuces framed by a gateway in the Cotswold stone wall. It is a sight to gladden the heart of every kitchen gardener, and you quicken your step in order to see more of this ebullient but well-ordered vegetable kingdom.

The kitchen garden is large: 0.5 hectares/over an acre of ground is under intensive cultivation, and in

A mellow Cotswold stone wall shelters the formal garden (at Le Manoir aux Quat' Saisons) where low-growing junipers and flowering herbs encircle the fountain pool.

addition there is an orchard of apples and wall-trained pears plus a delightful walled herb garden. All occupy an ancient site which is certainly Saxon and probably older. There has been a kitchen garden at the Manor House of Great Milton, eight miles south-east of Oxford, for hundreds of years. Yet the style of gardening practised at Le Manoir today is not solely traditional. Some of the horticulture is innovative and, in the view of many gardeners, revolutionary.

The gourmet garden cook at Le Manoir lacks any formal training and is largely self-taught. Raymond

Left: Young globe artichoke plants in the kitchen garden. Right: A box of freshly-picked baby courgettes, each with its large velvety flower still attached.

Blanc has been described as 'the best chef in Britain' and his brilliantly creative cooking has gained every accolade and distinction. He says that the qualities of his food are considered in the order: 'taste, texture, harmony; then I present the food. I love beauty but I don't think of the picture on the plate first. I believe there is a right order, and if you start with the finest, freshest ingredients, that is honesty.'

For Raymond Blanc, the finest freshest ingredients come from his own garden. 'When I was a child – at home in France – you were encouraged to eat and appreciate vegetables, right from the earliest age,' adding, as we admire the immaculate rows of vegetables in his English garden, 'And I always ate them all up.'

The gardening day at Le Manoir begins early, with the head gardener, Albert Ring, and his three assistants gathering the garden produce for the kitchen. In the summer they start with the courgettes (zucchini). Nothing illustrates more vividly Raymond Blanc's belief in cooking with the youngest, freshest vegetables than the story of Le Manoir's courgettes.

These baby marrows, which are also known as zucchini, are grown in three widespan plastic tunnels, each 18 m/60 ft long. Basically, the courgette is an easy vegetable to grow. 'Courgettes germinate so well,' explains Albert. 'You sow 100 seeds and you often get 100 plants. When each plant has four true leaves we plant them, four feet apart, in holes filled with well-rotted stable manure. Then all the plants need is water and more water.'

In the high heat and humidity of the plastic tunnel, the courgette plant grows fast and comes into flower within a month. Most gardeners remove and discard the plant's sterile male flowers and leave the female flowers to develop the courgette at its base. An attentive gardener will notice that there is one day in the development of each courgette when the female flower is in perfect condition, in full bloom, and the slim, bright-green courgette below it is 7.5 cm/3 in long. That is the day when the gardeners at Le Manoir pick the vegetable.

Cutting courgettes in flower is a delicate operation. The petals of the tender, yellow blooms are easily torn on the sharp edge of a courgette leaf or on the prickly stem of the male flowers. To harvest this vegetable successfully in temperatures approaching 50°C/120°F shows true horticultural devotion. However, the work is not yet complete. As well as the courgettes with their flowers attached, the male flowers are also harvested. In Raymond's kitchen, these are stuffed and cooked in a Blanc-style variation of a traditional Provençal dish.

Grown in this way, one plastic tunnel produces courgettes in flower from mid-April until October. The vegetables and flowers are picked every day, cropping, through the season, a total of 8000 baby courgettes from the same plants. No prudent French gardening cook could ask for a more productive plant. And when you consider that, at the start of the season, courgettes in flower, in top London markets, can command a price of £1.20 each, the culinary and financial wisdom of growing your own is clear.

With the courgettes picked, and wiping the perspiration from their brows, Albert and his crew are ready to move into the main kitchen garden to continue their cropping. Are the leeks ready to dig? Not yet, in the view of most ·British gardeners, but in Raymond Blanc's eyes these pencil-slim leeks, no thicker than your little finger, each pearly-white base topped with narrow blue-green leaves, are perfect. They will be trimmed, washed and steamed, or they may be cooked in a small amount of herb-infused liquor and served just as they are – perfection on the plate. Prepared this way, all the fresh, mild flavour of a baby leek is captured for the palate and there is none of the coarse, slightly abrasive taste of the large and over-mature vegetable.

Growing next to the leeks is a row of beetroot (beet), their pretty red-veined leaves only 12.5 cm/5 in high. Albert pulls up a sample to see

if this popular root vegetable is ready for the kitchen. 'They should be about the size of an old-fashioned gob-stopper,' he says, rubbing off some of the fine soil still clinging to the tiny crimson globe that's no bigger than a quail's egg. He nods to his assistants and they proceed to pull more baby beetroot. 'Once a vegetable is ready to eat, we pick them every day. A fifty-foot row like this will only last two weeks. So we are sowing more seed every two to three weeks to be sure of a succession. In my own garden at home, I sow one crop of beetroot or perhaps two, whereas here we'll sow five or six times during the season. And although there's a fair bit of weeding, there is no thinning to do, because the thinnings go to the kitchen.'

The beetroot (beet) seed is sown thickly in a 10 cm/4 in wide row and, given a warm spring and summer and a moist humus-rich soil, the vegetable grows to Le Manoir cuisine size in under eight weeks. Running my hand over the satiny-smooth beetroot leaves that at this stage resemble lamb's lettuce, I asked Albert whether the kitchen uses the leaves. 'No, funnily enough, they don't. At home, my wife cooks them like spinach and they taste delicious. I think I'll suggest that to Raymond,' he chuckles. 'Mind you, I do sometimes grow a new vegetable and send it up to the kitchen and suggest they try it. They usually like it.' Last year Albert grew some tiny silver-skinned onions for the first time – and they liked those. Remembering that Raymond believes that 'curiosity creates success in any endeavour – wanting to know, continuing to ask questions', I felt that Le Manoir had found a gardener worthy of its cooking.

Traditional French cooking esteems the root vegetables that in Britain we regard as low-status food only a few notches up from cattle feed. Indeed, in the fields around my Devon home, turnips and swedes (rutabagas) are grown after the barley harvest for sheep to graze during the winter. My farming neighbours are generous in allowing me to help myself to these deliciously sweet roots before they grow large enough for animal feed, but they regard this as odd gastronomic behaviour because their own preference is usually for frozen peas.

So it is no surprise that Raymond Blanc, from Franche-Comté, likes lots of root crops in his garden. Carrots and turnips are grown in the conventional way with seed sown fairly thickly in a single row. As with the beetroot, carrots and turnips are not thinned but are pulled as soon as their roots reach the most desirable size. Baby carrots are 5-7.5 cm/2-3 in long, and the small turnips measure 2.5-5 cm/1-2 in across. Provided that the soil is moist, pulling these small vegetables out of the ground is not difficult. It is important to keep the root intact and the stalks unbroken because the Blanc style is to serve the vegetables as unspoiled as possible:

the root is gently washed and left intact and the leafy stalks are trimmed to about 2.5 cm/1 in in length because the stalks of very young vegetables are delightfully tender with a delicate taste.

In this gourmet garden, leaving the root on the vegetable is particularly highly regarded. Most dramatic perhaps is the case of the Florence fennel. This aniseed-flavoured vegetable, with its basal layers of curving celery-like white flesh that grows into a hollow stalk, up to 60 cm/2 ft tall, with feathery-green foliage, is highly decorative and delicious. But it must be said that not everyone enjoys its fairly powerful aniseed flavour. However, Raymond Blanc has discovered how to charm even the most reluctant eater.

Florence fennel is sown fairly thickly, outdoors, in a single row. Rather to his surprise, Albert finds that the seed of this Italian vegetable germinates easily in this Oxfordshire garden. Once again the seedlings are not thinned, and after eight weeks the plant is looking most attractive with about 15 cm/6 in of delicate fern-like foliage above the ground. In my Devon garden I would now thin the vegetable and allow the roots to grow for six to eight weeks longer, watering them generously in the hope that the fleshy base would swell and begin to resemble the heads of

Florence fennel on the shelf of the supermarket. Even in the balmy climate of the south-west of England, this is not always achievable because this Mediterranean vegetable loves the sun.

Nevertheless, at Le Manoir, and despite the vagaries of an English summer, they can produce plenty of their own heads of fennel. Because at the tender age of eight weeks, and still as slender as macaroni, the Florence fennel is carefully loosened from the ground with a small garden fork and pulled free of the soil so that the fine thread of root is unbroken and the complete plant goes to the kitchen. There, the feathery fronds are cut off and used in other dishes – a little seafood mousse perhaps, or a dish of lobster or, most inventively, made into a pale almond-green sorbet for serving midway through the many courses of a *menu gourmande*.

On the southern side of the courgette (zucchini) tunnels lie the beds of globe artichoke. It would, of course, be unthinkable for a Frenchman to own a fine kitchen garden and not grow the queen of vegetables. Its flower – which is also known as the 'edible thistle' – is one of the palate's most sensational treats.

The globe artichoke plant is spectacularly beautiful, its glaucous-blue, curving leaves so deeply serrated that the plant looks tropical. Yet the vegetable can be grown very successfully in most areas of Britain and

over a long season. Indeed, Giacomo Castelvetro in his classic book *The Fruit, Herbs and Vegetables of Italy*, published in 1614, says, 'In Italy our artichoke season is in the spring, unlike England, when you are fortunate enough to have them all the year round.'

Globe artichokes can be grown from seed or from one-year-old plants. The latter come into full production sooner than seed-grown plants, and after three to four years the mature plants can be divided to produce a further supply. At Le Manoir the plants were divided rather earlier than advisable, which has delayed the full production of globes. There is now, however, a healthy number of plants, and from next year there should be plenty of globes to cut for the kitchen.

Raymond Blanc's cooking is particularly distinguished by his inspired use of herbs. Not only does he use herbs in a conventional way as, for example, by adding them finely chopped to a sauce or dressing. But he also succeeds in capturing the very essence of a herb by infusing the plant in a liquid such as a well-reduced stock, or a warm vinaigrette, or an unfamiliar vegetable oil like those made from grape seeds or the avocado. For these methods of preparation the herbs must be in the peak of condition and so, like any good gardening cook, he grows his own.

His herbs are grown in three places in the garden: under-cover in a plastic tunnel, outdoors in a sheltered bed, and in the walled herb garden on the west side of the house.

Growing plants in the protected conditions of a plastic tunnel or even in a cold frame is an excellent way of extending the seasons. At Le Manoir, tender herbs such as tarragon and herbs like chives – which when grown quickly have a more delicate flavour and finer texture – are grown in the tunnel. In spring and late summer when conditions outdoors are not so favourable, rows of coriander and chervil are also grown there. No extra heat is needed, for the protection from the chilling Cotswold winds increases the heat of the sun to produce highly-favourable conditions.

Albert takes full advantage of the tunnel by growing rather special leaves for salads in every available space: mâche or lamb's lettuce, and the pretty round-leaved claytonia or miner's lettuce, with its small white flowers produced as if on stilts, on a fine stem above the leaf.

Sugar snap peas are grown in the tunnel, not for the mangetout-type (edible) pods that I grow in my garden, but for the pretty graceful shoots. 'We pick these shoots as soon as they carry one flower,' says Albert as he picks me one and examines the curling tendrils and white flower. 'But I really don't know what they do with them in the kitchen. Perhaps they blanch them or just use them as decoration.'

Until Raymond Blanc took over the Manor House at Great Milton, the walled herb garden was a livestock yard for the home farm. Mellow Cotswold stone walls reflect the heat into the courtyard, making it an ideal site for growing herbs. Walking into the garden on a sunny afternoon, the scent of flowering thyme, rosemary and marjoram is marvellously intense and the perfumed air trapped here produces an enviable microclimate.

At the drive end of the garden, a small glasshouse is devoted to basil plants where they are persuaded by the high heat and plenty of moisture to flourish as if they were in Italy. Each morning a gardener picks this lovely clove-scented herb, leaf by leaf, to be taken straight to the kitchen before the perfume evaporates and the herb flags.

The borders in the centre of the garden contain summer herbs grown in restaurant quantities, in rows: here are chervil and dill, flat-leaf parsley and coriander. A variety of mints – apple mint, spearmint, pineapple mint and ginger mint – have been moved from the long bed at the foot of the wall where they grew so abundantly that they intermingled to an alarming extent. They are now planted in a shadier position, each kind confined by growing it in a half-dustbin, 45 cm/18 in deep and with no base, and sunk into the ground up to the rim.

In full sun and surrounded by gravel paths, a charming island of thyme displays at least a dozen varieties of this highly aromatic herb. Thyme flowers are picked for the kitchen along with tiny sprigs of mint, no more than 2.5 cm/1 in across, and these are used to garnish cool, smooth summer sorbets.

How a constantly creative cook like Raymond Blanc, who devises new recipes every week, translates his culinary needs into the more slowly-evolving world of the kitchen garden is fascinating and instructive for any gourmet gardener. But it would be a mistake to think that this trade in ideas was in one direction only. In fact, the stimulus of seeing how vegetables, fruits and herbs grow, how at certain stages their consistency, flavour and form are perfect for a particular dish, is of central interest to Raymond Blanc, so that the garden and its produce often become the starting point for many of his creative ideas.

Albert Ring, head gardener at Le Manoir, is only a little rueful about running the best kitchen garden in the village: 'There's nothing we grow here that's big enough for the village show.' And the epicure in us all thrills to hear that, at last, good gastronomic sense is triumphing. As Albert says, 'This is not like an ordinary garden. How things taste is what really matters.'

SALADE AUX LÉGUMES *CROUSTILLANTS* ET HERBES DU JARDIN AUX FILETS MIGNONS D'AGNEAU

A selection of salads, deep-fried vegetable ribbons and fillet of lamb scented with herbs from the garden

4 lamb fillets (skinless, boneless loins cut from 4 small racks of lamb)

a little rosemary

VEGETABLES:

2 shallots, sliced

2 small turnips, finely sliced

115 g/4 oz celeriac, finely sliced

115 g/4 oz aubergine (eggplant), cut into 3 mm/⅛ in julienne

2 small courgettes (zucchini), finely sliced

115 g/4 oz leeks, cut into fine julienne

oil for deep-frying

SALAD:

4 basil leaves

4 small sorrel leaves

8 mint leaves

4 coriander (cilantro) leaves

2 sprigs of dill

8 marjoram leaves

2 sprigs of rue

1 shallot, finely chopped

2 large handfuls of salad leaves: 'Oak Leaf' lettuce, endive frisée (curly endive), red radicchio, lamb's lettuce (corn salad), batavia (escarole)

20 leaves of rocket (arugula)

VINAIGRETTE:

2 tbsp water

2 tbsp olive oil

1½ tbsp balsamic vinegar

1 tbsp Fino or sherry vinegar

salt and freshly milled pepper

sugar (if necessary)

Roast the fillets of lamb in an oven preheated to 200°C/400°F/Gas Mark 6 until medium rare. Leave to rest. Reserve the cooking juices.

Deep-fry the vegetables at 170°C/325°F: cook the shallots, turnips, celeriac, aubergines (eggplant) and courgettes (zucchini) for 3 minutes each, and cook the leeks for 45 seconds. Drain the vegetables on paper towels and season with pepper.

Mix together the ingredients for the vinaigrette.

Roughly chop the herbs and toss with the salad leaves and finely chopped shallot. Dress lightly with the vinaigrette. Add half the deep-fried vegetables and toss gently to distribute the dressing.

Arrange the salad in the centre of four plates, piling the leaves into a mound. Cut each lamb fillet into five slices, season with salt and pepper and place around the salads. Arrange the remaining deep-fried vegetables on top and around the salad. Serve the cooking juices separately, scented with a little rosemary. Serve straight away. *Serves 4*

Navarin de Turbot et Coquilles St Jacques aux Petits Legumes de Notre Jardin

*Fillets of turbot and scallops, served with baby vegetables from
our garden*

4 fillets of turbot each weighing
     150 g/5 oz

salt and freshly milled black pepper

2 tbsp melted butter

4 large (sea) scallops

12 baby carrots

12 mangetouts (snow peas)

8 baby courgettes (zucchini)

1 red sweet pepper

24 small courgette (zucchini) flowers

24 sprigs of purple basil, or leaves of red
     radicchio torn into 24 pieces

BRAISING STOCK:

45 g/1 ½ oz shallots, finely sliced

25 g/¾ oz/5 tsp butter

45 g/1 ½ oz button mushrooms, finely
     sliced

4 tbsp dry vermouth

6 tbsp water

SAUCE:

2 tbsp double (heavy) cream

30 g/1 oz/2 tbsp butter, diced

2 tsp chopped chives

squeeze of lemon juice

Season the turbot with salt and pepper, brush with melted butter and set aside. Cut each scallop into 4-5 slices and set aside.

Wash and trim the carrots, mangetouts (snow peas) and courgettes (zucchini). Seed and slice the red sweet pepper. Steam or cook each vegetable separately in time for the finishing of the dish. Blanch the courgette (zucchini) flowers and basil or radicchio in boiling salted water for 15 seconds, then refresh in cold water, drain and set aside.

In a flameproof casserole, sweat the shallots in the butter without allowing them to colour. After 2 minutes, add the mushrooms and sweat for a further minute. Deglaze with the vermouth, reduce by half to remove acidity, then add the water.

Place the fish on top of the shallots and mushrooms, cover the pan with a lid slightly ajar and bring to the boil. Place the casserole in a prchcatcd ovcn at 220°C/425°F/Gas 7 to cook for 6 minutes. Remove and allow to rest for 5 minutes.

Strain the cooking juices into another pan and bring to the boil. Add the cream, then whisk in the cold butter. Correct the seasoning.

Poach the sliced scallops in the turbot sauce then, at the last moment, stir in the chopped chives. Correct the seasoning with salt, pepper and lemon juice.

Arrange the courgette (zucchini) flowers and the slices of scallop around the outside of four plates. Place the vegetables and the basil or radicchio in the middle and put the turbot on top. Spoon the sauce over and serve straight away. *Serves 4*

ASSIETTE ET SORBET DE FRUITS D'*ÉTÉ*

Summer fruits and sorbet

TULIPES:

200 g/7 oz white marzipan

1 tbsp sifted plain (all-purpose) flour

2 egg whites

RASPBERRY OR STRAWBERRY SORBET:

450 g/1 lb/1¹/₂ pints ripe raspberries or strawberries, washed

115-150 g/4-5 oz/¹/₂-²/₃ cup caster (superfine) sugar

juice of ¹/₂ lemon

RASPBERRY OR STRAWBERRY COULIS:

325 g/11 oz/1 pint ripe raspberries or strawberries

100 g/3¹/₂ oz/¹/₂ cup caster (superfine) sugar

juice of ¹/₄ lemon (optional)

APRICOT COULIS:

400 g/15 oz ripe apricots

150 ml/¹/₄ pint/²/₃ cup water

100 g/3¹/₂ oz/¹/₂ cup caster (superfine) sugar

juice of ¹/₄ lemon

1 tbsp kirsch

TO FINISH:

selection of summer fruits: raspberries, strawberries, loganberries, tayberries, kiwi fruit, peaches or nectarine, red currants

4 sprigs of pineapple mint or slivers of zest of lime

To make the tulipes, blend the marzipan with the flour and egg whites in a food processor until smooth. Spoon about one-quarter of the mixture on to a lightly buttered non-stick baking sheet. Use a spatula to spread the mixture into a round with four petals, about 15 cm/6 in across. Make three more rounds of the mixture (you may have a little of the mixture left over which can be used for making petit fours.)

Bake the tulipes in an oven preheated to 180°C/350°F/Gas Mark 4 for 5 minutes. Remove from the oven, and use a spatula to lift one biscuit (cookie) from the baking sheet on to a cold work surface. Gently raise the petal sides to make the shape of a tulipe. Shape the remaining tulipes and leave to cool. Store the baked tulipes in a lidded container in a dry place.

To prepare the raspberry sorbet, place the fruit with the sugar in a bowl and leave overnight in the refrigerator. Purée the fruit in a food processor, then force through a fine nylon sieve to remove the seeds. Add lemon juice to taste. Churn in a sorbetière (ice cream maker) until firm and smooth. Or spoon into a lidded plastic bowl and freeze until firm; scoop into a food processor and whizz until smooth; and return to the freezer until needed.

To make the raspberry coulis, purée the fruit with the sugar in a food processor. Pass the purée through a fine nylon sieve. Taste and enliven, if necessary, with lemon juice. Store in a covered container in the refrigerator.

Wash and drain the apricots. Halve and stone, and cut each half into three. Put the fruit into a pan with the water, sugar and lemon juice. Cover and bring to the boil. Reduce the heat and simmer for 5 minutes or until the juice turns into a light golden syrup. Test to see if the apricots are cooked, then leave to cool.

Purée the contents of the pan in a food processor and pass through a fine nylon sieve. Stir in the kirsch. Taste and correct the flavour with a little more sugar or lemon juice, if necessary. Store in a covered container in the refrigerator.

To serve the dish, slice or halve some of the summer fruits on to four plates. Arrange a scoop of sorbet in a tulipe, garnish with a sprig of mint and place on the plate. Spoon some raspberry coulis and some apricot coulis on to the plate. If you wish, use a needle or a skewer to feather one coulis into the other. Complete the garnish with some red currants or slivers of lime zest (rind) and serve straight away. *Serves 4*

GLOBE ARTICHOKE
Cynara scolymus

A PERENNIAL PLANT WHICH PROBABLY ORIGINATED IN SOUTHERN EUROPE OR North Africa, the globe artichoke has been prized for centuries. During the first century AD the Roman writer, Pliny the Elder, recorded that globe artichokes were the most expensive vegetable of his time. Of course, growing your own globe artichokes is the cheapest way to obtain this fine vegetable.

Fortunately, you don't need a separate kitchen garden to grow the vegetable. Its splendid foliage makes the globe artichoke an attractive plant to set amongst shrubs and perennials in a flower border or simply in a small island bed in a lawn.

Propagation is by seed or by plant. Seeds germinate easily but are not always true to type. However, you can always discard weaker specimens and take cuttings from the better plants. Seed varieties widely available are 'Green Globe', 'Green Globe Improved' and 'Green Ball'. Both France and Italy have bred some fine strains of globe artichoke. I recommend the Breton variety, 'Vert de Laon', and from Italy, the beautiful purple-flushed variety, 'Violetta di Chioggia'.

Globe artichoke seed sown in March and April will sometimes produce small edible heads in the following September or October. The plants are relatively easy to grow and are tolerant of a wide range of conditions. However, they prefer a deep, light or sandy soil in a sunny position. Globe artichokes are inclined to rot away during a cold, damp winter if planted in heavy soil in shade.

Alternatively you can start by buying well-rooted plants from a reputable nursery during the autumn or spring. Plant the artichokes 80 cm/2½ ft apart in humus-rich soil and water generously. A rough mulch of forest bark (bark mulch or white pine needles) or garden compost helps to conserve necessary moisture. Grow the plants for one year, cropping the globes as they appear. The following year you can divide the plants by splitting them or by removing the offsets just below the ground, making sure that a section of root is still attached.

The main flowerheads develop from June onwards. To increase the size of the main globes, remove the smaller heads on the side shoots. These are also edible. In most recipes, heads of globe artichokes are boiled in salted water with a slice of lemon for twenty to thirty minutes until a leaf can be detached easily. Drain well and serve the artichokes hot with melted butter, hollandaise sauce or with thick cream mixed with finely chopped tarragon.

Eating a whole globe artichoke is delightfully leisurely. Pull off a leaf, dip it in the butter or sauce and eat the fleshy part of the base of the leaf by scraping it against your teeth; discard the rest. Also discard the hay-like choke, or *foin*, of indigestible fibres which becomes the thistle-shaped flower of the plant if left to grow. The most valued part of the globe artichoke lies underneath the choke. This is the bottom, or *fond d'artichaut*, all of which is delicious.

FLORENCE FENNEL
Foeniculum vulgare subsp. *vulgare* var. *azoricum*

G IACOMO CASTELVETRO TRIED TO TELL US, IN 1614, that Florence fennel improves the taste of bad wine. 'Our villainous Venetian wine-sellers solicitously offer innocent or simple-minded customers a piece of fennel to eat with their wine, or a few nuts, insisting that otherwise they might do themselves harm by drinking wine on an empty stomach . . .' The vegetable also aids the digestion, he wrote, in *The Fruit, Herbs and Vegetables of Italy*, a treatise that was written for the English but, sadly, remained unpublished for over 350 years.

The bulbous fennel plant, with its curved fleshy layers, shares with its slender herbal brother the flavour of aniseed. The plant originated in the Mediterranean area; Italy became its natural home and most of the best fennel recipes are Italian. Fennel's delicious flavour and digestive qualities persuade Italian cooks to often serve the vegetable quite simply: raw and cut into slivers with a piece of grainy Parmesan or Pecorino cheese at the end of a meal.

Pale green and cream Florence fennel not only charms with its looks, but it tastes wonderful too: serve it raw or blanched in salads, steamed or braised, or baked with Parmesan cheese, or puréed in a soufflé or a sauce. Its aniseed flavour, which I sometimes heighten with a splash of Pernod, makes it a perfect match for fish, but white meats and poultry also benefit from its gently pervasive aroma.

I am surprised to find how well Florence fennel grows in Britain – in the south, at any rate. Sow seed thinly in late spring in a deep, fertile soil in full sun. Thin to 10 cm/4 in apart and use the seedlings in the kitchen – Raymond Blanc steams and serves them whole. Keep the plants weed-free and water in drought conditions. It's a good idea to apply a liquid organic feed in mid-summer. Crop from July onwards.

When you grow your own Florence fennel you have the advantage of all the feathery top growth which can be used in the same way as the fronds of herb fennel. Use the long, hollow stalks in stocks. Any surplus can be dried for adding to the coals of a barbecue to perfume the smoke while grilling fish, meat or vegetables.

*Bright yellow courgettes grow quickly in warm
weather and are soon ready to pick.*

COURGETTE *or* ZUCCHINI
Cucurbita pepo

THE MINIATURE VEGETABLE MARROW KNOWN IN FRANCE AND BRITAIN AS THE courgette and in Italy and the United States as the zucchini is a member of the Cucurbitae family which includes the large variety of melons and squashes.

In Britain, the vegetable marrow – its name was intended to distinguish it from bone marrow in recipes of the time – was a relative latecomer, being introduced during the second half of the nineteenth century. Lucy H. Yates, in her delightful *The Gardener and the Cook*, published in 1912, gives one of the earliest recipes in an English cookery book for 'Italian vegetable marrow, in Italy called the Zucchini'. She adds, 'It is this gathering whilst small and young which is the whole secret of getting the best out of marrows.' Marcel Boulestin, in his 1931 What *Shall We Have Today?*, also advocates cutting the courgettes when only 7.5 cm/3 in long.

Mrs Yates describes how her French cook, Charlotte, has a 'most dainty, relishable and thrifty use' for the surplus male flowers of the plant. 'Early in the morning, while yet the dew is upon them, she searches for them, and on her dresser you may afterwards find them placed cup downwards, to prevent them from closing.' Charlotte fills each flower with a mixture of cooked rice, a little minced chicken and garden herbs, ties the petals with thread to make a tiny parcel and then braises them in a light broth.

Sow courgette seed in compost, two or three to a pot, under glass in March and April. It is a good idea to place each seed – they are large enough to handle – on its side when sowing. When each plant has two true leaves, plant outdoors in a warm, sheltered position or under glass in moderately rich soil, and water generously in hot weather.

Pick the courgettes or zucchini continuously and remove the male flowers for the maximum crop.

The most reliable varieties include the F1 hybrids 'Green Bush' which matures early and 'Zucchini'. I also recommend the attractive yellow-skinned varieties 'Eldorado' (F1) and 'Burpee Golden Zucchini'.

BROCCOLI *and* CALABRESE
Brassica oleracea Botrytis group

BROCCOLI AND CALABRESE ARE TWO OF THE MOST DELICIOUS MEMBERS OF THE brassica family. They are relatively easy to grow, and just a few plants can produce a handsome amount of green or purple curds. Calabrese is the name given to broccoli that matures during the summer months.

All brassicas like a rich, slightly alkaline soil so, if necessary, a light dressing of lime should be applied three to four weeks before planting. Ideally, brassicas should follow legumes – peas and beans – so that they can take advantage of the nitrogen reserves in the soil. Well-rotted compost should have been dug into the ground during the previous season. The soil should be slightly firmed before planting. Sow seed of calabrese in a shallow drill in the seedbed in mid-spring. Sow broccoli in the same way three to four weeks later.

Transplant the seedlings to the prepared ground, planting them 30 cm/12 in apart and watering them in well. Calabrese heads are like small green cauliflowers; they are usually ready to cut forty to fifty days after planting. If you cut the top head of calabrese when about 15 cm/6 in long, the side shoots will start to sprout. For their superb flavour, I recommend the varieties 'Express Corona' F1, 'Autumn Spear' and the beautifully-sculpted lime green heads of 'Romanesco'.

Broccoli produces smaller heads of curds than calabrese, with a cluster of small tender leaves around each stalk which are also eaten. The well-established varieties 'White Sprouting' and 'Autumn Sprouting' are admirably reliable. The variety 'Nine Star Perennial' produces white heads over a period of several years, provided that you regularly crop the curds.

Both broccoli and calabrese are best steamed or cooked in salted boiling water until tender but still firm when pierced with a knife and retaining their bright green colour. Serve with melted butter, hollandaise sauce with chopped tarragon or a bitter-orange sabayon sauce.

Garden pea, Mangetout (edible pod pea), Snap pea
Pisum sativum

A DISH OF FRESHLY-PICKED GARDEN PEAS, SHINING WITH MELTED butter and flavoured with finely chopped mint, is one of the great luxuries in life. And one that, increasingly, is denied almost everyone except the gardening cook. Because the sugars in the vegetable start to convert to starch from the moment they are picked, nothing can match the flavour of peas that progress from the pod to the pan to the plate within minutes. That legendary 'fresh pea' taste simply evaporates if the vegetable is kept waiting before it is cooked.

The garden pea (which is also known as the green pea, English pea and shelling pea, or petit pois in the case of the French variety with very small peas) is a fine specimen of the vegetable domain – everything about it is appealing. The plant is reasonably easy to grow, preferably in full sun, in a slightly alkaline soil that is rich in humus. The pea is a member of the Leguminosae family and therefore shares with all varieties of beans the attribute of fixing in the soil the nitrogen from the air. This means that the prudent gardener leaves pea plants in the ground for as long as feasible before pulling them up.

The sought-after part of the plant are the round, green seeds encased in their fleshy pods. One of the advantages of growing your own vegetables is that the pea pods of organically-grown peas can also be eaten – they make a lovely fresh-tasting soup. A further bonus is that both the shoots and the flowers of unsprayed pea plants can be eaten. Cut the shoots about 12.5 cm/5 in long, steam them and serve, as in the Far East, as a delicacy – they go especially well with fish. The fragile white flowers make a decorative last-minute addition to a salad.

More than 2000 years ago, the Greeks and the Romans cultivated the pea plant to produce fresh greens for the table as well as crops from the variety of white field pea which, when dried, provided a pulse (a dried legume) for eating during the winter months. In 1573, Thomas Tusser wrote in his *Five Hundrede Points of Good Husbandrie* that in January, the gardener should:

*'Dig garden, stroy mallow, now may you at ease,
And set (as a daintie) thy runcival pease.'*

After the Restoration of Charles II, peas began to be grown widely in England and a dish of peas was regarded as particularly suitable as a 'dainty dish for the ladies'. In the last century Thomas Jefferson, in his garden at Monticello in Virginia, took pride, along with his neighbours, in producing a picking of peas as early in the season as possible. At the same time in Britain, seedsmen offered a vast number of different varieties of peas to enable a succession of cropping.

Other members of the pea family well worth growing are the flat-podded mangetout and the fatter snap pea with larger peas. Both are eaten whole – the pod and the peas are left intact, just the ends are removed – and the pods are steamed or stir-fried and served as a most delicious green vegetable.

Recommended varieties of peas include 'Hurst Beagle', 'Sweetness' and the dramatic-looking 'Purple Podded Pea' (which has green peas). For Petit Pois, grow 'Waverex' and 'Little Marvel'. Good varieties of mangetout pea include 'Carouby de Maussane' and 'Oregon Sugar Pod'. The best snap peas are 'Sugar Snap', 'Sugar Rae' and 'Sugar Bon.'

Ideally, dig the ground for peas and add compost in the previous season; ground that is over-manured produces too much leaf and few pods. Peas like a slightly alkaline soil so add lime if necessary. Sow peas about 5 cm/2 in apart in drills 5 cm/2 in deep. To prevent field mice from stealing the peas, sow some dill seed in the same drill. Provide pea sticks or netting for support, and ensure the plants do not dry out, particularly when in flower.

TURNIP

Brassica rapa

'THE SMALL TURNEP GROWES BY HACKNEY IN A SANDY GROUND, AND THOSE that are brought to Cheapside market from that village are the best that I ever tasted,' wrote John Gerard in 1597. The turnip as a garden vegetable intended for the table preceded its use as a crop for animals. It was the land-owner Lord Townshend who changed the face of British husbandry when, in 1730, he introduced the idea of feeding livestock with a winter feed of turnips. His revolutionary theory was adopted only slowly during the eighteenth century and in the meantime he acquired his nickname of Turnip Townshend.

The Greeks and Romans cultivated and cooked the turnip. But it was always regarded as a low-status vegetable. In their sumptuary laws, the ancient Aryans bracketed the turnip with onions and garlic, mushrooms and beans, as food forbidden to the upper classes yet allowed to their servants and minions. It seems to me that only the French with their customary good sense appear to really understand the turnip; they know how to grow them and they cook them in more delicious ways than any other nation. Indeed, John Gerard acknowledges that many of his opinions were influenced by his friend, Jean Robin, keeper of the royal gardens in Paris.

The turnip is an easy-to-grow vegetable, tolerant of a poor sandy soil and suitable even for cultivating among shrubs and flowers in a mixed border. Sow seed every three to four weeks from early spring, and thin the plants to 10 cm/4 in apart. The best turnips grow quickly so, if possible, add plenty of moisture-retaining garden compost to the soil. I find these varieties of turnip particularly good for the table: 'Early Snowball', 'Purple Top', 'Milan', 'Green Globe,' 'Veitch's Red Globe' and 'Golden Ball', which is a delicious yellow-fleshed turnip.

Once again, the gardening cook has every advantage: not only a crop of bright green leaves, which make a fine cooked vegetable – highly esteemed in Italy and Spain – but also young turnips which can be harvested, at their best, when they are small and sweet and perfect. At this size, the turnip does not need to be peeled, just trimmed and scrubbed. Baby turnips can be steamed or braised in stock, or cooked in butter and served with a few snipped chives. Golf-ball-size turnips make a wonderful dish steamed with baby carrots, tiny ears of sweetcorn and finger leeks, then tossed in a green-flecked herb butter and served in a crisp filo pastry case.

Tennis-ball-size turnips usually need to be peeled. Then grated raw and mixed with Greek-style yoghurt, they make a refreshing kind of cole-slaw. Or they can be cooked slowly in some of the classic dishes of French country cooking. The natural alliance of rich meat with turnips as, for instance, in the dish of carnard aux navets, makes a virtue of the fact that turnips enable us to digest fat. Larger, older turnips need to be puréed and then returned to the pan and stirred over moderate heat to dry the purée. I have made white bread by replacing some of the flour with puréed turnip (puréed potato also works well); it makes a light, fine-tasting loaf. John Evelyn described something similar, although it sounds as if his loaf contained no flour: 'And here should not be forgotten, that wholesome, as well as agreeable sort of bread, we are taught to make, and of which we have eaten at the greatest Persons Tables, hardly to be distinguish'd from the best of Wheat.'

WALNUT

Juglans regia

THE MAJESTIC WALNUT TREE NEEDS A BIG SPACE; IT CAN REACH A height of 12 m/40 ft, though taking a leisurely twenty years to do so. In time, an English walnut can grow up to 30 m/100 ft. But if you are planting up your garden for your heirs – or simply reckon that a decade from now you'll enjoy eating your own walnuts – then I recommend this beautiful tree.

The common walnut, *Juglans regia*, named after Jove or Jupiter – the most powerful of the Roman gods – is the variety usually sold by nurserymen, and it has been grown in Britain since the fifteenth century. John Parkinson, in *The Ordering of the Orchard*, recommended walnut trees to be planted around a fruit orchard as a windbreak. Olivier de Serres, the seventeenth-century French horticulturist, extolled the virtues of the tree and even today the drive to his family estate in Villeneuve-de-Berg is an avenue of magnificent walnut trees.

Most of the walnuts we eat at Christmas have been grown in France or Italy and then dried in kilns until pale brown. English walnuts are harvested green, in August and September. Some are eaten straight off the tree as wet (young) walnuts. Others are pickled in vinegar for eating with cold meats during the festive season.

Walnut trees should be planted when dormant, during the winter. They are tolerant of a wide range of soils although rarely prosper in a cold position with heavy ground.

Nurserymen sell both the common walnut and the black walnut, *Juglans nigra*. Recent European hybrids include the variety 'Buccaneer' which is highly productive and self-fertile and the variety 'Broadview' produces high quality nuts but the tree needs 'Buccaneer' as a pollinator.

Pear
Pyrus communis

A history of the pear could fill a large volume, so packed is it with incident, people and varieties. The classical writers Cato and Virgil wrote about pears and Pliny the Elder wrote, 'Of all the varieties of pears, the Crustumian is the nicest.' During the seventeenth century, De la Quintinie, the great gardener to the Sun King, identified the Winter Bon Chrêtien pear as the Roman Crustumian. Many of these early pears resembled the European wild pear, with its dry, crisp flesh which requires cooking to be palatable. During the sixteenth century, although popular, pears were still regarded as indigestible, hence the contemporary expressions: 'Pears without wine are poison' and 'After a peare, wine or a priest'.

In Britain, details of pear trees that had been planted long before the Norman Conquest, to mark boundaries, were recorded in the Domesday Book of 1086. During the thirteenth century, there was a burst of interest in gardening. At that time the queens of England, Eleanor of Provence, the wife of Henry III, and Eleanor of Castille, who married Edward I, were both keen gardeners, and were responsible for planting many new orchards of French pears.

However, a home-grown cooking pear that became highly popular was the Warden, raised about 1388 by the Cistercian monks of Bedfordshire. 'And a Warden pie's a dainty dish to mortify withal', runs a line in the Ingoldsby Legends.

In France, Olivier de Serres wrote his masterpiece, *Le Théâtre d'agriculture et mesnages des champs*, and promoted the growing of more pears. It was, however, the king's attorney, Le Lectier, who fostered such interest in pears that growing, raising their seedlings and eating pears became a craze in France during the early seventeenth century.

Until then, pears had been grafted on to either hawthorn or wild pear stock. But these trees grew tall. In 1676, John Rea advised that by growing pears on quince stock the trees would be smaller and more manageable. Most of today's pear trees for garden culture are grafted on to Quince A rootstock, which produces moderately vigorous growth, or Quince C rootstock for more dwarf trees.

Belgium became pre-eminent in the development of the pear in the eighteenth century when Nicolas Hardenpont, a priest at Mons, spent thirty years sowing pear seeds and raising promising seedlings. He specialized in developing 'beurré' or butter-tasting pears, and in 1750 introduced the fine pear, 'Glou Morceau'. But it was in the Berkshire village of Aldermaston that was found a seedling which became the 'Williams' Bon Chrétien', or Williams' for short, named after the Turnham Green nursery, Williams, which distributed the young trees. In 1797, the pear was taken to America and in 1817 acquired another name when Enoch Bartlett of Dorchester, Massachusetts took over an estate and sent out the existing pear trees under his own name. This early season juicy pear, known as the 'Bartlett', is now widely grown, especially in the US and is tinned (canned) on a large scale.

During the nineteenth century the lovely 'Doyenne' or 'Comice', and the 'Conference' pears were introduced. The latter pear will even set a crop on its own, but production is higher if a pollinator is near.

Pears flower a fortnight or so ahead of apples and their blossom can easily be destroyed by harsh winds or low temperatures. Although the sight of light snowfall on my pear blossom is beautiful I know that it is usually disastrous for my crop. To ensure successful germination of the pear flowers it is necessary to plant one or more pear trees nearby so that the bees and flying insects can fertilize the flowers. A catalogue of pears from any good fruit nursery will give advice on the best trees for pollination. Pears flourish in a warm, sheltered, slightly dryish climate. Light pruning usually gives the best results. Choosing a pear tree is a delightful task. In his *Handbook of Fruits*, Edward Bunyard lists over 150 varieties of pear and says 'the list might easily have been quadrupled'. Any devotee of the fruit with room in their garden will find growing a pear tree or two a true joy.

CHERVIL
Anthriscus cerefolium

Culinary use: aniseed flavour, a constituent of the French herb mixture 'fines herbes', chopped leaves in egg and fish dishes; whole leaves in pieces in salads, valuable as a garnish.

Cultivation: annual herb with delicate white flowers, height up to 45 cm/18 in; grow in moist soil in half-shade.

BASIL
Ocimum basilicum

Culinary use: spicy clove flavour, chopped leaves added at the last moment to sauces and dressings, essential herb in Italian pesto sauce; whole leaves in salads especially tomato.

Cultivation: half-hardy annual herb with several varieties, small white flowers should be removed to promote leaf growth, height 30 cm/12 in; grow in moist, well-drained soil in sheltered position in full sun or light shade.

PARSLEY
Petroselinum crispum

Culinary use: flat-leaf parsley more aromatic than curly-leaf variety, leaves and stalks in a classic 'bouquet garni', essential flavouring in many soups, sauces, and stocks, vegetable and fish dishes; whole and chopped leaves as a garnish; roots useful for adding flavour to slow-cooked meat dishes.

Cultivation: hardy biennial, yellow-green flowers best removed unless wanted for seed, height 30 cm/12 in; grow in moist, fertile soil in full sun or light shade.

THYME
Thymus vulgaris

Culinary use: strongly aromatic herb, many varieties, a constituent of a classic 'bouquet garni', sprigs and chopped leaves in soups, stocks and stuffings, onion and vegetable dishes, meat and fish.

Cultivation: evergreen with white or lilac flowers, height 5-30 cm/2-12 in; grow in well-drained, light soil in full sun.

Left: Thickly sown chives are grown in rows like a vegetable. Right: A glimpse of the kitchen garden seen through the Cotswold stone arch of the formal garden.

JELLIED SUMMER BORTSCH

450 g/1 lb raw beetroot (beets), skinned and chopped

1 carrot, sliced

1 stalk celery, chopped

white part of 1 leek

1 small onion, chopped

1 clove garlic

1 litre/1¾ pints/1 quart water

bunch of thyme

salt

300 ml/½ pint/1¼ cups good jellied chicken stock or beef consommé

1½ tbsp powdered unflavoured gelatine

juice of 1 lemon

3 tbsp red wine

GARNISH:

few leaves of lamb's lettuce (corn salad) and red radicchio

150 ml/¼ pint/⅔ cup soured cream

1 tbsp finely chopped chives

Cook the beetroot (beet) with the carrot, celery, leek, onion and garlic in the water with the thyme and some salt for 30-40 minutes or until the beetroot is cooked.

Add the stock or consommé and simmer for 5 minutes. Soften the gelatine in the lemon juice and red wine in a large jug and strain the vegetable liquid from the saucepan over the top. Reserve the vegetables.

Stir the wine mixture until the gelatine has dissolved. There should be about 1 litre/1¾ pints/1 quart. Cool the soup by standing the jug in cold water, then chill until just starting to set.

Select some of the reserved vegetables and arrange in a large glass dish or six smaller ones – or you can use moulds and turn out the soup when it is set. Pour over a little of the jellied bortsch and chill until firm. Continue filling the dish in this way – it is a matter of choice how much vegetable you include.

I sometimes enrich the bortsch with chopped hard-boiled eggs or slivers of cooked ham, some baby gherkins and a few chopped spring onions (scallions), when I want to serve the soup as a more substantial course.

Chill the bortsch until set. Serve, spooned from the bowl (or turn out the moulds) and garnished with lamb's lettuce (corn salad) and red radicchio. Spoon some soured cream on one side and sprinkle with chives.
Serves 6

CHINA GRILL SPINACH

*I was introduced to this deliciously simple way of serving fresh
spinach at the China Grill Café in New York where it appears
on the menu among the vegetable courses. But we could not
restrain ourselves and ate it as an appetizer – it's so good.*

450 g/1 lb fresh garden spinach

sunflower oil for deep-frying

sea salt

Pick the spinach on a dry day and, if possible, choose leaves that do not need washing. If you have to buy spinach, then wash well in cold water, drain and dry the leaves on a clean cloth. Remove the stalks.

Heat the oil to just below frying temperature, approximately 180°C/360°F. Test fry by dropping a leaf into the oil. (Take care because the spinach can spit: it is a good idea to wear oven gloves while you are frying.) The spinach is cooked when it puffs up and is still bright green (approximately 30-60 seconds). Use tongs to lift out each leaf and drain well on paper towels. The spinach crisps as it cools. Continue frying the leaves, a few at a time, and place on a large oval meat plate.

Serve with a bowl of crystalline sea salt. *Serves 4*

TOMATO, BASIL AND ORANGE SORBET

*This sorbet makes a refreshing first course to a meal on a hot
summer's day.*

450 g/1 lb ripe, full-flavoured tomatoes

1 slim clove garlic

1 bay leaf

pared zest (rind) of 1 orange

1 tsp sugar

¼ tsp salt

4-6 medium-size sweet oranges

1 tsp chopped basil

dash of Cointreau

4-6 sprigs of basil, to garnish

Quarter the tomatoes and put in a saucepan with the garlic, bay leaf, zest of orange, sugar and salt. Bring to the boil, then cover and simmer gently for 20-30 minutes or until the tomatoes are cooked.

Pour into a nylon sieve and push through the pulp, discarding the tomato skins, zest (rind) and bay leaf.

Thoroughly wash the oranges and dry them. Cut the tops from the oranges and scoop out the flesh into a food processor, discarding any pips (seeds). Whizz to a purée. Stir the orange purée into the tomato mixture with the chopped basil. Taste and check the seasoning, and add the Cointreau. Freeze the mixture until firm. Freeze the orange shells and lids.

Turn the sorbet into a food processor and mix until smooth. Spoon the sorbet into the orange shells, replace the lids and garnish with the sprigs of basil. Serve straight away. *Serves 4-6*

*Perpetual spinach is slow to bolt and its leaves
can be harvested over a long season.*

The distinctive overlapping leaves of a mature bulb of Florence fennel with its feathery foliage.

SMOKED HALIBUT AND STURGEON WITH GREEN CREAM

150 ml/¼ pint/⅔ cup soured cream

2 tbsp chopped chives

1 tbsp chopped dill

2 tbsp chopped parsley

1-2 tbsp lime or lemon juice

salt and freshly milled pepper

115-150 g/4-5 oz smoked halibut, sliced

115-150 g/4-5 oz smoked sturgeon, sliced

watercress or American land cress, to garnish

Spoon the soured cream into a bowl and stir in the chopped chives and dill. Pound the parsley in a mortar and pestle with the lime or lemon juice to make a paste and mix into the cream. Season with salt and pepper and chill until needed.

Arrange the sliced smoked fish on four plates. Spoon some of the green cream beside it and garnish with watercress. Serve with thinly sliced rye bread or pumpernickel and un-salted butter. *Serves 4*

PORK WITH PEARS AND PERNOD

Pernod's aniseed flavour offsets the richness of the pork and the sweetness of the pears wonderfully well.

4 1 cm/½ in slices of boneless loin of pork

60 g/2 oz/4 tbsp butter

salt and freshly milled pepper

juice of 1 lemon

4 ripe dessert pears

1 tbsp Pernod

4 tbsp double (heavy) cream

finely chopped fennel, to garnish

Trim any surplus fat from the meat. Sear both sides of each slice in one-third of the butter. Arrange the meat in a single layer in an oven dish, season with salt and pepper and sprinkle with half the lemon juice. Cook the meat under a hot grill (broiler), or in an oven preheated to 190°C/375°F/Gas Mark 5 for 15-20 minutes.

Meanwhile, peel and quarter the pears. Core and slice lengthways on to a plate. Pour over the rest of the lemon juice. Melt the remaining butter in a pan and sauté the pears for 3-4 minutes or until softened. Add the Pernod and cook for 1-2 minutes. Then stir in the cream and the meat juices from the pork.

Arrange the sliced pears neatly on top or beside each piece of pork and spoon over the sauce. Garnish with chopped fennel and serve straight away. *Serves 4*

Sweet-tasting baby carrots are harvested carefully to retain the full length of their tapering roots.

SWEET CARROTS

This is Eliza Acton's recipe for a light, creamy purée of carrots. Serve the vegetable with grilled (broiled) or roasted meat or to accompany a hot vegetarian dish.

450 g/1 lb carrots, scrubbed or peeled

salt

30 g/1 oz/2 tbsp butter

1 tsp sugar

90 ml/3 fl oz double (heavy) cream

Slice the carrots thickly and place in a pan with a little salt and cold water to cover. Bring to the boil and cook, covered, for 10-20 minutes or until tender. Drain well (the cooking liquor can be kept as vegetable stock for soups) and purée the carrots in a food processor or push them through a vegetable mill on its finest setting.

Return the purée to the pan and stir over moderate heat for 5-10 minutes until all surplus water has evaporated. Add the butter and sugar and gradually mix in the cream, stirring all the time until the purée is thick. Season to taste with salt and spoon the purée into a hot serving dish. *Serves 4*

Note: Eliza Acton suggests serving the purée with small bread croûtons, but the purée is delicious on its own or garnished with a few sprigs of chervil.

FIVE FRUITS TART BOURDALOUE

115 g-175 g/4-6 oz/1-1½ cups each of 5 summer fruits: strawberries, raspberries, black currants, red currants, blueberries, tayberries, dessert gooseberries, apricots, peaches, nectarines

6 tbsp apple or red currant jelly, warmed

PÂTE SUCRÉE:

175 g/6 oz/1¼ cups plain (all-purpose) flour

90 g/3 oz/6 tbsp vanilla-flavoured sugar (see below)

90 g/3 oz/6 tbsp unsalted butter

3 egg yolks

CRÈME BOURDALOUE:

600 ml/1 pint/2½ cups milk

3 egg yolks

90 g/3 oz/6 tbsp caster (superfine) sugar

35 g/1¼ oz/¼ cup cornflour (cornstarch)

35 g/1¼ oz/¼ cup plain (all-purpose) flour

2 egg whites

1 tbsp orange curaçao or Cointreau

To make the pâte sucrée, have all the ingredients at room temperature. Sift the flour on to a marble surface or into a wide bowl. Make a well in the centre and add the sugar, butter and egg yolks. Work the ingredients together using your fingertips and form the dough into a ball. Wrap and chill for 30 minutes.

Roll out the pastry dough on a floured board and use to line a 25-28 cm/10-11 in flan tin (tart pan), 4 cm/1½ in deep. Prick the bottom of the pastry case and chill well.

To bake the pastry case, line it with paper and fill with dry beans. Bake in an oven preheated to 200°C/400°F/Gas mark 6 for 15 minutes. Remove the paper and beans and bake for 5-10 minutes longer or until golden and crisp. Cool in the tin.

To make the crème bourdaloue, heat almost all the milk until boiling. Blend the rest of the milk with the egg yolks, almost all the sugar, the cornflour (cornstarch) and flour.

Pour the hot milk on to the egg mixture, whisking all the time. Return to the pan and cook, stirring, for 4-5 minutes or until thickened. Cover the pan and stand it in cold water. Stir the crème now and again until cool. Whisk the egg whites until stiff. Fold in the remaining sugar and orange curaçao, then fold into the crème. Spoon into the pastry case and smooth level.

Arrange the fruits in circles on top of the crème and brush over the warmed jelly to glaze. Set aside until cold. *Serves 8-10*

Note: for vanilla-flavoured sugar see page 55.

Red currants glistening in the summer sun.

RASPBERRY, RED CURRANT AND ROSE GERANIUM JELLY

Serve this prettily-scented jelly on muffins or toast at special breakfasts or teas.

225 g/8 oz/1 pint raspberries

450 g/1 lb/1½ pints red currants

white sugar

6-8 rose geranium leaves

Measure the raspberries and red currants into a pan and slowly bring to the boil. Simmer for 10 minutes or until the fruit has yielded its juice. Pour the mixture into a jelly bag or fine cotton strainer. Suspend the bag over a bowl and leave overnight until all the juice has dripped through. Don't be tempted to speed up the straining by squeezing the bag – this will make the jelly cloudy.

Measure the fruit juice into a pan and add 450 g/1 lb/2 cups sugar for every 600 ml/1 pint/2½ cups of liquid. Stir over low heat until the sugar has dissolved, then raise the heat and bring to the boil. Cook for 3 minutes. Apply the cold saucer test to check for setting point: a teaspoon of jelly cooled on a saucer should not run together when you draw your finger through it.

Place two or three rose geranium leaves in each small, hot jar and pour in the jelly. Stir to distribute the leaves, cover and label. *Makes about 350 g/12 oz*

CHAPTER FOUR

PUMPKIN *and* SQUASH, SWEETCORN, MARIGOLD, PURSLANE, SALSIFY *and* SCORZONERA, CRAB APPLE, ROCKET, MEDLAR, NASTURTIUM, GOOSEBERRY, SAGE

AN ELIZABETHAN KITCHEN GARDEN IN SUFFOLK

HINTLESHAM HALL

WHITE LEAD APPLES AND PEARS SWING FROM LONG CHAINS AT THE front of Hintlesham Hall. These stylish though inedible fruits add a nice period detail to the peach and white Georgian façade of the Elizabethan house. But, for all its wedding-cake prettiness from the front, I prefer the view of the house from the garden. From here the warm red bricks and tall Tudor chimneys face east over the lawn to the small lake and the gentle Suffolk landscape beyond. And the house that was built by Sir Thomas Timperley, when he retired from court circles – a little abruptly – in 1578, remains wonderfully unspoilt.

The lake in the formal garden at Hintlesham Hall provides ideal growing conditions for water-loving bog plants, grasses and bushes with edible fruits.

In the sixteenth century, East Anglia was home to some remarkable gardeners. Thomas Tusser lived and farmed at Cattawade in the valley of the River Stour about six miles south of Hintlesham. His *One Hundred Pointes of Good Husbandrie*, written in rhymed couplets, was published in 1557, and expanded sixteen years later to 500 points. It became the most influential gardening guide of the century. Also, from 1540 onwards, many skilled Flemish and French gardeners, fleeing from religious persecution in their own countries, settled in Norfolk and Suffolk and started market gardens.

The original Elizabethan garden at Hintlesham Hall probably lay close to the house and, like the present garden, was enclosed. Dr John Hall, a botanist and surgeon, described his garden in 1563 as hedged with honeysuckles, cornus, sweet briar, box, and blackthorn intertwined with briony, ivy and wild vine. In some of the larger gardens the hedges of trellised fruit trees and climbing roses were planted as a maze. At Hintlesham there is a fine clipped beech hedge with two oval entrances, each with a picket gate. Inside is a potager that Ruth and David Watson have slightly enlarged from the garden that the previous owner, Robert Carrier, laid out nearly twenty years ago.

Its design of geometrically-shaped beds separated by gravel paths is based on one of the simpler knot gardens that were the height of fashion during the sixteenth century. The Elizabethans were besotted with pattern as a decorative style: the herringbone brickwork and plaster-pargetting of their houses provided a splendid setting for the carved oak and ornate embroidery of their interiors. This passion for pattern reached its horticultural apogee in the complicated knot gardens and mazes of yew and box that were fashionable at that time.

Sir Thomas Timperley would doubtless have been familiar with the Tudor splendours of Hampton Court and the Palace of Nonsuch, and then,

as now, it was considered socially desirable to emulate the styles practised at court. Although no record exists of the original garden, we know from contemporary books on gardening and cooking which plants were grown at the time. So in the admirable interests of historical continuity, Ruth Watson grows mainly those vegetables and herbs, fruits and flowers that grew in the garden 400 years ago.

Each lozenge-shaped bed is devoted to one or two different herbs, vegetables or flowers. One of the most pleasing effects is the choice of companion plants: fennel is surrounded by rosemary, salad burnet is garlanded with the feathery moss-green foliage of southernwood, a bed of purple-leaved opal basil has a border of small-leaved green basil, and the spiky smoke-grey curry plant *Helichrysum angustifolium* is edged with marjoram. The contrast of leaf shape and perfume in these herbal alliances is delightful and an idea well worth adapting if you grow herbs.

A long half-moon border is crammed with nasturtiums, their yellow and orange flowers glowing, jewel-like against the beech hedge. In some of the centre beds, runner beans climb up tripods on sticks and, at their feet, sprawling plants of cherry tomatoes – a post-Elizabethan vegetable – ripen on a layer of straw. Around the margin grow clumps of the French marigold, *Tagetes patula*, which Elizabethan gardeners knew as the 'velvet flower'. Neatly clipped box edging gives a truly Tudor feel to a bed of wild strawberries, one of the most favoured fruits of the time.

'The gooseberry, respis, and roses all three
With strawberries under them trimly agree'

according to Tusser, illustrating the Elizabethan fondness for growing flowers and fruit together. Respis are raspberries.

We know from William Lawson's works published early in the seventeenth century that the kitchen garden was the housewife's responsibility. At Hintlesham, Lady Etheldreda, the daughter of Sir Nicholas Hare, Master of the Rolls under Queen Mary I, would have been in charge of the kitchen garden. Here she would have grown, for both culinary and medicinal purposes, plants like rounceval peas, skirret, salsify, scorzonera and quince. The study of herbs, or simples, and their attributes was central to a well-run Elizabethan household and books on the subject were popular. In 1568, William Turner dedicated his splendid herbal to the Queen herself. Ten years later, *A Nievve Herball or Historie of Plantes*, (an English version of a French translation by Clusius of Rembert Dodoens) was published by Henry Lyte. And in 1597, John Gerard's celebrated *The Herball or Generall Historie of Plantes* appeared.

The names of herbs and their properties were such common knowledge that Shakespeare could refer to them far more freely than any modern playwright. Canon Ellacombe has demonstrated that a garden composed of herbs and plants mentioned in Shakespeare's work would be surprisingly comprehensive and would include such culinary plants as parsley, bay, thyme, lavender, medlar, quince, rosemary, rue, pansies, marigolds, violets, gillyflowers (carnations) and, most famously, 'that which we call a rose, By any other name would smell as sweet'.

Through a picket gate at the far side of the potager, Ruth Watson grows more vegetables and herbs in narrow strips. This is a garnishing garden where decorative salad leaves, flowers and herbs are grown for easy picking. Alan Ford, Hintlesham's chef, uses all these plants in his dishes and makes a particularly delicious herb sorbet from them.

Yellow- and green-leaved purslane and the spicy leaves of salad rocket – both once widely grown – flourish here with dill, coriander and chervil, angelica, hyssop and thyme to create a charming herbal patchwork. Half the sage and chives are left untrimmed to allow them to produce their blue and mauve flowers. And a few plants of dill, fennel and coriander are left to flower so that the seed can be dried for the kitchen.

This garnishing garden also acts as a nursery which can be raided for plants needed to fill unexpected gaps in the main garden. Similarly, Gertrude Jekyll kept tubs of what she called 'fillers' for placing in gaps in her garden at Munstead Wood.

Asparagus grows in a narrow bed close to the hedge. The dozen or so crowns are not intended to keep Hintlesham in asparagus for the eight weeks of the season; this asparagus is grown for the tender tips which are lightly steamed to keep their bright green colour and are added to a dish at the last minute. Castelvetro, in his treatise of 1614, disparaged the English asparagus of the time, '. . . when I see the weedy specimens of this noble plant for sale in London I never cease to wonder why no one has yet taken the trouble to improve its cultivation.' Perhaps at Thomas Timperley's Hintlesham Hall, they did.

Globe artichokes grow in solitary splendour, their glaucous-blue sculpted leaves displayed to perfection. This Italian vegetable was quite familiar to Elizabethan gardeners who were advised by Charles Estienne, in *Maison Rustique or the Countrey Farme*, to soak the seeds – which resemble those of sweet peas – for three days before planting 'in the iuce of Roses or Lilies, or oyle of Bay, or of Lavander'. Then 'Plant Artichoks in the new of

the moone about our Ladie day in Lent' and give them 'a whole plot by themselves', which in the case of one Wimbledon garden of the time became a separate 'hartichoak garden' of 100 square metres/120 square yards.

The recipe book of Elinor Fettiplace, recently edited by Hilary Spurling, and the more well-known *Delightes for Ladies* by Sir Hugh Plat and Gervase Markham's *The English House-Wife*, record the considerable cooking and preserving involved in a well-organized Elizabethan household. Among the recipes for the preserving of cherries, raspberries, apricots, pears and quinces and the instructions for the candying of flowers, there are several ways of preparing globe artichokes.

Even more exotic to today's gardener is gardening advice for growing saffron, sometimes written as 'saferowne'. Lawson's *The Country Housewife's Garden* said that saffron should be grown in a separate plot, which was sometimes known by the romantic name of a 'saffron garth'. This costly spice was highly valued in Elizabethan cooking and medicine and the crocus, *Crocos sativus*, whose stamens are dried to produce saffron, were grown on such scale by the monks at Walden in Essex that the town became known as Saffron Walden.

The saffron crocus, whose corms increase by underground runners, is still grown in England by Roy Paske, a nurseryman from Newmarket in Suffolk (see the appendix for details). How delightful it would be to see a saffron garth at Hintlesham again.

One boundary of the kitchen garden is formed by an avenue of espalier fruit trees, mainly apples and pears, each with a square bed at its base filled with a flowering herb. The starry blue flowers of borage, the white lacy umbels of chervil and the yellow-centred daisies of feverfew look well against the grass of the old orchard. Here there are some magnificent old apple and pear trees. In the time of the Timperleys there would have been crab apples too, for making verjuice, the sharp-tasting juice widely used in cooking. And, of course, one would have found cherry trees – the most sought-after fruit of the time.

'When you take over an old garden, everything is a surprise,' remembers Ruth Watson. 'For example, Bob Carrier grew many more annual plants than I can cope with – all the sowing and bedding-out takes so long. So I have planted more perennial herbs and fruits. But I doubt that even Bob knew what varieties these very old trees are. Yet there's still a lot of fruit from them.'

The problem of identifying the varieties of old fruit trees is of interest to the Royal Horticultural Society at Wisley. Harry Baker, the Society's Fruit Officer, tells me that they offer a most valuable service to

members of the society. It is necessary to send the RHS several examples of the fruit at ripening time and the members of the Fruit Committee, which includes some highly distinguished and experienced gardeners, invariably succeed in naming the variety of your tree. (See appendix for details).

A fruit that is readily identifiable to just about everyone is the fig. Two well-established trees grow against the south wall of the house. Although allowed to grow unchecked for some years, the trees are now being pruned back into production, because a fig whose roots are not confined tends to produce branch and leaf rather than fruit.

Among the belt of mature trees planted on the north side of the garden to protect it from the bitter winds stands a sweet chestnut. And I realize that in the past many more nut trees would have been planted in this garden. The Elizabethan country housewife made a 'Sucket of greene Walnuts' by pickling them in a mixture of honey and vinegar. Hazelnuts were stored in clay pots buried in the ground. Walnuts were kept in good condition until eaten at Christmas by packing them amongst the dry mush left when crab apples have been crushed to produce verjuice. And sweet chestnuts were 'kept all the yeare' by drying them on the floor of the brick bread oven when the baking was over. The same method of drying chestnuts was used until early this century in the farmhouses of the Ardeche in France. When needed for cooking, the dried nuts are soaked in warm water until softened.

After spending a long time in this delightful potager and orchard, I walked out through the picket gate and up the lane until I came to a long high brick wall. At the gateway I looked in and was immediately transported through three centuries of horticulture to the huge nineteenth-century kitchen garden that belonged to Hintlesham Hall. Sadly, this magnificent garden is now empty except for a few fruit trees. But there is always hope; Ruth Watson has plans to restore it. But that's another story.

SUFFOLK LOBSTER WITH LIGHT CUCUMBER AND CHERVIL SAUCE SERVED WITH PASTA RIBBONS

4 lobsters, about 700 g/1½ lb each, poached and shelled

1 cucumber (English hothouse cucumber if available)

60 g/2 oz/4 tbsp butter

2 shallots, finely chopped

2 tbsp chopped chervil

3 tbsp champagne

2 tbsp dry white wine

150 ml/¼ pint/⅔ cup fish stock

300 ml/½ pint/1¼ cups double (heavy) cream

salt

cayenne pepper

4 portions of fresh pasta

Cut the cucumber in half lengthways and then into quarters. Cut away the seeds and divide the cucumber into 4 cm/1½ in lengths. Use a short, sharp knife to trim each piece of cucumber into a torpedo shape. Reserve all the trimmings and the seeds of the cucumber.

Melt half the butter in a pan and stir in the shallots, half the chervil and the cucumber trimmings. Cook over moderate heat until translucent.

Add 2 tbsp champagne and the white wine and boil to reduce by two-thirds. Add the fish stock and reduce over high heat until the liquid is syrupy. Add the cream to the pan and reduce until the sauce thickens. Liquidize the sauce and pass through a fine sieve into a clean pan. Reduce again until the sauce is of the desired consistency. Stir in the remaining champagne and chervil and season to taste with salt and cayenne pepper.

Melt the remaining butter and gently cook the 'turned' pieces of cucumber; do not allow to colour. Meanwhile, cook the pasta in a large pan of salted boiling water; drain. Lift the cucumber from the pan and toss the pasta in the cucumber-flavoured butter. Heat the lobster in a steamer or in some fish stock.

Slice the lobster and arrange on four plates. Divide the pasta between the plates and spoon the cucumber and chervil sauce around it. Garnish with the 'turned' cucumber. *Serves 4*

RARE BEEF WITH SESAME SAUCE AND SPINACH AND PURSLANE SALAD

225 g/8 oz Scottish fillet (tenderloin) steak

sea salt and freshly milled black pepper

young salad leaves including spinach, yellow and green purslane, rocket (arugula), radicchio, endive frisée (curly endive), 'Lollo Rosso' lettuce

white part of 1 leek, cut into fine julienne

1 carrot, cut into fine julienne

1 stalk celery, cut into fine julienne

150 ml/¼ pint/⅔ cup vinaigrette

toasted sesame seds

DRESSING:

1 tbsp sesame oil

7 g/¼ oz/fresh root ginger, peeled and finely chopped

7 g/¼ oz garlic (2-3 cloves), chopped

1 shallot, chopped

toasted sesame seeds

1 tbsp mirin (sweet sake used only in cooking)

½ tbsp sake

1 tbsp yellow bean sauce

150 ml/¼ pint/⅔ cup veal stock

vinaigrette to taste

Season the beef with salt and pepper. Heat an ungreased cast-iron pan until very hot. Add the beef and seal on all sides until it forms a crispy skin. Transfer the beef to a plate and allow to cool, then refrigerate.

To make the dressing, heat the sesame oil in a pan and sweat the ginger, garlic, shallot and sesame seeds until soft, but do not allow to colour. Add the mirin and sake and boil to reduce by two-thirds. Add the yellow bean sauce and veal stock and reduce by two-thirds again. Liquidize the sauce and allow to cool. Whisk in vinaigrette until the desired flavour is obtained. Season with salt and pepper.

Slice the beef as thinly as possible and arrange on four plates. Season with salt and pepper.

Toss the salad leaves with the julienne of vegetables and dress with the vinaigrette. Arrange the salad at the top of the plate. Pour the sauce around the bccf and sprinkle with toasted sesame seeds. *Serves 4*

PEARS POACHED IN SAFFRON AND LEMON

8 ripe dessert pears such as 'Doyenné du Comice'

450 g/1 lb/2 cups sugar

900 ml/1½ pints/3¾ cups water

juice of 2 lemons

pinch of saffron filaments

1 tbs arrowroot

DECORATION:

nasturtium flowers

sprigs of salad burnet or mint

a little raspberry coulis (optional)

Peel the pears, leaving them whole, and remove their cores from the base of each fruit.

In a pan large enough to hold the pears, dissolve the sugar in the water with the lemon juice over medium heat. Bring to the boil and add the saffron and the pears. When the liquid has returned to the boil, lower the heat so that the pears poach very gently for about 20 minutes or until tender.

Carefully remove the pears, which should be a beautiful shade of yellow. Taste the cooking liquid and add more sugar or lemon juice according-ly. Blend the arrowroot with a little water and add, stirring, to the pear liquid. Cook, stirring, for 1-2 mi-nutes or until the sauce is clear and glossy. Pass the sauce through a fine sieve and leave to cool.

Arrange two pears on each plate. Spoon the sauce over the fruit and garnish with nasturtium flowers and a sprig of salad burnet or mint. If you wish, you can pipe and feather some raspberry coulis, as in the photo-graph. *Serves 4*

PUMPKIN *and* SQUASH
Cucurbita pepo, C. maxima, C. moschata

THE PUMPKIN AND THE SQUASH ARE RE-lated to the melon and cucumber. They are all members of the large Cucurbitaceae family although the pumpkin and squash are easier to grow outdoors.

Both summer and winter squashes are still regarded as an American vegetable in Britain – but the interest is growing. Dorothy Hartley says, in *Food in England*, that the pumpkin was never very popular in England whereas it has, of course, an important role in the American Thanksgiving dinner.

The squash plant takes up less room than a pumpkin and therefore may be of more interest to the gourmet gardener. Seedsmen are now offering a wider range of squash varieties – in the past I had to depend on American friends sending me interesting seeds. The patty pan squash has yellow, white and green-skinned varieties. I like this squash because its shape makes it a natural container: slice off the top and discard the seeds and pulp. Then spoon out the flesh and cook it with garlic, saffron and cream, you can make a delicious, subtle soup for serving in the patty pan case. Place the lid on top and serve the natural tureen – one to each person with a bowl of hot, buttery croûtons.

The crook-neck squash, the acorn squash with its attractive fluted shape and the hubbard squash are all excellent table squashes. One of the most delicious is the spaghetti squash, also known as vegetable spaghetti. When cooked – it can be boiled or baked, but puncture the skin first – the spaghetti squash is cut in half and the fine tagliatelle-like threads are spooned out of the skin and tossed with melted butter and black pepper. Sprinkle with freshly grated Parmesan cheese and serve as a vegetable course – or in place of pasta.

Many of the summer squashes store for several months in a cold place. Winter squashes like the oval buff-skinned 'Butter-nut' and the orange-skinned 'Little Gem' will store until Easter.

Sow squash seeds in pots of compost under glass during late spring. Plant out when all danger of frost is gone, leaving 60-75 cm/24-30 in between the plants. Squash do best in a fertile soil in full sun. Water generously in hot weather and pick the squash as soon as large enough to eat, to bring on the rest of the crop. During August pinch out the growing tips to allow the fruit to complete growing before the first frost.

Pumpkins are grown in just the same way as squash. They form even larger plants and it is usually a good idea to pinch out their shoots once each plant has no more than four fruits formed. Tuck dry straw or cardboard under each fruit to keep the skin clean. Cut the fruits and store them in a cold place until needed for making pumpkin pie and the traditional big lantern for Hallowe'en. I like the pumpkin varieties 'Hundredweight', 'Connecticut Field' and 'Triple Treat' – whose name is surely a Chinese whisper version of Trick or Treat? Also do try the miniature pumpkins like 'Jack be Little'. I serve them stuffed with a mixture of crab, green coriander and spiced pumpkin purée as a lovely supper dish.

SWEETCORN
Zea mays

WILLIAM COBBETT, WHO HAD LIVED IN AMERICA, GREW sweetcorn in Britain. He wrote, 'This is a very fine garden vegetable . . . mine never fails to come to perfection in England, be the summer what it may.'

Sweetcorn is a native of South America and the plant was widely grown by North American Indians. My mother is Canadian, and I grew up with this delicious vegetable growing in our English garden. The 'corn', as we knew it, was served almost too hot to handle and running with melted butter. My brothers and I loved gnawing at the cobs of rich golden grains and sucking every trace of butter from the seed husks. I still enjoy this – a cob or two of sweetcorn makes a first-rate lunch on a warm autumn day spent gardening. It's a very satisfying food. Sweetcorn tastes particularly good grilled over charcoal on a barbecue. In Cyprus, along the seafront in Larnaca, small stalls sell freshly-grilled cobs of sweetcorn that taste smokey and sweet; how agreeable it was to stroll on the beach in late September, nibbling the sweetcorn and watching the sun go down over the Mediterranean.

For serving with other foods, I strip off the kernels by running a sharp knife down each side of the cob. Then cook the kernels with cream and butter to make a very good accompaniment to spiced sausages or ham. Or make American corn fritters or a corn bisque. In Europe, the Italians appreciate this vegetable the most as it is grown to produce the yellow cornmeal for polenta.

Sweetcorn has become easier to grow recently because there is a new family of fast-maturing super-sweet F1 varieties which are well worth trying. Sweetcorn straight from the garden to the pot to the plate really is astonishingly good. The sugar has not converted to starch and the vegetable is milky and luscious. Sow seed two to a pot in mid spring, in a temperature of 18°C/65°F, under glass or on the windowsill. Remove the weaker of the two seedlings and, after hardening off, plant outside in a deep, fertile soil in full sun during early summer. Plant in blocks, 60 cm/2 ft apart, because the flowers of sweet corn are fertilized by the wind and so some of the plants might get missed in a single row. As the plants grow, earth-up the stems to help prevent wind rock.

The cobs are ready to eat when the silky tassels at the end of each ear have turned brown. Strip off the leaves and plunge the cobs into unsalted boiling water; and cook for 7 minutes, or longer, until the kernels are tender. They should be juicy and sweet, not coarse and dry. Spread butter over the cobs and serve straight away. Recommended varieties of sweetcorn are: the super-sweet 'Candle' F1, 'Earlibelle' F1, 'First of All' F1, and 'Honeydew' F1, which produces small 15-17.5 cm/6-7 in cobs ideal for children. US varieties include 'Sugar Buns' and 'Platinum Lady'.

MARIGOLD
Calendula officinalis

Culinary use: petals and flowers in salads, garnishes, custards, butter, homemade cheeses; young leaves in salads.

Cultivation: hardy annual with orange and yellow flowers, height 30 cm/12 in; grow in well-drained fertile soil in full sun.

PURSLANE
Portulaca oleracea

Culinary use: leaves and flowers in salads; the cooked leaves make a green sauce for vegetable dishes; young leaves added to fruit compotes.

Cultivation: half-hardy annual with green or yellow leaves and flowers, height 15-30 cm/6-12 in; grow in moist, fertile soil in full sun.

SALSIFY
Tragopogon porrifolius

SCORZONERA
Scorzonera hispanica

IT'S EXTRAORDINARY HOW FOOD AND GARDENING WRITERS GO ON ABOUT THESE two root vegetables as if they were something special. Yes, they have rarity value – they are not for sale in every greengrocers – so when you do see them in the 'gourmet vegetable' department of supermarkets, they cost quite a lot. I have grown both these vegetables several times during the last twenty years and although every plant is interesting from the gardener's point of view, as a cook I do not find either salsify or scorzonera even mildly irresistible. Furthermore, I've never met anyone who has detected the slightest flavour of oysters in salsify, which is also known as the oyster plant. Waverly Root says of the vegetable: 'I notice that its partisans tend to describe its flavor as "delicate," which may be a giveaway. Certainly nobody would call it aggressive. Salsify does not force itself upon the attention, which may be the reason why it has never, at any time or in any place, occupied a particularly important rank in gastronomy.'

Even given these considerations, it is worth growing the plants now and again, for they are part of the fascinating history of food. Salsify has a long, tapering white root with a white skin. Scorzonera has a long slim white root with a black skin. These are early autumn vegetables, so sow seed in a moderately rich, deeply-dug soil during the spring. Thin the seedlings to 7.5 cm/3 in apart and keep weed-free. Salsify produces long, narrow leaves and scorzonera has wider blade-shape leaves – both, when young or blanched, can be eaten in salads. Dig the vegetables from late summer onwards. Discard the mature leaves and scrape or peel the roots.

Cook in boiling salted water with a good splash of milk to keep the vegetable white, and serve with a well-flavoured béchamel sauce. Incidentally, I like their daisy-like yellow flowers and add them to salads.

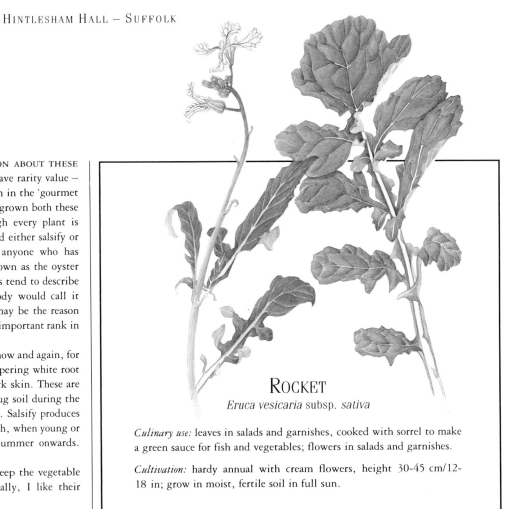

ROCKET
Eruca vesicaria subsp. *sativa*

Culinary use: leaves in salads and garnishes, cooked with sorrel to make a green sauce for fish and vegetables; flowers in salads and garnishes.

Cultivation: hardy annual with cream flowers, height 30-45 cm/12-18 in; grow in moist, fertile soil in full sun.

CRAB APPLE
Malus

IN MANY NURSERY CATALOGUES THE CRAB APPLE APPEARS IN THE FLOWERING TREE section. Which is reasonable since most of the varieties are grown for their pretty cup-shaped flowers and autumn colour rather than their fruit. Some crab apples, though, appeal to both the eye and the palate. And it's the trees with larger fruits which are of interest to the cook – the blossom that appears in April and May is a fabulous bonus.

Modern varieties of crab apple have been developed from the ancient wild form, *Malus silvestris*. The crab apple makes a small attractive tree which is easy to grow although in areas of heavy rainfall the common apple diseases of scab and cancer can occur when the tree is planted in a poorly drained soil.

Looking back I think I planted one crab apple in every garden I've owned. The tree is a delight and I can't recommend it too highly. The fruit needs to be cooked to be edible. It makes a beautiful clear sharp jelly, with an amber or red colour depending on the fruit, that is an excellent accompaniment to roast game and cold ham. I also pickle the fruit every autumn with cider vinegar, sugar and spices.

The crab apple with the largest fruit is 'John Downie'. The tree grows up to 3.5 m/12 ft, and its white flowers produce oval 5-7.5 cm/2-3 in long fruit that has a golden-yellow skin flushed with red. The fully ripe fruit is red all over. The variety 'Golden Hornet' is a joy, it grows to 3 m/10 ft and has white blossom and spectacular round bright yellow fruit which stays on the branches until Christmas. The form, 'Dartmouth', is most handsome, it grows to 3.5 ml/12 ft, produces fragrant white flowers and large crimson fruit.

MEDLAR
Mespilus germanica

GILLIAN RILEY HAS RENDERED A GREAT SERVICE TO EVERY GARDENER WITH A sense of history: she has recently provided us with the first English translation of *The Fruit, Herbs and Vegetables of Italy* by Giacomo Castelvetro. This happy book was written in 1614 while Castelvetro was a member of the household of Sir Adam Newton in Eltham yet, sadly, two years later, Castelvetro died, 'poor, ill and unhappy'.

A bed of flame-coloured nasturtiums glow in the evening sun at Hintlesham Hall.

The entry for medlars is particularly charming. 'They ripen, as the proverb says, with a little time and a little straw. Medlars are quite well known in England, and well liked for their pleasant flavour. They are eaten raw after meals, with or without sugar.' Castelvetro then desribes the Italian game of 'Ventura' that is played on the feast of St Martin, the night of 10 November when, by tradition, the first of the season's wines are sampled.

To play 'Ventura', the father of the family hides each of three coins inside a ripe medlar which are then shaken into a basket of the fruit. The youngest child at the gathering distributes two fruit to everyone present; two medlars are set aside for the poor – if they contain money, it is given to the first beggar who calls – and the last two fruit in the basket are given to the child. Castelvetro remembers 'the indescribable joy I once felt on finding the money in a fruit. When this cheerful commotion has died down, the medlars are eaten and the wines sampled.'

In Britain, port is the wine associated with medlars, for in the past, when medlars were more common, they were consumed together at the end of an autumn dinner. In the British climate medlars rarely ripen on the tree. So they must be 'bletted' or left to decay slightly by storing them in a cool place, spread out on straw, until they have softened.

Medlars are an acquired taste. I find their soft, light brown flesh has a delicious and unusual flavour – like a slightly winey custard – and they make a good accompaniment to a Wensleydale or a Caerphilly cheese. Alternatively, the unripe fruit can be used to make a fruit jelly for serving with game. Or a thick purée of the fruit can be turned into an old English butter or cheese, which is eaten in slices at the end of a meal.

The russet, brown fruit of this decorative tree has a noble history: Pliny writes of three varieties of medlar. The best-flavoured variety offered by fruit nurseries today is the 'Nottingham', which is possibly the same variety as the highly-rated 'Neapolitan' of the last century.

Any bon viveur with room in their garden should plant a medlar if only to prevent the fruit from disappearing entirely. The pretty blush-white cup-shaped flowers appear in May, and the intriguing-looking fruit, with their five conspicuous calyx lobes, are ready to pick in late autumn. The fruit has been the subject of ribaldry for centuries. In Shakespeare's time the medlar was known as the open-arse, and he refers to the fruit in both *Romeo and Juliet* and in *As You Like It*. Chaucer refers to the fruit in *The Reeve's Tale*, and according to the Westminster Abbey Customary of 1270, the gardening monks were required to produce medlars and other fruits for the monastery every year.

The medlar is a hardy, slow-growing tree with a maximum height of 5-6 m/15-18 ft, though the *Oxford Book of Food Plants* states that 'the size of the tree is proportionate to that of the fruit'. The tree tolerates a wide range of growing conditions, but prefers a well-drained soil in a sheltered position because its spreading habit can make it vulnerable to wind damage. In my Devon garden, I have planted a medlar on a grassy bank so that the drooping branches dip low towards the ground; in the autumn the tree looks beautiful as the leathery leaves redden and the golden-brown windfalls scatter on the dewy grass.

NASTURTIUM
Tropaeolum majus

Culinary use: the petals and flowers in salads, garnishes, to flavour white wine vinegar; chopped flowers and leaves in nasturtium butter for pasta and cooked vegetables; young leaves in salads; seed heads pickled in vinegar as a substitute for capers.

Cultivation: hardy annual with orange, yellow, cream and red flowers, dwarf and climbing varieties, height 20 cm/8 in; grow in poor, well-drained soil in full sun.

Although there are several varieties of sage, the grey-leaved variety has the most pronounced flavour.

GOOSEBERRY
Ribes uva-crispa (R. grossularia)

THE GOOSEBERRY IS A PECULIARLY BRITISH FRUIT AND NOT ESPECIALLY VALUED anywhere else. Even the French, normally such good arbiters in the matter of food, regard the gooseberry as an acid fruit mainly suitable for eating with an oily fish like mackerel, hence its French name *groseille à maquereau*.

These days, the opinion of Mrs Beeton (1836-1864, author of *Book of Household Management*), that 'All sorts of gooseberries are agreeable when stewed, and, in this country especially, there is no fruit so universally in favour', is no longer true. Boxes of sharp green gooseberries are still sold, quite cheaply, during May. The fruit, usually from local gardens, is sold to those increasingly few people who enjoy gooseberry pie and gooseberry fool, and the enlightened cooks who make the exquisite gooseberry and elderflower jelly.

I can see that unless we learn to love the gooseberry, that it will disappear totally from our shops and leave just a few of us to cosset this lovely fruit in our gardens. The main reason for the decline in popularity of the gooseberry is because so few people have ever tasted the best of the species: the dessert gooseberry – that large, deep red fruit, its thin satiny skin enclosing a cushion of sweet muscat-flavoured jelly. I can remember baskets lined with leaves full of this glowing fruit, each one no larger than a quails' egg; when I was a child gooseberries were served at the end of a meal, as a treat.

Lawrence D. Hills, our most splendid pioneer of organic gardening, blames the decline of the dessert gooseberry on 'the rise of 'Careless' to almost our only variety. Though this is a good, large market variety making rather a spreading bush, it is essentially for cooking and bottling. When it ripens to creamy white it is not a flavour fruit.' Although the 'Leveller' is sold as a 'dual purpose' gooseberry for cooking and eating raw, it is really only suitable for a pie, in my view.

Now a real old-fashioned dessert gooseberry – the kind that Beatrix Potter's Tom Kitten is caught under – is 'Whinham's Industry'; its sparring partner is 'May Duke' and a comparable creamy-skinned dessert gooseberry is 'Whitesmith'. In areas troubled with mildew, the new 'Invicta', bred from 'Whinham's Industry' and the German mildew-resistant 'Resistenta' might be worth trying, but I have not tasted the fruit.

There are still over 200 varieties of gooseberry available in Britain, evidence of the flourishing Gooseberry Clubs of the nineteenth century (in fact, some still exist), which held competitions for the heaviest fruit. Edward Bunyard wrote: 'The plebian origin of the Gooseberry has been, I fear, a handicap to its appreciation at cultured tables . . . the fruit is well worthy of the gourmet's attention.'

The gooseberry is perennial, self-fertile and easy to grow. Plant from November to March (or in the spring in the US) in deep, fertile soil. Prune back to stimulate new growth, and in early summer give a mulch to conserve the moisture in the soil and keep down weeds. The fruit appears on two-year-old wood; prune back the fruiting spurs quite soon after harvesting the fruit. I find gooseberry cuttings taken in late summer root easily in sandy soil. Picking the fruit is far easier, and less painful, from a bush grown as a cordon or pillar. But the most attractive gooseberry bush is grown as a standard on a 60-90 cm/2-3 ft stem. These are available from a good fruit nursery, or you can train an ordinary bush into a standard by pruning off the lower branches every autumn until you have the shape you want.

SAGE
Salvia officinalis

Culinary use: whole leaves wrapped around pieces of veal or poultry and fried, in marinades and slow-cooked meat and game dishes; chopped leaves in stuffings, sausages, sauces; flowers in salads and garnishes.

Cultivation: hardy evergreen shrub with grey, purple or variegated leaves, blue flowers and scarlet-flowered pineapple sage, height 30-60 cm/1-2 ft; grow in light, well-drained soil in full sun.

ICED PUMPKIN SOUP WITH ALMONDS

This is a delectably pretty, gently spiced chilled soup.

700 g/1¹/₂ lb pumpkin flesh, deseeded

60 g/2 oz/4 tbsp butter

1 small onion, chopped

600 ml/1 pint/2¹/₂ cups light chicken stock

300 ml/¹/₂ pint/1¹/₄ cups milk

150 ml/¹/₄ pint/²/₃ cup single (light) cream

salt

grated nutmeg

GARNISH:

1-2 tbsp toasted flaked (sliced) almonds

few sprigs of variegated mint

Roughly dice the pumpkin. Melt the butter in a saucepan, add the onion and pumpkin and stir to coat with butter. Cover with a lid and lower the heat. Cook gently for 10 minutes, but do not let the butter darken.

Add the stock and simmer for about 10 minutes, then purée the contents of the pan. Reheat the soup with the milk and cream, and season to taste with salt and freshly grated nutmeg. Cool the soup, then chill.

Serve in wide soup bowls, garnished with toasted almonds and sprigs of variegated mint. *Serves 4-6*

GREEN TAGLIATELLE WITH NASTURTIUM BUTTER

This delicious green pasta dish is flecked with bright orange nasturtium petals and the peppery-tasting leaves.

225 g/8 oz fresh green tagliatelle

salt

1 tbsp olive oil

freshly grated Parmesan cheese

NASTURTIUM BUTTER:

about 12 nasturtium flowers

6 medium-sized nasturtium leaves, or 30 g/1 oz/¹/₄ cup watercress

75 g/2¹/₂ oz/5 tbsp unsalted butter, softened

Make the nasturtium butter first: set aside four nasturtium flowers to garnish the dish and chop the remaining flowers and the leaves, or the watercress. Blend into the butter and leave in a warm place.

Cook the tagliatelle in salted boiling water until al dente. Drain well and return to the hot pan with the olive oil and the nasturtium butter. Toss well, then transfer to a hot serving dish.

Garnish with the nasturtium flowers and serve with the Parmesan cheese. *Serves 2-4*

The jewel-like blooms of delicately veined nasturtium flowers and their peppery-flavoured leaves.

94

Small-leaved Greek basil, one of the characteristic flavours of the Mediterranean.

GENOESE PESTO

This wonderful blend of fresh basil, pine nuts, garlic and Parmesan cheese is one of the world's great sauces. For me, it is the only truly satisfying accompaniment to a bowl of plain pasta.

115 g/4 oz/2½ cups basil leaves

8 tbsp virgin olive oil

30 g/1 oz/⅓ cup pine nuts

2 medium-size cloves garlic, chopped

¼ tsp salt

60 g/2 oz/½ cup Parmesan cheese, freshly grated

60 g/2 oz/4 tbsp unsalted butter (optional)

Measure the basil, olive oil, pine nuts, garlic and salt into a blender or food processor and whizz until you have an even paste. Alternatively, pound the ingredients in a mortar with a pestle.

Gradually work in the Parmesan cheese and, if you wish, the butter. Have ready a large bowl of freshly cooked pasta. Thin the pesto with a little of the pasta cooking liquid and spoon over the sauce. Toss lightly and serve straight away. *Serves 4-6*

CRAB AND SWEETCORN CHOWDER WITH LIME AND CORIANDER LEAVES

2-3 medium-sized sweetcorn cobs (ears), to produce 225 g/8 oz/1¼ cups kernels

30 g/1 oz/2 tbsp butter

1 slim clove garlic or 1 slice of onion, chopped

450 ml/¾ pint/2 cups creamy milk

450 ml/¾ pint/2 cups water

2 tsp cornflour (cornstarch)

90 ml/3 fl oz double (heavy) cream

pinch of ground ginger

squeeze of fresh lime juice

salt and freshly milled pepper

175 g/6 oz/1½ cups cooked crabmeat

1 tbsp chopped fresh coriander (cilantro) leaves

GARNISH:

6 coriander (cilantro) leaves

long thin curls of lime zest (rind)

Cut the kernels from the sweetcorn by running a sharp knife down the sides of each cob.

Melt the butter in a pan and stir in the garlic or onion and the sweetcorn kernels. Add the milk and water and cook, covered, over a moderate heat for 10-15 minutes or until the sweetcorn is tender.

Purée the soup in a food processor and return to the pan. Add the cornflour blended with the cream and the ginger. Stir the soup and bring to the boil. Cook, stirring, until thickened. Season the soup with salt, pepper and lime juice.

Warm six soup plates and divide the crabmeat between them. Sprinkle the coriander into the soup and ladle into the plates. Garnish with the whole coriander leaves and curls of lime zest (rind). Serve straight away, with crusty bread. *Serves 6*

ELIZABETHAN SNOWE

Towering stems of fennel surrounded by the young grey-green spikes of rosemary.

Originally this light, foamy cream was spooned over flat gingerbread to look like snow. Then a sprig of rosemary was stuck in the middle to look like a tree and rosemary spikes decorated the edge as grass on a snowy morning. A lighter alternative is to serve the 'snowe' in ginger-flavoured brandy snap baskets.

3 egg whites

75 g/2¹/₂ oz/5 tbsp rosemary-flavoured sugar (see below)

150 ml/¹/₄ pint/²/₃ cup double (heavy) cream

2 tsp rose water

TO SERVE:

6 brandy snap baskets (or thin cooki baskets)

few rosemary flowers

Whisk the egg whites until stiff. Whisk in half the sugar, then fold in the rest.

In another bowl, whip the cream until stiff but still glossy. Mix in the rose water to taste. Fold the cream into the egg whites, taking care not to lose the air in the mixture.

Spoon the 'snowe' into the brandy snap baskets and decorate with the rosemary flowers. Serve straight away before the snaps soften. *Serves 6. Note: for Rosemary sugar see page 55.*

VEGETABLE MARROW COOKED IN A PAPER BAG

Nicholas Soyer was the grandson of Alexis Soyer, the innovative chef who presided over the Reform Club in London during the mid-nineteenth century. He wrote a small book called Paper-Bag Cookery, *and this is a slight adaptation of his recipe.*

2 small vegetable marrows (large zucchini or other squash)

175-225 g/6-8 oz/1¹/₂-2 cups cooked chicken meat or ham, chopped

1 shallot or small onion, finely chopped

2 tomatoes, chopped

115 g/4 oz mushrooms, chopped

1 tbsp plain flour (all-purpose) flour or fine breadcrumbs

dash of Worcestershire sauce

2 tbsp stock

salt and freshly milled pepper

small piece of butter

Peel the marrows, cut them in half lengthways and remove the seeds. Blanch in boiling salted water for 3 minutes, then drain well. Place each marrow 'boat' on a sheet of well-buttered non-stick baking paper (parchment) or foil large enough to enclose the stuffed marrow.

Mix the chicken or ham with the shallot or onion, tomatoes, mushrooms, flour or breadcrumbs, Worcestershire sauce, and stock. Season with a little salt and pepper. For speed, it is possible to use a food processor, but the mixture should not be chopped too finely.

Spoon the stuffing equally into the marrow halves and dot the top

*Clusters of glowing fruit on a 'Golden Hornet'
crab apple tree.*

with slivers of butter. Fold the paper or foil loosely over the top and secure the edges firmly by folding – or use paperclips or wooden clothes' pegs (pins) that can be removed before serving.

Place the packages on a non-stick baking sheet and bake in an oven preheated to 190°C/375°F/Gas Mark 5 for 35-50 minutes or until the marrow is tender.

Transfer to a hot serving dish and serve the packages straight away. *Serves 4*

SWEET-PICKLED GINGER CRAB APPLES

Sweet-pickled fruit and vegetables are ready to eat after a few days and are best served within two months. These crab apples go well with cold ham and poultry. For pickling, I recommend the fruit from the varieties 'Golden Hornet', 'John Downie' and 'Hyslop'.

300 ml/½ pint/1¼ cups cider vinegar or
    white wine vinegar

300 ml/½ pint/1¼ cups water

4 cm/1½ in/piece of fresh root ginger,
    peeled and sliced

5 cm/2 in piece of cinnamon stick

4 allspice berries

2 cloves

2.5 cm/1 in strip of zest (rind) of lemon

225 g/8 oz/1 cup white sugar

450 g/1 lb crab apples

bay leaves

Measure the vinegar and water into a stainless steel or glass pan. Add the ginger, cinnamon, allspice, cloves, zest of lemon and sugar and bring to the boil. Simmer for 5 minutes.

Meanwhile, wash and drain the crab apples. Remove any leaves, but keep the stalks intact. Steam the fruit, in batches if necessary, over simmering water for 8-15 minutes, depending on the size, until cooked but not mushy.

Pack the fruit into several small,

hot jars or one large jar. Add a bay leaf to each jar, placing it against the glass. Strain the boiling syrup on to the fruit. Cover and seal with an air-tight lid. Store in a cold place for at least 2 days before serving.

Note: To make Sweet-pickled ginger vegetables: instead of the crab apples, prepare the same weight of mixed vegetables, all cut to roughly the same size. I usually prepare a selection that includes florets of cauliflower and calabrese, carrots, turnips, courgettes (zucchini), shallots, cloves of garlic, celery, red-skinned apples, baby sweetcorn, French (fine green) beans, a few slices of peeled fresh ginger, and a sprig or two of rosemary or fennel.

Steam or blanch the vegetables and proceed as in the recipe above. *Makes about 1 kg/2 lb*

CHAPTER FIVE

APPLE, MUSHROOM, RASPBERRY, FIG, BLACKBERRY *and* BLUEBERRY, BAY, NUT TREES, SALAD BURNET, ONION *and* SHALLOT, GARLIC, JUNIPER, SPINACH *and* SWISS CHARD

A WOODLAND KITCHEN GARDEN IN DEVONSHIRE
GIDLEIGH PARK

ONE OF THE BIGGEST PROBLEMS ABOUT GARDENING AT GIDLEIGH Park, on Dartmoor, is the constant distraction of the view. Both the herb garden and the kitchen garden lie 212 m/700 ft above sea-level in a natural amphitheatre of the River Teign, which tumbles noisily over smooth granite stones only a few feet below. The grassy hillocks and dappled forest trees are brightened in the spring by swathes of purple rhododendron. And in summer, an expanse of impossibly flat lawn, dotted with croquet hoops, reflects the clear Devon light on to the grey stone terraces around the gardens.

The fine culinary herb garden at Gidleigh Park with its box-edged borders of aromatic herbs separated by gravel paths.

According to Professor W. G. Hoskins, the earliest evidence of cultivation in Britain is found on Dartmoor. The rectangular corn-plots and stone hut circles date from the Early Bronze Age, about 900-1400 BC. The hamlet of Gidleigh, which was founded in the eleventh century by Gydda, the mother of King Harold, is a peaceful collection of farms and cottages just half a mile down the twisting drive from Gidleigh Park.

In the dozen years since Paul and Kay Henderson arrived at Gidleigh Park, they have gradually colonized some of the 16 hectares/40 acres of woodland that

99

surround the house. And their gentle taming of the ancient forest that forms part of the Dartmoor National Park has provided the house with a handful of individual and delightful gardens.

The fine herb garden has been constructed at the eastern end of the terrace that skirts the house. Each border, edged with clipped box, is set amongst gravel paths, and in the centre, the intertwining initials of Gidleigh Park have been planted in the style of a knot garden. Strolling here before breakfast or lunch, or in the cool of the evening while you sip an apéritif, is a quiet pleasure. The scents of the herbs are released into the still air and drift through the open windows of the house. A mop-headed

bay tree grows in a circular bed surrounded by daisy-flowered feverfew; a rectangle of variegated sage plants, all trimmed to the same height, makes a mellow-toned tapestry, and a triangular bed of lemon mint is a sea of pale lilac, spear-shaped flowers against the bright green shafts of sorrel leaves.

One of the long narrow beds is used for growing herbs and salad vegetables to be used as garnishes – pretty russet leaves of oak-leaf lettuce, fan-shaped young coriander and flat-leaf parsley – all of them near enough to the kitchen for their last-minute addition to a dish. Tall columns of lime-flowered fennel and two fig trees trained against the wall of the house

*Right: Spikes of rosemary and cotton lavender
thrive on a grey limestone wall on Dartmoor.
Left: A low aromatic cushion of different sages
clipped to a uniform height.*

lend a Mediterranean, even a Californian, note in one corner of this herb garden. After just a few years, this garden has a well-established feel.

A narrow path leads from the herb garden to the kitchen garden which is terraced against the hillside. Shaun Hill, the remarkably gifted chef at Gidleigh Park, is an enthusiastic gardening cook. He conducted me on a tour of the kitchen garden with a non-stop commentary of what is growing and why. 'To me cooking is a natural extension of things that grow, and so I like to be involved in the garden. In my free time I really enjoy pottering around in my garden at home, growing unusual vegetables and plants.'

'A lot of our vegetables are grown organically by an enthusiast down in the valley and they arrive freshly-picked every day. So here, we mainly grow soft fruit like black currants, red currants, raspberries and alpine strawberries – this garden is fairly high for Devon and quite often the moorland mist does not clear until late morning.'

The fruit grows on the higher slopes of the garden where it collects both radiant and reflected sunlight. Further down, in the damper, shadier part of the garden, rows of spinach look fresh and sparkling in the morning light. The smallest, most tender leaves can be used in green salad. The rest of the crop is cooked briefly before serving. Both the tender-leaved annual spinach and New Zealand spinach, or tetragonia, do well in this rich woodland soil. A few plants of wild spinach, or orache, grow nearby, and I suggested that next year they grow some of the red orache with its crimson leaves which are a joy in salads.

In the kitchen garden there is a useful overflow of herbs from the herb garden: a long row of fine-leaved chives and a clump of fennel, some marjoram and lots of flat-leaf parsley. Last year Gidleigh grew some American land cress to back up their sometimes erratic supply of watercress. For although Gidleigh Park is delightfully isolated, in a hard winter the narrow Devon lanes are easily blocked with snow, and some months the watercress arrives only once a week. So Shaun frequently makes a purée and freezes it. 'The opposite of fresh is stale, not frozen,' he declares.

Nevertheless, the climate of Dartmoor can be unexpectedly rewarding for a gardener. 'There are two young olive trees growing in sheltered places in this garden', wrote Cecil Torr in *Small Talk in Wreyland*. 'The smaller one is from an olive that I picked up at Rapallo, 10 January 1910, when the olives were being shaken down. It is nearly four feet high now – September 1917. The larger one came here from Cornwall in a pot, and was planted out in the summer of 1904. It was then six feet high and very slender, and now is nearly fifteen feet high and nine inches in girth. It has not born olives yet.' Cecil Torr's garden was just 9.6 kilometres/6 miles due south of Gidleigh Park.

Across the river, in a clearing in the woodland, Keith Mansfield, the head gardener at Gidleigh, has created a new orchard. The collection of fruit trees would delight any epicure: two 'Vranja' quinces, two *Juglans regia* walnuts, a crab apple – 'John Downie', and a selection of dessert apples which includes 'Ellison's Orange', 'Sunset', 'Cox's Orange Pippin,' 'Worcester Pearmain' and 'Duke of Devonshire'. In addition there are trees of the king of English cooking apples, the 'Bramley's seedling', and some good varieties of dessert pears including 'Clapp's Favourite', 'Louise Bonne

well-flavoured field mushrooms, *Agaricus campestris*, and the tiny fairy-ring mushrooms, *Marasmius oreades*, appear overnight in the meadows below the house. In the light shade of the oak and beech trees can be found the meaty Cep, *Boletus edulis*, and the pale orange chanterelle, *Cantharellus cibarius*. Of this fungi Gertrude Jekyll wrote: 'In colour and smell it is like a ripe apricot, perfectly wholesome and when rightly cooked, most delicious in flavour and texture. It should be looked for in cool hollows in oak woods; when once found and its good qualities appreciated, it will never again be neglected.' So imagine her reaction when a certain M. le Cerf, author of *Cinq Champignons*, was visiting her garden. The story is told by Edward and Lorna Bunyard in *The Epicure's Companion*: as M. le Cerf made his way through the copse in her wild garden there was 'an awful moment when, he almost but not quite, put his foot on a chanterelle which had been coming to perfection under the epicurean eye of his hostess.'

The woodland at Shaun's kitchen door contains a rich bounty of foods for free. Wild raspberries and blackberries have seeded themselves in the water garden on the far side of the drive. Beech trees, whose flimsy young leaves make a charming addition to a green salad, comprise much of the woodland. Embedded in the hedge skirting the meadow are sloe (blackthorn) bushes, *Prunus spinosa*, with their blue-black fruit that traditionally flavours gin and colours it pink in time for Christmas.

On the higher, open stretches of moorland grows the Devon whortleberry, whose dialect name is hurtleberry; its botanical name is *Vaccinium myrtillus*. This small black fruit is known to the Hendersons and their countrymen as the bilberry, and it makes a very fine American pie.

Wild food is, of course, the most ecologically sound and 'green' food available. By extending our use of wild foods we not only enrich our diet but we are able to protect our otherwise endangered areas of natural beauty. In our highly developed world we need to cherish every wilderness.

I have noticed that since I began to harvest the giant puffballs, *Lycoperdon giganteum*, that appear every autumn near the compost heap in my garden, they have multiplied. In picking the fungi and carrying it into the kitchen, I release spores which fall and germinate in the orchard grass. And the hazelnuts from neighbouring hedgerows that I planted in my kitchen garden have produced young saplings that I am training into a nut walk. With care, it is possible to grow and harvest a wild food as if it were a garden crop with its attendant advantages of being wholly organic.

Wandering through the mossy glades in the water garden at Gidleigh Park, and admiring the natural effect that had been produced,

of Jersey,' the exotic-looking 'Glow Red Williams', 'Packham's Triumph', 'Gorham', 'Conference' and 'Dr Jules Guyot'.

In spite of the efforts of their two chief enemies, the rabbits and the bracken – both of which endeavour to reclaim any cleared ground on Dartmoor – these fine young trees are a cheering sight which would be well worth emulating if you have any ground to spare.

Shaun Hill's eclectic style of cooking leads him to search for unusual sources of food. Nothing delights him more than a day spent hiking across the hills to return laden with wild food. He is beginning to discover the best woodland places for collecting wild mushrooms. In late summer, the

had me wondering about creating a wild kitchen garden. How could it be accomplished? Then I remembered a handful of friends that had taken some steps in this direction. In North London, Sophie Grigson has a sloe (blackthorn) bush in the corner of her small paved garden for the beauty of its tiny star-like flowers and its blue-bloomed fruit which she uses to make sloe gin. A friend in Gloucestershire grows service trees and a couple of bullace *Prunus domestica* in her woodland garden to harvest their fruit. And, years ago, my mother dropped a basket of ripe wild blackberries in the shrubbery, only to discover a couple of years later that the plants which sprang from them produced marvellously luscious berries. Country people call wild blackberries brambles, and William Robinson said of them: 'A man might do a more foolish thing than get these together and grow them on some rough bank or corner. There is much beauty of leaf among the plants, and variety in the quality of the fruit.'

Inspired by the skill of the Hendersons in harmonizing their man-made environment with the surrounding unspoilt countryside, I saw that one could create an enchanting kitchen garden by unobtrusively planting some of the wild edible varieties of fruit, nuts and berries from which our cultivated varieties have been developed without losing any quality of taste. These plants would surely flourish in the damp shady conditions that are their natural habitat, and their unforced beauty would enhance any woodland garden.

The rowan or mountain ash, *Sorbus aucuparia*, with its flame-red berries which make an amber jelly that complements the flavour of roast game and moorland lamb, looks at its best growing wild – as it does in Scotland. The yellow-fruited 'Shepherd's Bullace' (Eastern European plum) and the 'Shropshire Prune' or 'Prune Damson', both forms of *Prunus insititia*, a forebear of our domesticated damson plum, would also be good choices. The 'Quetsche' is a rarely planted tree whose oval black fruit has the rich flavour of a Carlsbad plum when cooked. The myrobalan plum or cherry plum, *Prunus cerasifera*, has varieties with either red or yellow fruit, which preserved in a spiced vinegar makes a lovely preserve. Crab apples, the original wild apples of Great Britain, also make marvellous preserves. The cultivated varieties 'Red Glow', 'Golden Hornet' and 'John Downie' have much to commend them as beautiful trees in flower and fruit.

The wild cherry, *Prunus avium*, is an entrancing sight in full bloom. The tree is widely grown in Bavaria for its fruit, which flavours the fiery but excellent Schwartzwalder Kirschwasser. The Morello cherry, *Prunus cerasus*, is one of my most favourite trees, and the scarlet-fruited variety 'Kentish Red Cherry' is well worth growing because the fruit can be bottled in eau-de-vie or Armagnac to make a wonderful preserve.

Berries for a woodland garden would include the small delicate alpine strawberry, and even the tiny fraises de bois. The worcesterberry, *Ribes divaricatum*, is an American wild gooseberry related to both the gooseberry and the black currant, and is highly ornamental with its long arching branches. Both the blueberry, *Vaccinium corymbosum*, and the dewberry, *Rubus trivialus*, are popular American berries which, in my garden, prefer lightly shaded growing conditions. And the Scottish wild raspberry would feel totally at home in these surroundings.

Cutting down an elder tree, *Sambucus nigra*, is said to be unlucky. So why not plant them instead? The common elder grows freely in hedgerows

The creamy panicles of elderflower ripen into the dark shiny edible berries during August and September.

and cottage gardens. Its lacy, off-white flowers which appear in May and June make elderflower champagne, muscat-flavoured sorbets, jellies and gooseberry jam, and the shiny black berries of September have a unique and earthy flavour that goes well in a sauce with game or an old English sweet pie.

Nut trees prosper in a woodland garden. The hazel, the cob nut and the filbert, *Corylus maxima*, all grow well in most areas. The purple-leaved filbert 'Purpurea' is particularly attractive. And the sweet chestnut, *Castanea*, makes a fine tree which is self-fertile. But the walnut, *Juglans regia* prefers to be planted in twos or threes. The loveliest nut tree in my opinion, however, is the almond, *Prunus dulcis*, whose delicate pink blossoms appear on the bare branches in late March or early April. The effect is truly stunning.

As I write these words, the great British winter storms of 1990 have wrought havoc in my Devon garden. There have been many casualties. Our 100-year-old plum tree has gone and a dozen of our ancient cider apple trees. It has been estimated that Britain has lost three million trees in one week of gales. And this on top of the horrendous damage of the 1987 hurricane. I shall, of course, replant. A treeless world is too dreadful to contemplate. But now I know what trees I shall choose. I am going to make a wild kitchen garden around the sloping lawn outside my kitchen window. There will be nut trees and wild damson plums and cherries and rowans and berry plants and wild strawberries and hurtleberries and brambles. And not only will this wild kitchen garden create a natural habitat for insects and birds, but in a small way I hope that it will help to restore some part of the wooded world we have lost.

PASTA WITH *WILD* MUSHROOMS

PASTA:

115 g/4 oz/³/₄ cup plain (all-purpose) flour

salt

1 size 3 or 4 (US large) egg

1 tbsp chopped fresh herbs

2 tbsp olive oil

SAUCE:

225 g/8 oz mixed wild mushrooms including chanterelles, black trumpets (horns of plenty) and morels

60 ml/2 fl oz vegetable stock or water

120 ml/4 fl oz double (heavy) cream

squeeze of lemon juice

15 g/½ oz/1 tbsp butter

GARNISH:

1 tomato, peeled, seeded and finely chopped

finely chopped chives

Sift the flour into a bowl with a good pinch of salt and add the egg. In a liquidizer, blend the fresh herbs with the olive oil. Add this to flour and egg mixture and beat well. The amount of oil you will need to use in making the dough may well vary according to the type of flour and the size of the egg you have used. Don't be afraid to use a little more oil if the mixture looks as if it needs it.

Turn the dough out on to a floured board and knead well until it is a smooth, elastic consistency. Cover with a damp cloth and refrigerate for at least 30 minutes to allow the dough to relax.

Roll out the dough until 3 mm/ ⅛ in thick and dust with flour or fine semolina if it becomes difficult to work. Trim the sides of the dough and cut into narrow ribbons. If you have a pasta rolling machine, this will simplify matters considerably.

To make the sauce, cook the wild mushrooms in the stock or water for a few minutes. Add the cream and a little lemon juice to sharpen the flavour.

Drop the pasta into salted boiling water and cook for 2 minutes. Drain and spoon into the middle of two plates. Spoon the wild mushrooms around the outside. Beat the butter into the sauce and pour over the pasta. Garnish with a little chopped tomato and a few chopped chives. Serve straight away. *Serves 2*

RAGOÛT OF SEA BASS WITH *BABY* VEGETABLES

*Shaun Hill says he prefers to use fillets from a larger fish rather
than several small fish.*

1 sea bass (or striped bass), about 1
   kg/2¹/₄ lb

bunch of baby carrots

8 baby artichokes

small bunch of baby leeks

225 g/8 oz/1¹/₂ cups shelled baby broad
   (fava) beans

1 shallot, chopped

120 ml/4 fl oz fish stock

1 sprig of basil

salt and freshly milled pepper

115 g/4 oz/1 stick unsalted butter

4 basil leaves, to garnish

Scale the fish by scraping your knife
from tail to head. Then remove the
fillets with a sharp knife and cut into
four neat pieces.

Wash and trim all the vegetables.
Place in a pan with the shallot, stock,
basil and a little salt and pepper. Add
the fish and gently bring almost to
the boil. Poach the fish for 5-7
minutes or until just cooked.

Divide the vegetables between
four soup plates and place the sea bass
on top. Whisk the butter into the
cooking liquor and pour over the
fish. Garnish each plate with a basil
leaf and serve straight away. *Serves 4*

CORN-FED PIGEON WITH SHALLOTS

4 corn-fed pigeons (squab)

salt and freshly milled pepper

a little olive oil

12 shallots, peeled

1 tbsp olive oil, for cooking

1 glass of red wine

300 ml/½ pint/1¼ cups home-made chicken stock

½ tsp arrowroot

POTATO GALETTES:

2 large potatoes

freshly grated nutmeg

groundnut (peanut) oil, for frying

Rub the skin of the pigeons with salt, pepper and olive oil. Roast the pigeons with the shallots and olive oil in an oven preheated to 200°C/400°F/ Gas Mark 6 for 25 minutes.

Meanwhile, for the galettes, peel the potatoes but do not put them in water after they are peeled, for if you soak the starch out of them, the galettes will not stick together. Grate the potatoes on the widest setting of your grater. Carefully season with nutmeg, salt and pepper.

Heat a little groundnut (peanut) oil in a frying pan until it is quite hot. Take a heaped dessertspoonful of the potato, compress it briefly in your hand and place it in the frying pan. Let it become golden and crisp on each side. Pat dry on paper towels and keep warm while you cook the remaining galettes.

When the pigeons are cooked to your preference, lift on to a plate with the shallots and keep warm.

Deglaze the roasting pan with the red wine and stock. Thicken with the arrowroot moistened with water. Boil hard for 2-3 minutes until clear and syrupy, then strain.

To serve, place one or two potato galettes in the middle of four warm plates. Arrange a pigeon on each and spoon the sauce over. *Serves 4*

CARAMEL AND APPLE TARTLETS WITH CARAMEL ICE CREAM

Shaun Hill writes: 'Caramel and apples is not a new combination. People have enjoyed eating them together from whenever toffee apples were dreamed up. This is my variation on that theme and it works well. The choice of apple is important. Cooking apples such as 'Bramley's seedling' are quite useless – too sour and inclined to disintegrate. A sharp but well-flavoured dessert apple such as Granny Smith is fine. I don't use Cox's Orange Pippin for cooking though they are great for eating if they are ripe. We have planted both these classic varieties in our orchard at Gidleigh Park.
'The ice cream contrasts nicely with the warm tart and caramel. If you have neither the time nor inclination to make it, use a spoonful of clotted (whipped) or very thick cream instead. Don't use ready-made pastry from a shop: it will give an unpleasant greasy aftertaste and spoil the dish.'

6 dessert apples (see above)

175 g/6 oz/1½ sticks unsalted butter

250 g/9 oz/1¼ cups granulated sugar

2 tbsp Calvados

150 ml/¼ pint/⅔ cup double (heavy) cream

SWEET PASTRY:

225 g/8 oz/1⅔ cups plain (all-purpose) flour

60 g/2 oz/¼ cup caster (superfine) sugar

150 g/5 oz/10 tbsp unsalted butter, softened

1 egg

ICE CREAM:

225 g/8 oz/1 cup granulated sugar

4 tbsp cold water

300 ml/½ pint/1¼ cups milk

300 ml/½ pint/1¼ cups double (heavy) cream

8 egg yolks

Make the ice cream first. Dissolve the sugar in the cold water and boil hard until it caramelizes. It will turn a light brown colour, just past golden yellow. Take the pan off the heat at this point and let it develop into a rich brown colour as it cools slightly.

Cover your hand with a cloth while you pour the milk and the cream on top of the caramel. Stir until the caramel has dissolved; if necessary, place over low heat to melt the caramel slightly. Pour the caramel cream on to the egg yolks, whisking all the time. Return the mixture to the pan and cook very gently, stirring constantly, until slightly thickened. On no account allow the mixture to boil or the custard will go grainy. Cool the custard, then pour into a sorbetière (ice cream maker). Or pour into a lidded plastic box, freeze until almost firm, whizz in a food processor and return to the freezer.

To make the pastry, sift the flour and sugar together into a bowl. Rub in the butter and egg with your fingertips. Form the dough into a ball, wrap and rest in a cool place for 1 hour.

Roll out the dough on a floured board to 3 mm/⅛ in thickness. Line six 10 cm/4 in tartlets tins. Rest them in a cool place for 1 hour. Then place foil and beans in each pastry case and bake blind in an oven preheated to 180°C/350°F/Gas Mark 4 for 10 minutes. Cool the pastry cases in their tins, then transfer to a wire rack.

Peel and core two of the apples and cook in a covered pan for 2-3 minutes until they start to disintegrate; purée. Spoon this purée into the tartlet cases.

Cook the butter and sugar, preferably in a copper pan which spreads the heat most evenly, until the mixture caramelizes, i.e. turns a rich brown colour. Add the Calvados and cream (take care because it might spit), remove from the heat and stir until blended. Set aside.

Peel and core the remaining apples. Poach for 2 minutes in water to cover, then slice them thinly and fan them across the apple purée.

Place a tart on each plate. Coat with the caramel sauce, and serve with a scoop of caramel ice cream. Decorate the plate with a few extra slices of poached apple. *Serves 6*

Note: for our photograph, Shaun placed the ice cream in a tulipe, but this is not essential.

like the 'Bramley's Seedling' and 'Cox's Orange Pippin' have been chance seedling apples raised by amateur gardeners. The romance of the apple remains, and every child who plants a pip (seed) must hope for the perfect fruit.

Although, compared with a century ago, many fewer varieties of apple are now available, the choice is still wide with new introductions all the time. When considering planting apple trees it's worth consulting the catalogues of the best fruit nurseries. In a small garden a family tree is a good idea. And it's not a new idea – the practice of grafting several varieties of apple on to one tree was recommended by Mascall in 1575.

Apple trees are best planted during the winter (or early spring) when they are still dormant. Dig a hole at least 90 cm/3 ft across and 60-90 cm/2-3 ft deep and fork well-rotted compost into the base. Sprinkle some bone meal into the soil, position the tree and stake it securely, then replace the soil, packing it fairly firmly around the roots and trunk. Keep the ground free of weeds for three to four years, then you can grass over the bed or underplant with bulbs.

If you have the room there is nothing nicer than growing an epicurean orchard with fine old varieties of apples that are scorned by commercial growers yet are still available to the amateur gardener. Dwarfing stocks make such an orchard a possibility. You not only have the joy of the blossom, the beauty of the ripening fruit and the delight of picking and eating it at the right time, you also have the deep satisfaction of knowing that by planting these forgotten fruits our pomological heritage is being preserved. 'Kissin' don't last, apples do' as we say in Devon. Or as more poetically in the *Song of Songs*, 'Stay me with flagons, comfort me with apples; for I am sick of love.'

APPLE
Malus domestica

'No fruit is more to our English taste than the apple,' wrote Edward Bunyard in *The Anatomy of Dessert*. His essay was written thirteen years after his classic *Handbook of Hardy Fruits*, in which he classified dessert and cooking apples into families defined by shape, colour and flavour. Bunyard's splendid scheme formed the basis of our most important collection of apple trees at the National Fruit Trials at Brogdale.

The apple is, of course, the fruit of myth and legend – the fruit from the tree of knowledge, our first fruit. The cultivated apple has been grown for over 3000 years and with over 3000 varieties. They are all descended from the wild Crab apples, *Malus sylvestris* and *Malus pumila*. A present-day example is the variety, 'John Downie'. Named varieties of apple date from 1204, when the 'Pearmain' is recorded in a deed of the Lordship of Runham in Norfolk.

From the time of Henry VIII, the number of varieties of apple grew steadily. There has always been a trade in fruit trees, mainly apples and pears, from France. However, British hybridizers introduced hundreds of new varieties during the eighteenth and nineteenth centuries. Yet some of the most lasting and popular varieties

MUSHROOM
Agaricus bisporus

Mushroom gardening started over 2000 years ago when the Japanese began to cultivate their shiitake mushrooms. Then Columella, Pliny and Virgil all referred to mushrooms growing in gardens. The fungi was so highly appreciated that Roman hosts sometimes flambéed the vegetable on the dinner table in front of their guests.

In Britain, domestic mushroom cultivation flourished in the era of the estate garden prior to 1914. A turn-of-the-century gardening book states, 'Where to Grow Mushrooms: They may be grown in ridge-shaped beds out-of-doors, in cold frames, in cellars or outhouses, in caves, under the staging of greenhouses, or on the floors of greenhouses. During autumn, winter, and early spring, a cellar where the temperature does not fall below 50 deg. will suit the growth of Mushrooms admirably.' The author then gives detailed instructions for the construction of a hot bed made with horse manure on which mushrooms could be cultivated from midsummer until the following spring. Indoor cultivation was also common, and during the nineteenth century

Right: A solitary Shaggy Ink Cap, Coprinus comatus, *also known as the Lawyer's Wig, an edible wild mushroom. Left: All over Britain wild mushrooms appear in well-grazed fields and meadows from late Summer onwards.*

mushrooms were so highly regarded that special outhouses were built against the cool north wall of the kitchen garden.

In France in the seventeenth century, Olivier de Serres, the father of French agriculture, and later the botanist, Marchant, demonstrated that cultivated mushrooms could be grown on well-rotted horse manure in a controlled temperature and humidity. This led to the start of the new industry of mushroom-growing in the disused quarries near Paris. The mushrooms became known as champignons de Paris, a term still used in France for mushrooms grown on a hot-bed.

The only kind of mushroom-gardening that I've done successfully has involved a mushroom kit. These are sold by seedsmen and comprise a cardboard box or plastic bucket of sterilized mushroom spawn mixed with peat. The instructions are given on the side of the kit and, when properly followed, should result in the handsome crop of delicious home-grown mushrooms that you can cut at button size upwards, depending on the age of the mushroom.

I daresay most good cooks can keep up with the rate of mushroom production from a growing kit. There are so many excellent ways of cooking the vegetable in soups and casseroles and fricasées. Surplus mushrooms can be steamed and preserved in olive oil with bay leaves and thyme. Or they can be dried very simply. Thread the caps on to fine string, leaving a small gap between each one. Hang the garland in a warm place for five to seven days until all their moisture has evaporated. Take them off the string and store in an air-tight container. To cook dried mushrooms, soak them in warm water for thirty minutes or until softened, then add them to soups and casseroles – with the soaking water if appropriate.

RASPBERRY
Rubus idaeus

IF I HAD TO CHOOSE BETWEEN THEM, I'D GROW RASPBERRIES RATHER THAN strawberries in my garden. I suppose raspberry canes with alpine strawberries tumbling over their feet might be the perfect solution. The raspberry is a woodland perennial, happiest growing in light shade with a moist rich soil. Even the cultivated raspberry loves a mulch of dead leaves and conditions close to its natural habitat. Our native wild raspberry has small, sweet fruit with a good flavour and a lot of charm. But the cultivated varieties soon win you over with their larger berries with fewer seeds and no loss of flavour. And recent research has resulted in raspberries that fruit heavily over a longer period and in more adverse conditions.

Seeds of the wild raspberry have been found in glacial deposits near Edinburgh and among Early Bronze Age excavations at Stonehenge. The wild plant is widely distributed over the northern hemisphere and its medicinal qualities were noted by the Greeks and Romans. During the fourth century, Palladius describes the raspberry as a cultivated fruit. But the fruit does not appear in Charlemagne's list of plants to be cultivated on his domain, nor does it appear in the 1391 *Forme of Cury*, which lists English fruits and vegetables. Although Turner's *Herbal* of 1568 includes the fruit, the passage is a quote from Pliny. Just five years later, Thomas Tusser does give cultural advice for what he calls 'repis'.

Both red and white (actually yellow) raspberries were described by Parkinson in 1629. And during the eighteenth century, named varieties became known, including the yellow-fruiting 'Golden Antwerp' still available today. One gardening writer recommended binding together the long whippy canes in a plait – an idea which I must try. The question of how to support raspberry canes occupied William Forsyth, gardener to George III and George IV. He suggested the system still in use today, of providing stakes at each end of the row and with wires run between them. Fortunately, though, an increasing number of the present-day varieties have been bred with shorter, stouter canes that need no support.

If you have little space in your garden for more than one variety of raspberry, I would suggest 'Glen Clova', a highly reliable early to mid-season variety whose bright red fruit ripens over a long period. Recently, the Scottish Crop Research Station has developed a 'Glen Clova' cross, called 'Glen Moy' which is heavy-cropping with a good flavour, and the canes are thornless, which makes 'Glen Moy' a good choice for planting close to paths or among flowers. Another smooth-stem, well-flavoured raspberry is 'Glen Prosen', but I have not grown this variety.

Gourmet gardeners with room for more fruit will certainly want an autumn-fruiting variety. For years I have grown 'September', but it has now been ousted in my affection by 'Autumn Bliss', whose short sturdy canes need no support and whose fruit ripens during August and runs through to late September – blissful indeed. Real raspberry fanciers also crave a few yellow-fruiting varieties. There are three to choose from: the historic 'Golden Antwerp', said to be the sweetest, the well-known 'Golden Everest', and the recently-introduced 'Fallgold'. If a raspberry that has been crossed with a blackberry to produce black raspberries appeals, then look out for the varieties 'Blackie', and 'Starlight' with its attractive red canes.

Plant raspberry canes, in rows or patches 45 cm/18 in apart, from November to March whenever the soil is workable. Dig the ground deeply and work in plenty of well-rotted manure or compost. If you have a heavy, clay soil work in plenty of peat and acid compost. The fruit prefers an acid soil; too much lime can lead to chlorosis which, if serious, may need to be treated with sulphate of ammonia or sequestrene. In early spring, cut down the top growth on newly-planted raspberries to encourage root production. Provide support for tall-growing varieties. Prune summer-fruiting raspberries during late autumn and autumn-fruiting varieties during the early spring.

Although I have included some recipes, I doubt that anyone needs to be told how to serve raspberries. Just enjoy them.

FIG
Ficus carica

THE FIG IS AN ANCIENT FRUIT WITH A MYTHICAL PAST. ITS LEAVES CLOTHED ADAM and Eve, and records date the tree from the Egyptian Fourth Dynasty, nearly 5000 years ago. This voluptuous fruit was developed from the wild variety native to Western Asia. Cato described six varieties and Pliny gave an account of twenty-nine in cultivation. And in 1826, at least seventy-five varieties figured in the Horticultural Society garden at Chiswick. Today there are twenty varieties of fig tree for sale; 'Brown Turkey' with its bronze skin is the most widely grown outdoor variety, while the yellow-green 'Brunswick' and the delectable pale-green 'White Marseilles' are mainly grown under glass. All these varieties are self-fertile and can be grown on their own.

Running across the British Isles – somewhere north of Watford but I'm not sure where – there is a fig line: above it figs will not fruit outdoors. I have been fortunate in being able to grow figs in three south of England gardens where, with scarce attention, they have all done well. If only the fig trees growing against the National Gallery in Trafalgar Square were as neglected as mine then perhaps they would fruit too.

Fig trees are more common in old gardens where they are planted against a warm south-facing wall. During the sixteenth century, one of the earliest trees in England grew in the garden of the Archbishop's Palace in Lambeth, close to the present-day Museum of Garden History. In Mediterranean countries where fig trees still grow wild, up to three crops of fruit are produced every year. In Britain one pickable crop is more usual. But what a harvest of luscious, scented, purple fruits. Nothing compares with the deeply sensual pleasure of eating a warm fig straight from the tree. If more people knew about it there would surely be more fig trees around. Even in poor fruit years the fig tree is useful. The large leaves throw a charming green shade for sitting in, and I often adopt the Mexican trick of adding a single fig leaf to the cream or milk for custards and creams to give them the leaf's extraordinary vanilla-like flavour.

The tree prefers to struggle. My present fig tree grows among cobbles in an old farmyard. The soil is poor and drains quickly and the stone wall behind the tree reflects all the heat of the midday sun. When planting a tree in fertile soil consider sinking an old dustbin or metal drum into the ground and planting the roots inside it. The tree is

then more likely to fruit rather than produce solely branch and leaf. This habit does make the fig a good subject for growing in a strong container like a old metal-bound barrel.

Figs do not grow true from seed – it is better to take cuttings. These root easily if planted in late summer in a sandy compost. Keep them shaded and don't let them dry out. In the following spring, repot the cuttings singly, and in autumn, if large enough, transplant to a permanent site. Little aftercare is needed. Simply prune to the desired shape in midwinter and pray for a hot summer.

Although figs are simply delicious eaten plain, they also make a fine accompaniment to prosciutto and Parma ham. This combination of sweet and salty flavours has long been favoured. During the first century AD, Pliny the Elder wrote, 'A plan has lately been devised to use a fresh fig instead of salt when eating cheese'. But one of my favourite ways of serving fresh figs comes from Provence where a friend makes a raspberry cream by mixing a purée of the fruit with some crème fraîche; then freshly gathered figs are quartered on to a plate and the pale pink cream is splashed over them to resemble an impressionist painting. This happy marriage of cool cream with the warm fruit tastes sensational.

BLACKBERRY
Rubus fructicosus

EFFICIENT MISCREANTS CHECK IN A MIRROR BEFORE LEAVING THE SCENE OF THE crime, but it took me some time to realize it. Only when older, and then for other reasons, do we understand how revealing the eyes and the mouth can be. And so childhood forays to the cultivated blackberry that grew out of sight behind the climbing roses were invariably detected by my mother. And my portion of blackberries served at mealtimes was adjusted accordingly.

These days I've almost given up hope of ever tasting a Veitchberry again. In my memory those were the best blackberries I've ever eaten – large and sweet and running with juice. My parents had bought the plant from the famous Veitch nursery and the Veitchberry was one of nearly 500 plants developed by their talented hybridizer John Seden (1840-1921). Sadly, it now seems to be only rarely cultivated.

Even if you normally depend on hedgerows and roadsides for supplies of September blackberries, you may wish to plant an improved variety nearer home. Cultivated blackberries are larger and juicier than their wild cousins and are excellent served plain or with cream and sugar.

Most cultivated varieties retain the flavour of the wild blackberry and have the advantage of cropping earlier. 'Bedford Giant' produces fruit in late July and August, and 'Himalayan Giant' crops a fortnight later. And almost as vigorous is the recent introduction, 'Ashton Cross'.

Since the thorns are the most annoying feature of a blackberry, I favour the pretty, parsley-leaved variety, 'Oregon Thornless'. A thornless hybrid is usually less vigorous and this can be an advantage in a small garden. If you are short of space, beware the adjective Giant in the name of a plant – it usually refers to the full-grown size of the bush, not the fruit. There are two other thornless blackberries worth considering, both American – the 'Smoothstem' and the early-cropping 'Blackstem'.

These days new blackberries are launched like the autumn collections – with a flurry of photographs and lots of press attention. This is rich territory for the amateur who can introduce a new berry with a fanciful name to the gardening world; the 'Hildaberry', for instance, is named after the hybridizer's wife, and I believe that the

A mature standard bay tree in its own circular box-edged border.

name of another berry was based on an idealized description of the allotment (community garden) where it was discovered. It is called 'Fantasia'.

Not wanting to be left out of these berry contests, the fruit research stations weigh in with their champions. The celebrated East Malling Research Station crossed a blackberry with a 'Malling Jewel' raspberry and came up with the 'Sunberry' which according to their tests appears to produce gargantuan crops.

All cultivated blackberries are easy to grow, and they can be planted whenever the soil is workable from the end of September until March (or in the spring in the US). Ideally, they like a position in full sun but many are tolerant of some shade. If you can provide deep, loamy soil, they can develop a long root run. Allow 1.8-2.4 m/6-8 ft between the bushes and cut all growth down to 23 cm/9 in after planting. Then, as they grow, train the long whippy branches on to a trellis or wire frame in a fan shape so that the short fruiting spurs which grow along the branches are easy to reach. Give each plant a dressing of well-rotted manure or compost or a nitrogenous fertilizer each spring to ensure a good crop of fruit.

BLUEBERRY: HIGHBUSH
Vaccinium corymbosum

LOWBUSH
Vaccinium angustifolium

BOTH THE HIGHBUSH AND THE LOWBUSH FORMS OF BLUEBERRY ARE NATIVE TO North America. The lowbush variety grows wild on stretches of heathland in the eastern seaboard states of Canada and in Maine in the US. Lowbush blueberries produce smaller fruit with a more pronounced bilberry-like flavour which is delectable. The highbush blueberry is more amenable to garden cultivation. The plant likes a quick-draining acid soil, and in some sites it is necessary to incorporate peat into the ground. Alternatively, highbush berries can be grown in a container.

Buy named varieties of blueberry from a reputable nursery and plant in a sunny, sheltered position during the winter (or early spring in the US) while the plant is dormant. Although self-fertile, better fruiting results from planting two different varieties which should remain productive for forty to fifty years.

The highbush blueberry forms an attractive 60-90 cm/2-3 ft high, deciduous shrub with shiny oval green leaves that turn flame-red in the autumn. The pretty bell-shape flowers turn into the round navy-blue fruit covered in a grey-blue bloom. By planting early, mid-season and late varieties of the fruit, you can extend the blueberry season from July to September. I have grown the varieties 'Bluecrop', 'Berkeley' and 'Jersey', all of which produce well-flavoured fruit during August.

Blueberries are very good eaten raw, but their flavour intensifies when gently heated in a light sugar syrup. Blueberries go well in small fruit tarts, arranged on a layer of crème fraîche slightly sweetened with vanilla-flavoured sugar (see page 55).

BAY
Laurus nobilis

Culinary use: leaves in classic 'bouquet garni', to flavour soups, stocks and sauces — essential to bechamel sauce, marinades, slow-cooked meat and game dishes and pâtés, some cream puddings and rice dishes.

Cultivation: hardy evergreen tree with small white flowers, also a yellow-leaved golden bay, height .25-10 m/1-30 ft — bay can be clipped to keep it small; grow in rich, well-drained soil in a sheltered position in full sun or light shade.

Tawny-shelled cob nuts, traditionally eaten with a glass of port at the end of dinner.

NUT TREES: HAZEL
Corylus avellana

FILBERT
Corylus maxima

SWEET CHESTNUT
Castanea sativa

ALMOND
Prunus dulcis

*'The king of Spain's daughter came to visit me,
All for the sake of my little nut tree.'*

SO RUNS THE WELL-KNOWN NURSERY RHYME. AS A CHILD I USED OFTEN TO picture the fabulous little tree bearing its silver nutmeg and its golden pear. As an adult I find myself dwelling on the bruised ego of the poet. But, maybe I've got it all wrong and the writer is really boasting about his wonderful tree.

Indeed, anyone who grows a nut tree in Britain has good reason to boast. For it seems that we have only one native nut tree – the wild hazel, *Corylus avellana*, that grows in many hedgerows, producing the small, sweet nuts that are gathered by prudent squirrels. This tree is the forerunner of the cob nut.

'The distinction between cobs and filberts has been obscured in the course of breeding and selection,' says the *Oxford Book of Food Plants*. So that the nut we know and can sometimes buy as the 'Kentish Cob' is really a filbert. The distinguishing feature of both cobs and filberts is the frilly husk, or involucre, which in the filbert extends well beyond the nut, totally enclosing it as if gift-wrapped in green crêpe paper. Pick the nuts when green. Serve some with fruit as dessert – the kernels taste sweet and milky at this stage. Store the remainder of the crop in a cool, airy place for eating at Christmas.

Both filbert and cob trees are deciduous and easy to grow in most parts of Britain. Victorian gardeners planted nut trees in thickets to act as windbreaks and also to delineate different areas of the garden. Gertrude Jekyll planted a hazel nut walk in her garden at Munstead Wood. I sometimes dream of making a nut walk using both the purple-leaved (*Corylus maxima* 'Purpurea') and the green-leaved varieties, training their branches (prune in February or late winter) to meet in the form of a tunnel – but I haven't got round to it yet.

If you've only room for one nut tree then a filbert, pruned into a goblet on a short trunk and planted in a lawn, can look charming. Like the wild hazel – which Canon Ellacombe pointed out 'is the only truly wild British plant to flower before

March' – both the filbert and the cob produce lovely male catkins in the spring. The delicate red tracery of the female blooms when fertilized by the pollen from the catkins, produce the nuts. Plant hazels, filberts and cobs in the autumn in a sandy, slightly alkaline soil.

It's thought that the Romans introduced the sweet chestnut, *Castanea sativa*, into Britain. Of all the nut trees that we can grow, this, surely, has the most beautiful leaf – dark green and glossy with a toothed edge. In the autumn the leaves turn a burnished golden-brown and the spine-covered nuts – very like those from a horse-chestnut – fall to the ground. Unlike most nuts, the sweet chestnut is farinaceous rather than fatty. And so, for centuries, in the Ardeche region of France and in Corsica, the nuts have been ground into flour for bread. As a result, the sweet chestnut is known in country districts as the bread fruit. But these days, although it is delicious, few people make chestnut bread. Instead, the sweet chestnut in France has a sugary fate in the form of the luxurious marron glacé.

The sweet chestnut makes a large tree – it can grow up to 15 m/50 ft high. But since it makes a really splendid specimen, I would urge anyone who has room to plant one. It is important to buy from a good nurseryman who sells grafted or budded cultivars that are highly productive. Of course, you can grow a tree from a chestnut, but it takes a long time to bear fruit and the results could be disappointing. The sweet chestnut which is also known as the Spanish chestnut, can be grown in most soils and positions. It grows fast and carries creamy-yellow flowers in July.

114

To my mind, the most beautiful nut tree is the almond. A member of the peach family, this tree should be grown in a similar way, in a sheltered position. In cold districts you may well get the best results by fan-training the tree against a south-facing wall.

The sweet almond, *Prunus dulcis*, delights the gardener twice a year. In the spring the bare branches carry the deliciously pretty pink flowers. And when seen in bloom against a background of dark evergreens, an almond in full blossom is lovely enough to tempt any daughter of the king of Spain to visit you.

Then, in July, the tree produces the nuts, with their felty green covering. In France, some of the nuts are picked green for eating at the end of a meal, as a midsummer treat. The rest of the crop is left on the tree for two months after which they are picked and dried for winter use.

Almond trees are best planted in the autumn. They prefer a moist but not especially rich soil. And, like peaches, they benefit from some lime or rubble in the base of the planting hole.

SALAD BURNET (GARDEN BURNET)
Sanguisorba officinalis (syn. *Poterium sanguisorba*)

Culinary use: leaves in salads and garnishes, in fish dishes, to flavour white wine vinegar for salads, added to chilled wine cups and fruit compotes.

Cultivation: hardy, herbaceous perennial with pinkish-green flowers, height 30 cm/12 in; grow in well-drained soil in full sun or light shade.

ONION
Allium cepa Cepa group

'Let Onions, atoms, lurk within the bowl,
And, scarce suspected, animate the whole.'

THUS WROTE SIDNEY SMITH, THE EIGHTEENTH-CENTURY BON VIVANT CLERIC, who clearly understood that the powerful yet essential flavour of the onion needs to be kept in check.

The cultivated onion has been bred from the wild form native to the eastern Mediterranean and Asia. The Egyptians revered the vegetable, and Herodotus wrote that the Great Pyramid carried an inscription stating that 1600 talents had been paid for onions, radishes and garlic eaten by the workmen during its construction. The onion is now a valued and well-established vegetable in most areas of the world and there are few cuisines that do not use it. Dr Richard Bradley, the Cambridge botanist, wrote in 1718 that onions were more common in English gardens than any other vegetable. Most kitchen gardeners still regard the onion as an important crop.

Onions are grown from seed or from sets. Seed is normally sown under glass during January or outdoors in spring. Sow onions in a drill (line) and then thin. An exception is the Japanese onion which is sown in August – the exact date depends on where you live – for over-wintering. Japanese onions provide a most useful midsummer onion; the variety, 'Kaizuka', produces a flat yellow bulb, and 'Senshyu' is a round yellow-fleshed onion. Sets of Japanese onions are also now available from good-quality nurseries and stockists.

Onion sets are popular with the gardening cook. These baby onions have their growth arrested during the previous season and are stored at a controlled temperature. The dormant onions can be planted from Christmas onwards, in well-tilled ground, leaving the dry stalk above ground. Birds, mice and cats like pulling the sets out of the ground, so keep an eye on them and replace where necessary. Plant onion sets 10-15 cm/4-6 in apart in rows 30-37.5 cm/12-15 in apart. 'Stuttgarter' is an old reliable variety of onion set, but 'Turbo' is also good and produces a large Spanish-type onion.

Despite the popularity of the onion set, there is a wider choice of varieties in onion seed. I recommend the mild-flavoured red-skin onions, 'Carmen' F1 and 'Brunswick', and the small green-veined onion, 'Aviv'. 'White Lisbon' is the old favourite for spring onions, and 'Ishikura' is a Japanese non-bulbous onion, like a spring onion, with a useful long cropping time. I particularly like growing the Egyptian tree onion *Allium cepa* Proliferum group with its small bulbs produced above the ground at the end of the stalks.

All onions like a site in full sun in ground manured from a previous crop. Seed can be sown in groups, but it is important to keep onions weed-free, particularly during the early stages. From July onwards the top growth starts to shrivel and dry. When the stalks have yellowed, lift the onions on a dry day and leave on the soil, overnight. Then place them on slatted boards or on a wire rack in full sun so that the bulbs can ripen fully and the soil can be easily dusted off. Tie the onions in bunches or plaits. Or store the bulbs in net bags – my mother stores her onions in old pairs of tights which look amusing but work well. Hang the onions in a dry, cool place, out of direct sunlight, until needed.

GARLIC
Allium sativum

Culinary use: a characteristic flavour of Mediterranean, Chinese and Indian cooking, valuable in many hot and cold savoury dishes, salad dressings, vegetables and meat and fish dishes, affinity with potatoes and olive oil.

The health promoting properties of garlic have been well-known for thousands of years. The herb contains a sulphie of the radical Allyl, which is antiseptic and therefore combats bacterial infections. Garlic has also been recommended for treating high blood pressure, rheumatism and baldness.

Cultivation: hardy perennial with white star-shaped flowers, height 45 cm/18 in; grow as an annual in well-drained soil in full sun.

SHALLOT
Allium cepa Aggregatum group

THE SHALLOT IS AN IMPORTANT CROP IN THE GOURMET GARDEN because it is essential to good cooking. This vegetable is very rarely on sale in shops, yet the shallot is easier to grow than an onion. I usually plant shallot sets, either 'Giant Long Keeping Red' or 'Giant Long Keeping Yellow'. There is a ruddy brown-skinned variety 'Hative de Niort' which has an oval onion shape; it's often to be seen on the showbench, but I prefer the flavour of the other varieties.

The shallot is a refined form of onion which is unrivalled in the kitchen. Its flavour is finer than that of the onion and the flesh has a closer texture and is less watery. French cooking appreciates the vital distinction between a shallot and an onion and many of the classic sauces of haute cuisine require shallots.

Plant shallot sets in a sunny position in well-drained ground manured from a previous crop. Each bulb should be planted up to its neck (like an onion set) 20-25 cm/8-10 in apart with 30-37.5 cm/12-15 in between the rows. Keep the shallots free of weeds. Towards the end of summer the top growth dies down and turns yellow. Dig up the shallots and dry in full sun on chicken wire or newspaper for a few days. Remove any loose soil and store the bulbs in boxes in a cool, dry place.

Try cooking peeled shallots whole in butter or olive oil for serving with game and beef. Season a bottle of wine vinegar by adding one or two shallots.

JUNIPER
Juniperus communis

Culinary use: the berries in marinades, pâtés, terrines, sauces, stuffings, slow-cooked dishes of rich meats and game.

Cultivation: hardy evergreen shrub with white flowers, height 1-3 m/3-9 ft; grow in well-drained sandy soil in full sun.

SPINACH
Spinacia oleracea.

SWISS CHARD
Beta vulgaris subsp. *cicla*

DOES EVERYONE HAVE A SECRET RECIPE FOR IMPROVING our lot in life? The inimitable Groucho Marx, in the film *Animal Crackers*, asserts, 'This would be a better world for children if parents had to eat the spinach.' One would hope, though, that the spinach of our childhood – green, slimy and, worst of all, good for you – is disappearing fast. Nowadays, surely, parents have learned how to prepare this nutritious and delicious vegetable properly and are even keen to eat it themselves.

Everyone agrees that in the matter of spinach, freshness is all. Because crumpled and tired leaves have lost most of their goodness and much of their flavour, spinach picked fresh from the garden, washed quickly and tossed straight into the pan offers every gastronomic advantage. So even in a small garden, spinach is one of the most worthwhile vegetables to grow. And by sowing two or three varieties at different times, you can produce a supply for almost the whole growing season.

There are mainly two kinds of spinach. First there's annual spinach, *Spinacia oleracea*; good varieties are 'Norvak' and 'Long Standing Round' which are normally sown in the spring for summer crops. For winter eating in England it's a good idea to sow, in late August or September, the variety 'Sigmaleaf' which is a good non-bolting spinach.

Annual spinach can bolt and run to seed alarmingly quickly in a dry season and for this reason I really prefer the other main kind, perennial spinach, which is usually grown as a biennial. I grow spinach beet or, as an alternative to perennial spinach, Swiss chard, *Beta vulgaris* subsp. *cicla*, which is also known as seakale beet.

Swiss chard has been developed from spinach beet to produce large green leaves and thick white fleshy stalks, each of which is cooked and served separately. To claim that the stalks of Swiss chard taste like asparagus is overstretching one's culinary imagination, in my view. They don't; they taste like Swiss chard. But they are cooked and eaten with butter in the same way as asparagus.

The seed of Swiss chard is sold as such, or it may appear in catalogues as silver or seakale or perpetual spinach. Recently a red-stalked variety has become available, known as rhubarb chard, and one seed firm has produced a mixture called Swiss chard 'Rainbow' which has stems of red, orange, purple, yellow and white. I suppose that a saving grace of these amazing Technicolor developments is that if you don't fancy the vegetables on your dinner plate you can tuck the leaves into your flower arrangements.

Traditionally, Swiss chard is sown in late August and September to provide fresh spinach for Lenten dishes. The cooked leaves are still used as a replacement for meat in country cooking. With luck, during a mild winter in England there is a small picking of outer leaves available every week or so, especially if the plants are given the protection of glass or plastic cloches.

All spinach seed is best sown thinly in drills (lines) 2 cm/¾ in deep, about 30 cm/12 in apart. As soon as they are large enough to handle, thin the seedlings to 10 cm/4 in apart. Keep the plants weed-free, and water generously in dry weather. When you grow your own spinach, you'll discover that the small tender leaves can be eaten raw in salads. They are specially good served with diced crisp bacon and hot croûtons and dressed with the hot bacon fat mixed with a dash of wine vinegar. The larger spinach leaves taste better cooked.

Spinach originated in Persia, and it is interesting that Eastern spices, especially freshly grated nutmeg, do wonders for the flavour of cooked spinach. The cooked vegetable provides a soft-textured and harmonious background to eggs, fish and ham, which characterizes all those dishes termed 'Florentine'. The Italians also make very good spinach pancakes where a few tablespoons of puréed spinach are stirred into lightly beaten eggs and the mixture is then cooked in the same way as an omelette. For a picnic, try spinach pancakes stuffed with garlic- or herb-flavoured curd (cottage) cheese, or pile up several layers and cut them into wedges like a cake.

POTATO AND MUSHROOM ROLL

Creamed potato seasoned with fresh dill wrapped around a dark rich mushroom filling is a Russian-inspired idea.

700 g/1½ lb potatoes, peeled

salt and freshly milled black pepper

60 g/2 oz/4 tbsp butter

1 tbsp plain (all-purpose) flour

1 tbsp chopped dill

2 egg yolks

toasted flaked (sliced) almonds or browned breadcrumbs

FILLING:

60 g/2 oz/4 tbsp butter

1 clove garlic, chopped

350 g/12 oz/flat mushrooms sliced

squeeze of lemon juice

2 tsp plain (all-purpose) flour

60 ml/2 fl oz single (light) cream

freshly grated nutmeg

Cook the potatoes in salted boiling water. Drain and purée the potatoes in a vegetable mill on its finest setting into a mixing bowl. Season with pepper and mix in the butter, flour, dill and almost all the egg yolk. Set aside to cool to make the mixture easier to handle.

For the filling, melt the butter in a wide pan and cook the garlic and mushrooms with a little lemon juice until softened. Sprinkle in the flour and stir in the cream. Cook, stirring gently, until slightly thickened. Season with salt, pepper and nutmeg. Set aside to cool.

Dust a sheet of greaseproof (wax) paper with flour and roll out the potato mixture on it to make a rectangle measuring 30 × 20 cm/12 × 8 in. Roughen the top surface with the prongs of a fork and spread the mushroom mixture over, leaving a margin. Roll up as for a Swiss (jelly) roll, from a narrow end, using the paper to help you.

Unwrap enough to brush the top with the remaining egg yolk and sprinkle with the almonds or breadcrumbs. Chill the potato roll for 2 hours.

Bake in an oven preheated to 190°C/375°F/Gas Mark 5 for 30 minutes or until hot right through. Serve, cut in slices. *Serves 4-6*

RABBIT BRAISED WITH *WINTER* CABBAGE AND JUNIPER BERRIES

A slow-cooked and comforting dish, this is especially suitable for a chilly, winter evening.

1 rabbit, about 1-1.5 kg/2-3 lb, cut up

3 tbsp seasoned flour

45 g/1½ oz/3 tbsp butter

1 onion, sliced

1 clove garlic, finely chopped

1 teaspoon juniper berries, bruised

90 ml/3 fl oz dry (hard) cider

90 ml/3 fl stock or water

450 g/1 lb drumhead (solid head) green or white winter cabbage

salt and freshly milled black pepper

Beads of rain lie on the overlapping leaves of a late summer cabbage.

118

The lilac flowers of the mint, Mentha spicata, *are attractive and edible.*

Rinse the rabbit in cold water. If you are using a wild rabbit, soak it in salted water for 1 hour, then drain well. Roll each piece of rabbit in the seasoned flour.

Heat 30 g/1 oz/2 tbsp of the butter in a pan and brown the rabbit pieces all over. Remove from the pan and keep hot. Add the remaining butter to the pan and cook the onion and garlic over moderate heat for 4-5 minutes until softened but not brown. Add the juniper berries, cider and stock or water and simmer for 3 minutes.

Meanwhile, finely slice the cabbage and blanch in boiling salted water for 3-4 minutes. Drain well and transfer to the bottom of a hot casserole. Season with salt and pepper. Place the rabbit on top and pour over the cider and juniper mixture.

Cover the casserole with a tight-fitting lid and cook in an oven preheated to 170°C/325°F/Gas Mark 3 for about 1½ hours or until the rabbit is tender and the cabbage has absorbed the cooking juices. Serve with creamed potatoes mixed with chopped garden herbs. *Serves 4*

PETIT SUISSE CHEESES WITH BLUEBERRY SAUCE

225 g/8 oz/1½ cups blueberries

finely grated zest (rind) and juice of ½ lemon

2 good pinches of ground cinnamon

1 pinch of nutmeg

60 g/2 oz/¼ cup caster (US granulated) sugar

2 tbsp cold water

1 tsp arrowroot

1 tbsp kirsch

4 Petit Suisse cheeses

4 sprigs of mint, to decorate

Rinse the blueberries and put in a pan with the zest and juice of the lemon, the cinnamon, nutmeg and sugar. Add 1 tbsp of cold water and cook the fruit gently over moderate heat until the juice runs and the fruit is cooked.

Mix the arrowroot with the remaining cold water and add to the pan. Cook, stirring, until the sauce thickens and clears. Mix in the Kirsch and remove from the heat.

Turn each Petit Suisse cheese on to a small plate and spoon the blueberry sauce around it. Garnish each plate with a sprig of mint and serve. *Serves 4*

HEADS OF GARLIC PRESERVED IN OLIVE OIL

Whole heads of new season's garlic are highly delicious preserved in oil for autumn and winter use.

4-6 heads of garlic, with fat cloves

virgin olive oil

few sprigs of wild thyme

sprig of rosemary

2-3 bay leaves

black olives (optional)

English cooking apples, growing on an espalier-trained tree, with globe artichokes planted below.

Remove the outer papery layers from the garlic until the separate cloves are uncovered, but leave them intact. Brush a sheet of foil with olive oil and place in a roasting pan. Arrange the garlic on top, then wrap in the foil, folding the edges over.

Bake the garlic in an oven preheated to 190°C/375°F/Gas Mark 5 for 15-20 minutes or until the cloves are tender.

Transfer the heads of garlic to a wide-necked preserving jar and tuck in the herbs. Add olives if you wish, and pour in enough olive oil to cover. Fasten down the lid tightly and store in a cold place for 3-4 weeks or longer if preferred.

The garlic-flavoured oil is magnificent for adding to provençale dishes and salads. Add the cloves of garlic to soups and casseroles.

DEVONSHIRE APPLE PIE

PASTRY:

115 g/4 oz/3/4 cup plain (all-purpose) flour

30 g/1 oz/2 tbsp vanilla-flavoured caster (superfine) sugar (see below)

75 g/2½ oz/5 tbsp butter, softened

1 egg yolk

a little beaten egg or milk

FILLING:

2 slices of white bread, crustless

grated zest (rind) of 1 lemon

1 kg/2 lb cooking apples

115 g/4 oz/½ cup vanilla-flavoured sugar

150 ml/¼ pint/⅔ cup single (light) cream

Sift the flour and sugar into a wide shallow bowl. Make a well in the centre and add the butter and egg yolk. Mix together the ingredients, using your fingertips until you can form the dough into a ball. Wrap and chill for 30 minutes.

Make the bread into crumbs in a food processor or use a grater. Mix with the zest of lemon. Butter a 20 cm/8 in round shallow pie dish (pie pan) and spread the breadcrumbs over the bottom.

Peel and core the apples and cut into rings or slices. Mix with the sugar. Arrange the apples over the breadcrumbs and pour over the cream.

Roll out the pastry dough to fit and cover the pie. If you have any pastry left over, you can make a few leaves to decorate the lid of the pie. Prick the lid with a fork a few times to make steam vents and brush with beaten egg or milk.

Bake the pie in an oven preheated to 190°C/375°F/Gas Mark 5 for about 30 minutes or until the apples are tender and the pastry is golden. *Serves 6*

Note: for vanilla flavoured sugar see page 55.

MORELLO CHERRY STONE EAU-DE-VIE

This easy-to-make preparation has a fine kirsch-like flavour that is wonderful for flavouring cakes, creams and custards.

Morello cherry stones (for example, saved from the cherry recipe opposite)

eau-de-vie

Crack the stones and extract the kernels. Place the cherry kernels in a small jar or bottle. Pour in eau-de-vie to the top of the bottle and cork or seal the top.

Leave the jar in a warm kitchen for several weeks to allow the alcohol to acquire the flavour of the cherry kernels. Use the essence for flavouring biscuits (cookies) and cakes. Top up the bottle with fresh eau-de-vie now and again.

A Mediterranean corner of the Gidleigh Park herb garden where fennel and thyme grow together.

MORELLO CHERRY AND ALMOND CONSERVE

I pick my Morello cherries when they are flushed with scarlet. If, however, you prefer to allow the fruit to ripen until it is lustrous crimson, it's best to net the fruit to protect it from marauding birds.

1.1 kg/2½ lb/5 pints Morello cherries

225 g/8 oz/1 pint red currants

900 g-1.35 kg/2-3 lb/4-6 cups white sugar

45 g/1½ oz/⅓ cup blanched almonds, halved

Wash and drain the cherries. Stone the fruit, saving all the juice. Place the cherries and juice in a preserving pan.

Wash and drain the red currants and tip into a nylon sieve. Use a wooden spoon to gently push through the juice, leaving all the pulp in the sieve. Add the juice to the pan and cook the cherries over moderate heat until tender.

Weigh the contents of the pan and add an equal weight of sugar. Stir constantly over a low heat until the sugar has dissolved, then bring to the boil and cook the conserve until it reaches the setting temperature, 105°C/220°F on a sugar thermometer.

Remove from the heat and stir in the almonds. Pour the conserve into hot, dry jars. Cover and label. Makes about 1.8 kg/4 lb

PROVENÇALE AROMATIC OIL

This flavoured oil makes an excellent basis for a marinade for vegetables, fish and meat to be grilled on the barbecue. Mix the oil with a dash of wine or the juice of a lime, lemon or orange.

1 600 ml/1 pint/2½ cup bottle of virgin olive oil

1 clove garlic, peeled

2-3 sprigs of fennel

1 sprig of rosemary

1 small dried chilli pepper

1 tsp coriander seed

1 tsp green or black peppercorns

Pour 2-3 tablespoons of the olive oil into a cup. Add the remaining ingredients to the bottle. Try to distribute them in the bottle and, if necessary, use the handle of a wooden spoon to ease them into position in the bottle. Top up the bottle with the reserved oil and replace the cap.

Leave in a warm room for about 2 weeks, until the oil has absorbed the herb flavours. Then store in a cool place.

CHAPTER SIX

TOMATO, RADISH, CUCUMBER, CORIANDER, LETTUCE, SCENTED GERANIUM, CHINESE ARTICHOKE, MARJORAM, SWEET WILLIAM, MELON, HORSERADISH, BERGAMOT, ROSES, JERUSALEM ARTICHOKE, CHIVE, DILL, FENNEL

A LAKESIDE GARDEN IN CUMBRIA
SHARROW BAY

AT THE ENTRANCE TO THE OLD KITCHEN GARDEN AT SHARROW BAY, an oak and an ash tree grow beside each other, their roots entwined, their trunks united, until a few feet above the ground the two trees separate and grow in their individual way. This arboreal partnership is conveniently placed for any gardener who trusts in the old adage:

If the ash be out before the oak
We shall indeed be in for a soak
But when the oak's afore the ash
Then 'tis unlikely to be more than a splash.

Azaleas and blue iris flower in the long
mixed border along the foot of the ancient yew
hedge on the lakeside of the kitchen garden
at Sharrow Bay.

It is over forty years since Francis Coulson travelled down the narrow lane from Pooley Bridge and discovered the fine Victorian house of Sharrow Bay. 'As soon as I saw it I knew it was right,' Francis recalls, 'and that to be able to share the peace and beauty of the place with other people I would open a hotel. But everything was in a terrible state.' The rambling garden on the southern shore of Lake Ullswater was completely overgrown and the oak and the ash were mere saplings. 'They struggled to survive, the weeds were everywhere and the flowers had seeded themselves. It was a sea of lupins – wherever you looked the

123

A wooden trellis arch at the entrance to the kitchen garden.

garden was ablaze with pink and blue.' During the early years, the fine old kitchen garden was restored and brought back to working order. Its tapering, rectangular shape follows the curve of the lakeside, and through the protective belt of trees at the water's edge you can hear the ripple of small waves breaking on the pebble beach. The kitchen garden faces west and slopes down towards the water. Ancient yew hedges and dry stone walls offer protection from the prevailing winds, and divide the garden into the 'green rooms' that Vita Sackville-West and her husband Sir Harold Nicolson constructed in their famous garden at Sissinghurst Castle in Kent.

Roughly in the centre of the kitchen garden stands an old stone wellhead crowned with a wrought iron frame. On the surrounding lawn you can make out the varied greens of grassed-over borders that years ago produced all the vegetables and fruit for the house. Using a kind of horticultural detective work, the earlier design of the garden becomes clear. A row of mature apple trees, their well-pruned branches trained along horizontal wires, still acts as a natural screen between a path and a flower bed. Doubtless this screen was once longer and, probably, it was matched – in the symmetrical style of old gardens – with another on the other side of the dividing path.

As I stood near the wellhead and contemplated this lovely garden and how it had changed over the years, Hugh Palmer threw a coin into the well – perhaps to wish us luck with the garden photography ahead. We both listened for the splash as it hit the water. But instead there was a dull thud and we realized that the well was no more. It had been filled in, no doubt on grounds of safety and because the garden now has piped water with plenty of convenient taps.

We walked across to the wellhead and looked down, and laughed when we saw scores of coins lying on the mossy ground below us, where other visitors to the garden had had the same thought. And I realized that the well represents the history of the garden: that all gardens change, inexorably, with time, reflecting their owner's interests and energies. Gardens evolve just as trees grow, reach their life span and decay. The sheer excitement of gardening, the constant making of plans, the never-ending anticipation of the season ahead immerses one so completely in the experience that only rarely does one stand back and contemplate the pattern of it all. Here at Sharrow Bay some of the earlier patterns are still visible.

Francis Coulson remembers, 'To begin with, we grew all our own vegetables, especially salad crops, lettuces and herbs, and masses of tomatoes and cucumbers in the big glasshouses.' The largest glasshouse is

a magnificent Edwardian vine-house which stands at the far end of the kitchen garden against a red-brick heated wall. The flues can be seen at the base of the wall, each covered with a piece of Penrith stone. The chimneys, built along the top for the smoke to escape, are also protected from the rain by large stone slabs. The fine single-span glass roof slopes down from a height of 3.6 m/12 ft to end just 60 cm/2 ft from the ground. And the hot-air vents from the flued wall run in a straight line just below the glazing bars of the roof. Each vent is covered with wire gauze to prevent hot cinders or ash from escaping into the vine-house with the risk of starting a fire. Wooden shutters control the size of the warm air vents, and these are connected by a wire-and-chain pulley operated at shoulder height so that the gardener can control the degree of heat allowed into the house. Unfortunately, the grape vine is no more. These days the glasshouse is used for growing potted plants mainly geraniums and fuchsias, that are set out in the garden in early summer.

A second smaller glasshouse is used for raising seedlings of herbs and some vegetables like sweet peppers and edible flowers. Between the two glasshouses, the raised beds of a dismantled glasshouse have been planted with the furry-leaved Bowles's mint – said by mint fanciers to be the best

fresh garden herbs. Every day at lunch and dinner the menu contains dishes with at least a dozen herbs. Sorrel is served as a purée with the local salmon, dill is part of the Swedish dish of gravadlax, corn-fed chicken is cooked in cream with mushrooms and marjoram, and handfuls of parsley go into the parsley pie. Horseradish flowers and the herb's young tender leaves add a decorative flourish to a green salad. And tarragon, basil and mint have a major part to play in Francis's cooking.

In front of the cold frames, a border with a generous mulch of leaf mould and well-rotted compost contains rows of flowers grown specially for the kitchen. Nasturtiums and chrysanthemums, gladioli and marigolds not only bring colour and scent to the kitchen garden but their individual blooms are used as a garnish for salads and desserts.

Although edible flowers are being hailed as the latest discovery, this is simply a revival of an ancient and, it seems, forgotten food. Ever since man discovered the seductive taste of honey which derives, in turn, from flowers foraged by bees collecting their nectar, cooks have known that flowers have a flavour. In ancient Greece, the honey from Mount Hymettus – the name itself comes from the Greek word for honey – was prized for its flavour of wild herbs. In medieval England many dishes included flowers like those of rosemary and primrose, melissa and elderflower. The unknown author of *A Book of Fruits and Flowers*, published in 1653, has many recipes for syrups, pastes and conserves made with violets, marigolds, cowslips and roses. The book includes instructions for making a charming 'Sallet of all kinde of Hearbs' in which a dish of sliced cucumber and herbs, dressed with a vinaigrette, is garnished with a handful of freshly picked flowers.

At Sharrow Bay, there are roses in the kitchen garden and in the several magnificent pleasure gardens. There are roses in the rooms and on the tables. There are roses in the food and on the food, garlanded with crystallized petals. Even the plates are smothered with painted roses. Francis Coulson and his partner, Brian Sack, love roses.

In some borders roses grow amongst herbs, as in an Elizabethan garden. A pretty, scented old-fashioned rose with blush-pink blooms grows beside a grey-leaved rosemary bush, its pale blue flowers like miniature snapdragons. Clumps of cottage pinks – or gilliflowers – have been planted around them, and willow-leaved French tarragon luxuriates among this perfumed trio.

No flower has such a long and distinguished culinary history as the rose. Its scented petals have fascinated us since the flower grew wild in China over 4000 years ago. Cleopatra had rose petals strewn over the floor of her palace before welcoming Mark Antony. For the rose has been

for mint sauce – and a smooth-leaved spearmint. The upright slabs of stone around the mint bed keep this invasive herb under enviable control. Similarly, large clumps of horseradish in a corner of the kitchen garden are surrounded with paving. This is another colonizing herb that can run amok in a fertile garden unless limited in its root growth. The cream star-like flowers look attractive against the shiny dock-like leaves of the herb.

The Lake District winters can be prolonged and severe, so any growing area under glass is immensely valuable. A row of cold frames contains pots of tender half-hardy herbs. Tarragon and Italian or flat-leaf parsley flourish beside coriander with its pretty blush-pink flowers and two kinds of leaves. (Young coriander leaves resemble flat-leaf parsley; as the plant matures the leaves become feathery fronds similar to dill.) Clumps of golden-leaved marjoram and purple-flowered chives edge the path from the ivy-roofed toolshed to the vine-house. And against the heat-retaining stone wall, rosemary and bay have grown into large shrubs.

A cook who admits, like Francis Coulson, that, 'Vegetables are difficult to cook well – to catch the flavours and textures at just the right moment', naturally understands the simple yet rich effect of cooking with

125

regarded as the symbol of love, since its deep crimson petals were said to have sprung from the spilled blood of Adonis who was slain by a wild boar. Gradually, as this legendary plant moved westward across the northern hemisphere, gardeners not only cultivated the bush and picked the flowers, but they pulled the petals from the bloom to expose the scent to the air.

The perfume in a rose is an essential oil stored in tiny cells just below the outer 'skin' or cuticle of the petal. This scent, which is contained in the glucoside in the petal, is so near the surface that the slightest touch or bruising releases the perfume. Although rose perfumes can have various predominant notes such as clove, lemon or apple, the generally accepted 'rose scent' comes from the highly-perfumed damask rose, *Rosa* × *damascena*, introduced to Britain by Crusaders returning from Damascus.

Rose water and attar, or oil, of roses is made from fresh rose petals using a process of steam distillation. And it takes the blooms of thirty roses to produce just one drop of attar of roses. Red and pink roses are generally the most highly scented, and they are the best varieties for the gardening cook to grow. The blooms of the hybrid tea varieties 'Alec's Red', 'Crimson Glory' and 'Josephine Bruce', as well as the climbing rose 'Guinée', all give good results in recipes which call for rose petals.

Right: Luxuriant sprays of mint grow in a raised bed in cool and shady corner of the garden. Left: Mixed nasturtiums grown for the salad bowl.

One of the attractions of cooking with flowers is that there are so many ordinary garden subjects to choose from. Sometimes the whole flower can be used in a dish. For example, I like to mix a salad of crimson radicchio leaves and black grapes with some tiny, purple heart's ease pansies and a few yellow marigold petals strewn over the top. In midsummer I make a featherlight sponge cake or a snow-white angel cake, spread with thick cream scented with rose water and then decorated with crystallized rose petals.

Even the non-kitchen gardener, who only grows flowers, can bring some of his produce to the table, for the following garden plants have edible flowers: alyssum, begonias, chrysanthemums, coleus, cosmos, dahlias, geraniums (more correctly termed zonal pelargoniums), gladioli, hibiscus, lime (linden) flowers, mallows, marigolds, mesembryanthemums, monarda, nasturtiums, roses, sedums, primroses, and violets.

Herb growers have a wide choice of delightful edible flowers with a milder taste of the herb itself: basil, borage, chamomile, claytonia, chervil, chive, dill, elderflower, fennel, hyssop, lavender, lemon balm, lemon verbena, mint, pineapple sage, purslane, rocket, rosemary, grey-leaved sage, salad burnet, sorrel, sweet cicely, thyme, valerian and woodruff.

And the kitchen gardener can extend the range of his produce even further with the flowers of fruit and vegetables, remembering that the most important exceptions are rhubarb and the potato. If in doubt about the edibility of any flower, choose an alternative that you know is safe. The flowers of these fruits and vegetables are edible: apple, French bean, mangetout (edible pod peas), oriental vegetables, pea, pear, plum, radicchio, radish, salsify, scorzonera and strawberry.

The gardens at Sharrow Bay persuade one that the best kitchen garden is not just an area of useful food plants but a wider vision of nature that succours both the body and the spirit.

There sprang the violete al newe,
And fresshe pervinke riche of hewe,
And floures yelowe, whyte and rede:
Swich plentee grew ther never in mede,
Ful gay was al the ground and queynt
And poudred, as men had it peynt,
With many a fresh and sondry flour
That casten up a ful good savour.

(Geoffrey Chaucer's Translation of *Roman de la Rose*)

127

FEUILLETÉ OF LEMON SOLE ON A BED OF SPINACH WITH SALMON CAVIAR

115 g/4 oz weight puff pastry

beaten egg

350 g/12 oz fresh spinach

90 g/3 oz/6 tbsp unsalted butter

4 tbsp dry white wine

salt and freshly milled pepper

6 fillets lemon sole (sole or flounder)

SAUCE:

3 shallots, finely chopped

60 g/2 oz/4 tbsp butter

1 tsp chopped fresh root ginger

6 cardamom seeds, bruised

10 coriander seeds, crushed

1 bay leaf

300 ml/¹/₂ pint/1¹/₄ cups fish stock

300 ml/¹/₂ pint/1¹/₄ cups dry white wine

300 ml/¹/₂ pint/1¹/₄ cups double (heavy) cream

lemon juice

GARNISH:

1-2 tbsp salmon caviar

few sprigs of dill

Roll out the pastry on a floured board and cut into six rectangles. Place on a wetted baking sheet and brush the tops with beaten egg. Mark the tops very lightly with a knife. Bake in an oven preheated to 220°C/425°F/Gas Mark 7 for 15-20 minutes or until

well risen and golden brown. Keep warm on a wire rack.

Wash the spinach, then plunge the leaves into a pan of boiling salted water and cook for 2-3 minutes until wilted but still bright green. Drain and plunge the spinach into iced water, then drain well. Set aside.

To make the sauce, sweat the shallots in the butter and when soft stir in the ginger, cardamom, coriander and bay leaf. Add the fish stock and wine. Bring to the boil, then reduce over high heat until syrupy. Add the cream and reduce by half. Strain and season to taste with lemon juice, salt and pepper. Keep warm.

Melt 60 g/2 oz/4 tbsp of the butter in an oven dish and add the wine and a little seasoning. Place the fish in the dish, spoon over the liquid and cook in the preheated oven for 5-7 minutes or until the fish is just set. Remove from the oven and keep warm.

Melt the remaining butter and add the spinach, stirring gently until reheated. Season with salt, if desired.

To serve, slice each rectangle of puff pastry across in half and place the bases on individual plates. Cover each pastry base with spinach and place a fillet of sole on top. Spoon over a little of the sauce and cover with the lid of the pastry case. (A chef's trick is to brush the top of pastry case with clarified butter – but it is not essential.) Spoon more sauce around each pastry case and garnish with salmon caviar and a sprig of dill. *Serves 6.*

SADDLE OF VENISON MARINATED IN RED WINE WITH *FRESH* THYME

1 saddle of venison to serve six

225 g/8 oz wild mushrooms, sautéed in butter

watercress and raspberries, to garnish

MARINADE:

1 bulb Florence fennel

2 carrots

2 stalks celery

1 medium onion

2 cloves garlic

6 sprigs of fresh thyme

1 bouquet garni

6 black peppercorns

6 juniper berries

600 ml/1 pint/2½ cups red wine

SAUCE:

90-115 g/3-4 oz/¾-1 sticks unsalted butter

600 ml/1 pint/2½ cups venison stock

300 ml/½ pint/1¼ cups demi-glace sauce

1 tbsp red currant jelly

6 tbsp port wine

Remove the fillets and eye of meat from both sides of the saddle of venison. Trim all sinew from the meat and place in a mixing bowl.

To make the marinade, trim and wash the fennel, carrots, celery, onion

and garlic; peel if necessary. Add to the meat in the bowl with the thyme, bouquet garni, peppercorns and juniper berries. Pour in the red wine and turn the venison over in the marinade. Cover the bowl and refrigerate for 24 hours.

Strain the marinade into a pan, reserving the vegetables, and bring to the boil. Simmer for 5 minutes, skimming all the time. Place the meat on a plate and set aside.

Melt a little of the butter in a heavy-based pan and brown the vegetables from the marinade. Add the stock, demi-glace sauce, marinade, red currant jelly and port wine. Bring to the boil and simmer steadily until reduced to 300 ml/½ pint/1¼ cups. Strain through a fine sieve and keep warm.

Melt a little of the remaining butter in a roasting pan and seal the venison all over. Transfer to an oven preheated to 200°C/400°F/Gas Mark 6 and roast for 8-10 minutes, or longer if required not pink. Remove the venison from the oven and leave in a warm place for 3-4 minutes.

Meanwhile, over a low heat, gradually beat the remaining butter into the warm sauce, adding it in small pieces. Carve the venison into six slices per portion.

To serve, place a small heap of mushrooms in the centre of each plate, and arrange the slices of venison around it. Spoon the sauce around the meat. Garnish with watercress and raspberries and serve.
Serves 6

PARSLEY PIE

Francis Coulson says, 'We have Jane Grigson to thank for this
recipe – ours is a slight variation on it.'

PASTRY:

115 g/4 oz/³/₄ cup plain (all-purpose)
  flour

60 g/2 oz/4 tbsp butter

1 tsp icing (confectioners') sugar

beaten egg to mix

FINES HERBES MIXTURE:

3-4 tbsp chopped parsley

1 tbsp chopped chives

1 tbsp chopped tarragon

1 tbsp chopped watercress

1 clove garlic, chopped (optional)

grated zest (rind) of ¹/₂ lemon

FILLING:

2 shallots or 1 small onion, chopped

90 g/3 oz/6 tbsp butter

300 ml/¹/₂ pint/1 ¹/₄ cups cream

2 eggs, beaten

salt and freshly milled pepper

Sift the flour into a bowl and rub in the butter and sugar until the mixture resembles breadcrumbs. Mix to a soft dough with the beaten egg. Chill the pastry dough, then roll out to line a 24 cm/9¹/₂ in loose-bottomed flan tin (tart pan).

To make the fines herbes mixture, stir all the ingredients together in a bowl.

Cook the shallots or onion in the butter until golden and translucent. Cool, then spoon into the pastry case. Mix the cream and eggs into the fines herbes mixture, season well and pour over the onions.

Bake in an oven preheated to 190°C/375°F/Gas Mark 5 for 40 minutes. Serve hot or cold, garnished with extra herbs if desired. *Serves 6*

*Trusses of salad tomatoes starting to ripen ready
for harvesting.*

TOMATO
Lycopersicon esculentum

PERHAPS IT DID THE TOMATO NO GOOD AT ALL TO BE INTRODUCED INTO EUROPE as the 'Love Apple'. The name might sound like a present-day advertiser's dream, but the English of the seventeenth century were possibly alarmed by the prospect of consuming an alleged aphrodisiac at a family meal.

This fruit that we regard as a vegetable – its correct terminology even came to the attention of the US Supreme Court in 1893 – is a native of Peru, and it is now known by a derivation of its Mexican name, *tomatl*.

It is not mere chance that makes the tomato grown outdoors in a sunny clime taste better. The ripe, red fruit of the Mediterranean has a full, rich flavour with none of the tasteless wateriness of the tomato grown under glass by commercial growers. How could a tomato that is bred solely for looks and uniformity and fed on fertilized water be expected to taste of much? Fortunately, in the realm of tomatoes the gourmet gardener is at a tremendous advantage: tomatoes grown on rich garden compost have a wonderful flavour.

In fact, this tender perennial plant which is usually treated as an annual is quite easy to grow. Seeds sown in February or March can be planted outside in June and should produce fruit by the end of July. Alternatively, seed can be sown in heat from January onwards to produce plants for growing in a heated or cool greenhouse to fruit earlier in the season.

There are mainly three kinds of tomato for garden culture:
1. The large Mediterranean-type sometimes known as 'beefsteak' tomatoes which are excellent for slicing for salads and for cooking whole as stuffed tomatoes. Recommended varieties for growing outdoors or in a plastic tunnel are 'Big Boy', 'Marmande', 'Super Marmande' and 'Oxheart Giant'.
2. The widely grown medium-sized tomato with either a trailing, bush habit or a tall-growing vine that requires staking. Recommended red-skinned varieties are 'Herald', 'Harbinger', and 'Sleaford Abundance' F1. Well-flavoured yellow-skinned varieties are 'Golden Sunrise' and 'Yellow Perfection'; the orange-skined 'Ida Gold' and the striped tomato 'Tigerella' are also well worth growing.
3. The small 'cherry' tomato, *Lycopersicon esculentum* var. *cerasiforme*, with its superb flavour, is easy to grow and highly recommended. The red-skinned varieties 'Gardener's Delight', 'Tiny Tim' and 'Small Fry' are excellent and the recently introduced yellow-skinned 'Mirabelle' and pink tomato 'Whippersnapper' are also well-flavoured. If you prefer small tomatoes you may care to grow the smallest of the species, the doll's-house-size currant tomatoes, *Lycopersicon pimpinellifolium*, which grow wild in South Africa. Currant tomatoes have both red and yellow-skinned varieties.

The tomato is an ideal subject for growing in a container such as a large pot, tub or gro-bag. Plant in well-rotted garden compost and place in a sunny, protected position. Keep the soil moist and feed with a liquid seaweed or animal manure fertilizer every two weeks from midsummer until early autumn. Do not overwater the plants or the fruit will be large and tasteless.

Home-grown tomatoes taste so good that it is tempting to eat them absolutely plain, straight from the vine. The larger fruits make a glorious salad, sliced thinly into a wide dish with leaves of basil torn into pieces scattered on top. Season with sea salt and freshly ground black pepper and pour over plenty of a fruity virgin olive oil. Leave for fifteen to twenty minutes, then serve with newly-baked crusty bread.

RADISH
Raphanus sativus

I'VE GROWN RADISHES LONGER THAN I CARE TO REMEMBER. THEY WERE THE FIRST crop in my first garden when I was not yet three-years-old. Radishes are ideal for children to grow – they're easy and quick to mature. Seed sown in lightly raked ground during early summer and covered with a scattering of soil, should produce a crop of radishes – give or take a few stragglers – only twenty-one to twenty-eight days later.

The radish is one of the oldest cultivated vegetables, said to have been part of the daily diet of the Pharaohs' pyramid-builders. On the opposite shore of the Mediterranean, one ancient Greek devoted an entire book to the vegetable.

Shop-bought radishes have usually lost the juicy, spicy quality of those freshly pulled. And the pleasure of running your hand over the green leaves, looking for the tell-tale swelling just above the soil where radishes are ready to eat, is enough to make your mouth water. John Parkinson in *Paradisi in Sole Paradisus Terrestris*, wrote that radishes 'serve as a stimulum before meat; the poor eat them alone with bread and salt'. Poor or not, I can never resist one of the bunch, quickly rinsed under the garden tap and eaten straight away.

Radishes come in two shapes – round- or oval-rooted. Commercial growers concentrate on the bright, red globe variety. Sow 'Cherry Belle' or try 'Ribella' if you like this style of radish. It is very fast-growing and can be grown under cloches or in a garden frame from February onwards. It's also the best kind if you or the children around you like making radish roses: make three cuts crossways in the base of the radish, then soak in cold water for an hour and, hey presto – a rose. Personally, I prefer my radishes to look like radishes.

For flavour I choose the peppery, pink and white, oval-rooted 'French Breakfast' variety. Although I've never seen anyone in France eating radishes for breakfast, they are served as a first course at lunch. A bowl of freshly-scrubbed radishes, each with a short green handle cut from the stem, is served with butter for spreading on the radish, and a crust of baguette. Radishes also go well with a few slices of continental sausage or smoked ham. They are a salad staple in Britain, yet cooked radishes taste surprisingly good, like baby turnips. The young leaves and the seed pods are quite fun in a green salad.

Real radish addicts will be keen to grow the large-rooted winter radish, either the 'Black Spanish Round' or the pink 'China Rose'. Seed sown in July should give a crop towards late autumn or Christmas. In November, cover the plants with straw to protect from frost and dig the roots as required.

If you have little growing space the wisest plan is to sow a packet of mixed summer radish. All types of radish like a rich, deep soil in a well-sheltered position. Sow seed 5 mm/¼ in deep, in a row or a patch, between other vegetables or among flowers and shrubs. To ensure a succession of summer radish sow a few seed every fortnight and keep the ground moist.

CUCUMBER
Cucumis sativus

A FEW WEEKS AGO, I NOTICED A BEAUTIFUL SILVER AND IVORY OBJECT IN THE window of a local antique shop. An adjustable blade was mounted on a polished frame – it looked like a miniature mandoline for slicing food. But what kind of food? I went into the shop to find out. This handsome tool turned out to be a George III cucumber-slicer. It was lovely to hold, with exquisitely workmanship. I tentatively asked the price. '£1000 – it is most unusual', was the reply. I carefully replaced the rare and valuable slicer, thanked the owner and left. If a Georgian cucumber-slicer is rare, I found myself wondering, how common was the Georgian cucumber?

The cucumber is one of the oldest cultivated vegetables, with an almost cult following. The Israelites, wandering in the desert, complained to Moses about the deplorable lack of cucumbers (and melons and leeks). And the Emperor Tiberius insisted on a year-round supply of the vegetable. Whereas the cucumber was once a seasonal vegetable, your local supermarket now sells them every day of the year. Happily, though, the home-grown cucumber remains a seasonal vegetable – and tastes all the nicer for it too.

Cucumbers can be grown outdoors, or under glass. The nice old-fashioned ridge cucumber scrambling over the compost heap seems to be in retreat since the arrival of the affordable small greenhouse. However, there's a lot to be said for outdoor cucumbers – they taste terrific and they are easy to grow. The F1 hybrid Burpless varieties crop well, and the short, dark green pickling cucumber or gherkin is almost unobtainable unless you grow your own. And the round, pale green 'Crystal Apple' cucumber is decidedly interesting. 'It breaks the ice at parties,' according to one of my gardening friends.

Sow seed of outdoor varieties in pots, on the windowsill or under glass, in late spring. Or sow directly in the ground in early summer. All cucumbers require a fertile, humus-rich soil that stays damp. Transplant to 60 cm/2 ft apart when two true leaves have formed. If you are short of space, grow the cucumbers up a wigwam of four stout canes, tied together firmly at the top. Tie the plants to the canes every 15-20 cm/6-8 in so that the developing fruits are well-supported. Pinch out the side shoots when they have two leaves, and cut off the tops when they have grown too long for the canes. Cut the cucumbers as soon as large enough to eat to encourage further fruits.

The seed of indoor cucumber plants usually needs a minimum night temperature of 20°C/68°F to germinate. Gardeners with unheated greenhouses often buy chitted (already germinated) seed or small plants. The F1 all-female varieties of cucumber, like 'Femspot', 'Petita' and 'Fenumex', have made growing cucumbers under glass far more productive. Provided that you stop the side growths at two leaves, keep the compost damp and feed with liquid seaweed fertilizer every fortnight, you should be rewarded with a handsome crop of cucumbers.

In the kitchem, the cucumber is a versatile vegetable. They are highly delicious, just as they are – peeled or unpeeled – or in thinly-cut brown bread sandwiches, or dressed with yoghurt mixed with lemon, honey and mint as a cooling salad, or cooked slowly in butter with dill, or stuffed and braised. Best of all, perhaps, is a beautifully smooth, rich cucumber soup served chilled, in the garden, on a fine summer evening.

CORIANDER
Coriandrum sativum

Culinary use: whole and chopped leaves in sauces and salads, in Oriental cooking; as garnish, flowers in salads; roots in Thai and Chinese dishes; seeds in sauces, desserts, fruit syrups and cakes.

Cultivation: half-hardy annual with white flowers, height 30-60 cm/1-2 ft; grow in fertile, light soil under glass or in a sheltered position in full sun.

SCENTED GERANIUM
Pelargonium species

Culinary use: leaves to flavour sugar, syrups, fruit compotes, sorbets, ice creams and desserts, and as a garnish; flowers – fresh and crystallized – for decorating cakes, creams and puddings.

Cultivation: tender evergreen perennial with pink or white flowers, several varieties with different aromatic leaves, height .3-1 m/1.3 ft; grow in fertile, well-drained soil in pots in full sun or light shade.

LETTUCE
Lactuca sativa

IR MAX BEERBOHM ONCE COMPARED LIVING IN THE ENGLISH COUNTRYSIDE TO being in the middle of a lettuce. Green and damp, I suppose he meant, which is fair up to a point, provided that you overlook the wide range and colours of this popular vegetable that is grown all over the world.

Lettuce originally grew wild in Egypt. Herodotus tells us that lettuce was served to the kings of Persia in 500 BC; later, the Emperor Augustus popularized the vegetable by proclaiming its medicinal value. In 1614, Castelvetro wrote: 'Most of the salads we eat in summer are made from lettuce. The crisp, white 'capucina' is refreshing and at the same time induces the sweet sleep that the heat disturbs and dispels.' The soporific effect of eating too many lettuces was, of course, discovered to their cost by Beatrix Potter's Flopsy Bunnies.

No doubt, Mr McGregor, like other Victorian gardeners, took a pride in producing crisp, fresh lettuce all the year round by growing a succession of varieties in cold frames and under glass lights or cloches. The delightful gardening writer, Mrs C. W. Earle, noted in 1897 that seedling lettuces which are usually discarded when thinning make an excellent salad when mixed with finely chopped fresh herbs.

Present-day gardeners grow loosehead lettuce whose leaves resemble lettuce seedlings. Their small tender leaves are much favoured by salad connoisseurs – the leaf can be eaten whole, and because it does not need to be torn or cut into smaller pieces for a salad, the leaves stay more crisp.

The bronze-leaved 'Oak Leaf' lettuce, or *feuilles de chêne*, is a particularly delicious variety. Loosehead lettuces are quicker and easier to grow, and because you cut just their leaves and leave the plant to produce a second crop, they are often termed 'cut-and-come-again' lettuce. The traditional hearted lettuce takes time to develop its tightly-packed centre.

Recently there has been much attention given to the Italian lettuces whose leaves are as frilled and lacy as lingerie. Some are flushed with red, others are lime green, and the effect in the kitchen has been to considerably perk up the salad bowl. For as John Evelyn wrote, lettuce 'ever was and still continues the principal foundation of the universal Tribe of Salads; which is to cool and refresh'.

Lettuces are easy to grow. Sow seed 5 mm/¼ in deep in fertile soil, and thin or transplant when large enough to handle. When grown too slowly lettuce can develop a bitter taste, and it is worth remembering that because lettuce is 95 per cent water, it's important to keep the soil moist.

The best-tasting varieties of cabbage lettuce are: 'All Year Round', 'Continuity', 'Regina dei Ghiacci', 'Rougette du Midi', 'Tom Thumb' and 'Webb's Wonderful'. Cos or romaine lettuce: 'Little Gem', 'Rouge d'Hiver' and 'Winter Density'. Loosehead or picking lettuce: 'Biscia Rossa', 'Green Lollo', 'Green Salad Bowl', 'Lollo Rosso', 'Red Saladbowl', 'Ricciolina di Quercia' and also the packets of mixed loosehead or cut-and-come-again lettuce.

Although lettuce is most commonly eaten raw, braised lettuce is a delicious dish. Castelvetro recommends charcoal-grilled lettuce: 'Cut the solid heart into four parts, each well oiled and salted and peppered, and roast them on a grid over hot charcoal (not burning embers) and eat them sprinkled with orange juice. They are delicious, almost as good as asparagus.' Just so.

CHINESE ARTICHOKE
Stachys affinis

CECILIA MARIA PEARSE, IN *THE KITCHEN GARDEN AND THE COOK* (1913), describes the chinese artichokes as 'a curious little vegetable, only introduced into Europe from China or Japan during the last few years; the tubers are used either boiled or fried, and they have a nutty flavour.'

If you grow nothing else in your kitchen garden, do try a few of these bewitching little artichokes. You will be charmed by their flavour and their looks. Each pearly-white tuber grows up to 6 cm/2½ in long and the shape makes one think that they have been piped from a forcing bag (pastry bag) – almost like a row of beads. Simply wash the tubers carefully in cold water, place in a steaming basket with a bouquet of fresh herbs, and cook for five to six minutes or until tender. Turn in melted butter and finely chopped parsley. Chinese artichokes are also very good dressed with a nut oil or simmered in cream with a fresh bay leaf until tender.

Chinese artichokes are grown in the same way as Jerusalem artichokes, and as easily. Plant the tubers – which can be bought from a seedsman specializing in unusual vegetables, or look for them in a high-class delicatessen – about 2.5 cm/1 in deep in moist, fertile soil during the spring. At other times of the year, plant the tubers in pots in a cool greenhouse or sunny porch. Try to keep the soil moist but not wet and apply some organic fertilizer in midsummer. The top growth is similar to that of Jerusalem artichokes but grows only 60-90 cm/2-3 ft high. Dig the tubers from September onwards, and store some in dry sand for planting the following year.

MARJORAM
Origanum marjorana

Culinary use: sprigs and leaves in 'bouquet garni' for sauces, lamb and rich meats, in marinades, cheese and vegetable dishes, pizza and pasta, Italian cooking; young leaves and flowers in salads, tisanes.

Cultivation: hardy herbaceous perennial with pink flowers, several varieties plus wild marjoram or oregano, height 15-45 cm/6-18 in; grow in well-drained soil in full sun.

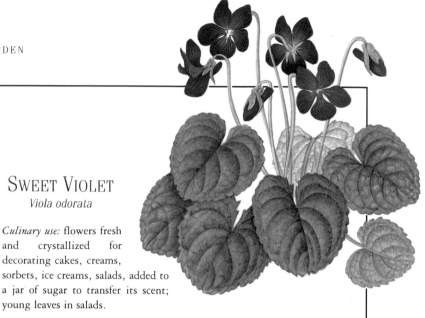

SWEET VIOLET
Viola odorata

Culinary use: flowers fresh and crystallized for decorating cakes, creams, sorbets, ice creams, salads, added to a jar of sugar to transfer its scent; young leaves in salads.

Cultivation: hardy perennial with purple-violet flowers, height 8-15 cm/3-6 in; grow in fertile, moist soil in a sheltered position in light shade.

MELON
Cucumis melo

ON 21 OCTOBER 1779, PARSON JAMES WOODFORDE VISITED HIS NEIGHBOURS, Mr and Mrs Kerr. In his usual endearing style, he described the food in his diary entry. 'We had for dinner a leg of pork, boiled, a Turkey rosted and a couple of Ducks. We had for Supper a couple of Fowls boiled, a fine Pheasant rosted and some cold things. Dinner and Supper served up in China, dishes and Plates. Melons, Apples and Pears, Walnuts and small Nutts for a desert.' It was a splendid day of eighteenth-century eating, with food and china that evidently impressed him, for everything would have been home-grown and home-made. What impresses me is the mention of melons – an exquisite fruit that is rarely seen in today's English gardens.

The melon had become far better known during the eighteenth century. For in 1699, John Evelyn wrote: 'That this Fruit was very rarely cultivated in England, so as to bring it to Maturity, till Sir Geo. Gardner came out of Spain. I my self remembring, when an ordinary Melon would have been sold for five or six shillings.' He says that the fruit might seem unusual in a book on salads, but that the ripe flesh is excellent with salt and pepper. Indeed, a ripe home-grown melon is delectable. The fruit is perfect eaten plain and still warm from the garden; or it goes well with walnut oil vinaigrette, and, of course, in many of the sweet dishes that have been devised since the fruit arrived in our islands.

It seems that melons were first grown in Britain during the reign of Edward I, and were forgotten, and then revived by Elizabethan gardeners. It is surely time to once again revive the home-grown melon. Happily, the new breed of F1 varieties has made successful melon-growing available to many more people. The quick-maturing varieties like 'Sweetheart' can be grown under glass as far north as Scotland, and even outside, in sheltered gardens in the south.

My melon-growing experience is limited compared with my mother who has grown the fruit for fifty years. In the early days, she sowed seed saved from shop-bought melons, since melon seed was rarely seen in catalogues. Now she swears by the 'Sweetheart' variety and every summer produces a score or more of these peach-fleshed, scented fruits. The variety 'Sweetheart' F1 is a cantaloupe melon, and in the same family are the varieties 'Early Sweet' F1, 'Ogen' and 'Charantais'. If you prefer melons with a pale green flesh, try the varieties 'Blenheim Orange', 'Emerald Gem' and 'Hero of Lockinge'.

My mother sows the seed in her greenhouse during March or April – one seed to a 7.5 cm/3 in pot, sown edge down, and covered with newspaper and a sheet of glass. Remove the covering when the seeds have germinated. And when the plants have two true leaves, transplant to the greenhouse border or to larger pots or even gro-bags. But she finds the melons do best in rich, fertile soil in an unheated greenhouse border, outside in a cold-frame or under cloches, Do not allow the plants to dry out but also do not over-water. Provided that the soil is rich, no extra feed is necessary; however, melon plants in pots benefit from a dose of liquid tomato fertilizer every month once the fruits have set.

It is important to pinch out the growing point after four leaves. Allow two side-shoots to form and stop these after eight to ten leaves. My mother allows four to six flowers on each plant, and provided that insects are able to fertilize the flowers these should all fruit. She harvests them from August until late September. And they taste truly wonderful.

HORSERADISH
Armoracia rusticana

Culinary use: grated root in sauces for beef, smoked fish, in vegetable dishes notably beetroot, avocado pears, salads; young leaves in salads; flowers as a garnish for salads.

Cultivation: hardy herbaceous perennial with white flowers, height 50 cm/18 in; grow in moist, fertile soil, preferably in a container or pipe sunk into the ground to confine its roots, in full sun or light shade.

BERGAMOT
Monarda didyma

Culinary use: leaves for tisanes, add to green China tea, wine cups, chilled fruit drinks; flowers in salads, as a garnish for desserts.

Cultivation: hardy herbaceous perennial with red, pink or purple flowers; height 30-60 cm/1-2 ft grow in fertile, moist soil in full sun or light shade.

ROSES
Rosa species

Culinary use: petals in creams, custards, junkets, syrups, sorbets, ice creams, to flavour sugar, as a garnish for cakes and desserts, crystallized for decorating sweet dishes.

Cultivation: hardy deciduous shrub with red, pink, white, yellow, orange flowers in many shades but the most useful and fragrant are usually red or pink, many named varieties, height 1-4 m/3-12 ft; grow in fertile, well-drained soil in full sun or light shade.

Far right: 'Salad Bowl' lettuces grow beside feathery fennel and baby turnips.

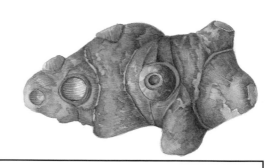

JERUSALEM ARTICHOKE
Helianthus tuberosus

APART FROM THE NAME, THE ONLY SHARED CHARACTERISTIC OF the globe and Jerusalem artichoke is a slightly smoky taste. The Jerusalem artichoke is a useful, low-starch root vegetable with knobbly edible tubers. The top growth can reach a height of 2 m/6½ ft and from midsummer produces charming yellow sun-flowers. The vegetable does not come from Jerusalem. Its name is derived from the Italian word *girasole*, meaning turning to face the sun, a typical movement of all sunflowers.

The flavour of the Jerusalem artichoke is delicious and is, in my view, superior to the over-rated scorzonera and salsify, two root vegetables which taste of very little but have fascinating names.

Jerusalem artichokes are cooked in the same way as potatoes, but only for eight to twelve minutes if fresh from the garden. They can be scrubbed or peeled and boiled in salted water with a splash of milk to keep them white. They are also excellent peeled, sliced and steamed, and served hot with a walnut oil vinaigrette or a well-flavoured béchamel sauce. I often use these root artichokes in salads, either cooked and diced or raw and grated, and mixed with lemon juice to keep them white.

Add diced celery and black olives to bring out their earthy flavour.

For years I grew a very knobbly type of Jerusalem artichoke acquired from a friend. But now a smoother variety called 'Fuseau' is available which reduces waste when peeling. Most gardeners buy Jerusalem artichokes only once, because the tubers multiply like made if left in the ground and, unless you are careful, can take over part of the garden. Plant the tubers about 10 cm/4 in deep in rows or a group, in well-drained, moderately rich soil, during the spring. Be sure to keep them free of weeds, but apart from this they require scant attention, hence they are great fun for children to grow. The top growth provides summer shelter for other plants or an informal screen to hide the compost heap. And you can even pick the flowers for decoration in the house.

Dig the roots as required at any time from September to early winter. Cut the top growth down to 30 cm/12 in in November to prevent wind damage.

CHIVE
Allium schoenoprasum

Culinary use: leaves used for their subtle onion flavour; chopped leaves in sauces and savoury butters, affinity with egg dishes, homemade cheese, salads, and as a garnish, flowers in salads and garnishes.

Cultivation: half-hardy perennial with purple flowers, related varieties: garlic chives, Chinese chives, Egyptian tree onion, Welsh onion, height 20-30 cm/8-12 in; grow in fertile, well-drained soil in full sun or light shade.

DILL
Anethum graveolens

Culinary use: whole leaves and sprigs in salads and stuffings; chopped leaves in sauces, in fish dishes, with fresh and pickled vegetables especially cucumber and gherkins; flowers in salads, to flavour wine vinegar; seed in fish and vegetable dishes, in breads.

Cultivation: half-hardy annual with white flowers, height .6-1 m/2-3 ft; grow in fertile, well-drained soil in a sheltered position in full sun or light shade.

MELON SALAD WITH RASPBERRY, NECTARINE AND MINT COULIS

1 large ripe 'Galia' or 'Ogen' melon

175 g/6 oz/1½ cups raspberries

3 ripe nectarines

3-4 tsp caster (superfine) sugar

3 tbsp virgin olive oil

1 tsp finely chopped mint or basil

salt

freshly milled green peppercorns

6 sprigs of mint, to garnish

Halve the melon and remove the seeds. Take out the flesh with a Parisienne spoon (melon ball cutter). Or cut the melon into segments, slice the fruit and reform on the melon peel.

Purée the raspberries with the nectarines (leave the skin on but discard the stones), then push through a fine nylon sieve. Sweeten the purée to taste and stir in the oil with the mint or basil and a little salt.

Spoon the coulis over the melon, grind on some green peppercorns and garnish with the sprigs of mint. Serve straight away. *Serves 6*

CHILLED CUCUMBER SOUP WITH DILL

If fresh dill is not available, this soup is equally delicious made with fresh mint or tarragon. Serve with small hot cheese sablés.

1 large cucumber (English hothouse cucumber if available)

30 g/1 oz/2 tbsp butter

1 clove garlic, chopped

300 ml/½ pint/1¼ cups chicken or vegetable stock

300 ml/½ pint/1¼ cups Greek-style plain yoghurt or buttermilk

salt

freshly milled green peppercorns

1 tbsp chopped dill

GARNISH:

3-4 tablespoons whipped cream

3-4 sprigs of dill

Wash and dry the cucumber and trim off the ends. Use a potato peeler to remove just under half the skin, then roughly chop the cucumber.

Melt the butter in a pan and stir in the garlic for 2 minutes. Add the cucumber, stir and cover with a lid. Lower the heat and cook for 5-8 minutes or until the cucumber is tender. Add the stock and bring to the boil, then remove from the heat and allow to cool.

Purée in a food processor, then mix in the yoghurt or buttermilk and season to taste with salt and green peppercorns. Stir in the dill and chill until ready to serve.

Ladle into chilled bowls or dishes (in hot weather set them on plates of crushed ice) and garnish each bowl with a spoonful of whipped cream and a sprig of dill. *Serves 3-4*

FENNEL

Foeniculum vulgare subsp. *vulgare*

Culinary use: whole leaves in stuffings for fish; young leaves and sprigs in salads, fish stock and garnishes; chopped leaves in sauces and in vegetable dishes; flowers in salads, vinegars and pasta; seeds in breads and yeast cakes; dried stems burned over charcoal under grilled fish.

Cultivation: hardy herbaceous perennial with green or bronze leaves, sulphur-yellow flowers, height .9-1.8 m/3-6 ft; grow in fertile soil in full sun.

A fine crop of summer spinach ready to cut for the kitchen.

SPINACH and *GREEN* PEPPER TART WITH WALNUT PASTRY

The crisp, nutty pastry of this tart makes an excellent contrast to the filling of spinach enlivened with green pepper and pancetta.

PASTRY:

60 g/2 oz/1/2 cup broken walnuts

200 g/7 oz/1¾ cups plain wholewheat flour

¼ tsp salt

90 g/3 oz/6 tbsp butter, softened

1 tbsp sunflower oil

4-5 tbsp cold water

FILLING:

450 g/1 lb fresh spinach

150 ml/¼ pint/²/3 cup single (light) cream

3 eggs

4 spring onions (scallions), chopped

freshly grated nutmeg

salt and freshly milled pepper

1 large green sweet pepper, seeded, diced and blanched

90 g/3 oz pancetta or smoked streaky (Canadian) bacon (optional)

Chop the walnuts roughly in a food processor. Add the flour, salt, butter and sunflower oil with 4 tbsp of the water. Process until binding together into a ball. Because flours vary, add the extra water, if necessary, to make the dough. Wrap the dough and place in the freezer for 10 minutes or chill for 30 minutes.

Butter a 25 cm/10 in fluted china or glass flan (quiche) dish. Roll out the pastry and line the dish. Prick the bottom all over with a fork and bake blind in a oven preheated to 200°C/400°F/Gas Mark 6 for 20 minutes.

Meanwhile, prepare the filling: wash the spinach and cook in the water clinging to the leaves until wilted but still bright green. Drain well in a sieve. Chop the spinach in a food processor with some of the cream until fairly fine. Add the remaining cream, the eggs, spring onions (scallions), nutmeg and salt and pepper and mix well. Stir in the green pepper and the pancetta and turn the mixture into the pastry case.

Replace in the oven and bake for 25-30 minutes. Serve the tart hot or cold. *Serves 6-8*

HOT BEETROOT (BEET) WITH HORSERADISH CREAM

The deliciously pungent flavour of horseradish makes an excellent foil to the sweet taste of freshly cooked beetroot (beet).

450 g/1 lb small beetroot (beet)

1 tsp vinegar

30 g/1 oz/2 tbsp butter, melted

salt and freshly milled pepper

1-2 tbsp freshly grated horseradish

150 ml/¼ pint/²/3 cup soured cream

¼ tsp finely grated zest (rind) of lemon

squeeze of lemon juice

1 tbsp finely chopped chives or parsley

Wash the beetroot (beet) under cold running water, taking care not to scratch the skin; leave the roots intact. Cover with cold water, add the vinegar and bring to the boil. Place the lid on the pan and cook gently on the top of the stove, or in an oven preheated to 180°C/350°F/Gas Mark 4, for 30-40 minutes or until tender. Remove from the heat, drain and peel.

Transfer the beetroot to a hot serving dish and pour over the melted butter. Season with salt and pepper and keep hot.

Mix the horseradish with the soured cream. Stir in the zest (rind) of lemon and add lemon juice to taste. Spoon over the beetroot and sprinkle the chives or parsley on top.
Serves 4

The golden green leaves and pink flowers of marjoram against the feathery foliage of southernwood.

WINTER RADISH AND CARROT SALAD WITH HERB MAYONNAISE

Red and pink summer radishes were a popular salad vegetable in Victorian times. This may explain the enthusiasm for the autumn- and winter-cropping Long Black Spanish radish which was sometimes cooked and served as a hot vegetable but more often was eaten raw.

300 g/10 oz carrots

1 or 2 winter radishes

2 tbsp finely chopped mixed fresh herbs: parsley, chives, chervil, marjoram

150 ml/¼ pint/⅔ cup mayonnaise

lemon juice or milk

Scrub or scrape the carrots and grate into a salad bowl.

Peel the winter radish thinly and grate finely. Mix with the carrot.

Mix the herbs with the mayonnaise. Thin with lemon juice or milk and pour over the grated vegetables. Toss gently until well mixed and serve within 1 hour while still crisp.
Serves 4

CABBAGE COOKED IN CREAM WITH WHISKY

Most members of the brassica family respond well to being cooked slowly with butter, goose fat, olive oil or cream. In this recipe, the beautiful crinkle-leaved Savoy cabbage almost melts into the nutmeg- and whisky-flavoured cream to make a luxurious and comforting dish.

1 small Savoy cabbage

salt

30 g/1 oz/2 tbsp butter

1 shallot or clove garlic, finely chopped

150 ml/¼ pint/⅔ cup double (heavy) cream

2 tbsp Scotch whisky

freshly grated nutmeg

139

Discard any damaged outer leaves of the cabbage and cut it into quarters. Trim away the thickest part of the stem, but leave enough to hold the leaves together. Rinse the cabbage in cold water and blanch in salted boiling water for 4 minutes, then drain well.

Melt the butter in a flameproof casserole dish and cook the shallot or garlic for about 3 minutes until softened but not coloured. Place the pieces of cabbage on top and pour the cream mixed with the whisky over the leaves. Grate a little nutmeg over the dish and cover with a tight-fitting lid.

Bake in an oven preheated to 180°C/350°F/Gas Mark 4 for 30-40 minutes or until the cabbage is cooked and has absorbed most of the cream. Some cabbages produce quite a lot of water, so if there is still too much liquid in the dish, boil to reduce it over high heat for a few minutes. *Serves 4*

Punnets of small, sweet alpine strawberries ready to be taken to the kitchen.

BRAISED LETTUCE

Nearly every Victorian cook book has a recipe for Stewed Lettuce. Most of them give a rather long cooking time by today's standard. This is my version of a delicious Victorian way of braising lettuce that goes admirably well with grilled (broiled) poultry, lamb or beef.

2 well-hearted lettuces like 'Little Gem'

60 g/2 oz/4 tbsp butter

1-2 tbsp sherry or herb-flavoured vinegar

Trim the stalk of the lettuce, discard any limp outer leaves and, if necessary, wash the lettuce. Cut each lettuce in half lengthways.

Melt the butter in a pan large enough to hold the lettuce halves in a single layer. Add the lettuce and turn over until coated with butter. Then place them cut side down and cover with a lid or buttered paper.

Cook over moderate heat, or in an oven preheated to 180°C/350°F/Gas Mark 4, for 10-15 minutes or until the lettuce is cooked but not mushy. Transfer the lettuce to a hot serving dish. Add the vinegar to the pan and mix with the cooking juices. Simmer for 1 minute, then pour over the lettuce and serve. *Serves 2-4*

STRAWBERRY TARTLETS

PASTRY:

150 g/5 oz/10 tbsp butter

60 g/2 oz/¼ cup caster (superfine) sugar

1 egg

115 g/4 oz/¾ cup plain (all-purpose) flour

115 g/4 oz/¾ cup self-raising flour

FILLING:

175 g/6 oz cream cheese

45 g/1½ oz/3 tbsp caster (superfine) sugar

1 tsp powdered unflavoured gelatine

1 tbsp cold water

120 ml/4 fl oz/½ cup double (heavy) cream

small strawberries or alpine strawberries

Midsummer roses in full bloom, their petals will be crystallised for sorbets and ice creams.

For the pastry, cream the butter with the sugar and beat in the egg. Mix in the flours to make a soft dough, but do not overhandle. Chill the dough for 30 minutes.

Roll out the pastry dough on a floured board and line 8-10 cm/4 in tartlet tins. Prick the bottoms of the pastry cases and bake in an oven preheated to 190°C/375°F/Gas Mark 5 for 12-15 minutes or until golden brown and crisp. Cool in the tins, then transfer to a wire rack. (These pastry cases can be frozen and thawed when needed.)

Cream the cheese with the sugar. Soften the gelatine in the cold water, then dissolve over gentle heat. Mix into the cheese mixture in a fine trickle. Whip the cream constantly until fairly stiff and fold into the cheese mixture.

Spoon some of the cream cheese mixture into each pastry case and arrange sliced or halved strawberries on top. *Serves 8-10*

ROSE PETALS

The most scented roses tend to be red and pink, and the deeper the hue the greater the fragrance. Rose petals can be eaten straight from the bush provided that no sprays have been used. Pick the petals before mid-morning if possible, when their scent is strongest.

Crystallized rose petals: remove the white base of each petal since it can taste bitter. Brush both sides of each petal with lightly whisked white of egg and sprinkle with caster (superfine) sugar until evenly coated. Place the petal on a sheet of non-stick baking paper (parchment) resting on a wire rack. Leave the sugared petals in a warm place for 3-4 hours until dry. Use for decorating creams, junkets and custards. Crystallized petals store well for up to a week in a tightly closed container, although they taste at their best the same day they are made.

Rose-scented sugar: layer fresh, dry rose petals and caster (superfine) sugar in a glass jar, leaving a small space at the top. Shake the jar when you remember, to distribute the scent. Sieve the sugar and use in recipes and for sprinkling on cakes, biscuits (cookies) or yoghurt.

Rose-scented honey: gently warm a jar of honey with a handful of fresh, dry rose petals, stirring now and again. Remove from the heat and leave in a warm place for 5 hours, then strain the honey back into the jar. Rose-scented honey is excellent on hot toast or muffins or stirred into yoghurt.

Rose petal vinegar: cover a jar of highly-scented fresh, dry rose petals with white wine vinegar and cover tightly. Leave in a warm place for 2-3 days, then strain off the vinegar and use in salad dressings and sauces.

Rose petal sandwiches with rose petal butter: cut some unsalted butter into dice and place on a piece of greaseproof (wax) paper. Surround with fresh, dry rose petals, wrap in the paper and leave in a cold place for 24 hours. Discard the petals: the butter should have absorbed their scent. Make sandwiches from a sliced brioche loaf, spread with rose petal butter, cover with a layer of fresh rose petals and place a layer of rose-buttered brioche on top. Cut the sandwiches into fingers and sprinkle with rose-scented sugar.

CHAPTER SEVEN

SEAKALE, LEMON VERBENA, ENDIVE *and* SCAROLE,
HYSSOP, ORIENTAL VEGETABLES, CHICORY, DANDELION,
VEGETABLE SPAGHETTI, BORAGE, CLAYTONIA *and* WINTER
PURSLANE, ELDER, APRICOT, QUINCE

A VICTORIAN KITCHEN GARDEN IN THE ENGLISH SHIRES

HAMBLETON HALL

IT WAS ALMOST LIKE ST TROPEZ OR ST MORITZ AROUND HERE IN THE nineteenth century,' explains Tim Hart, referring to England's smallest county, Rutland, now subsumed by neighbouring Leicestershire. 'In the season, everybody came for the hunting. The local shops were some of the smartest outside London because all the swells were here. And many of them built country houses and hunting lodges. Hambleton was one of them.'

Benjamin Disraeli, Queen Victoria's favourite minister, described the new-found wealth of middle-class Victorians as 'an explosion of prosperity'. He died

The Victorian gothic entrance to Hambleton Hall is emblazoned with the words: Fay ce que voudrais *cut into the stonework above the door.*

in 1881, the same year that Hambleton Hall was built in local Pendle stone. The house is a classic Victorian residence with the comfortable – and now, highly luxurious – air of a large rectory. Oddly though, its lakeside position is relatively recent – Rutland Water was created only a decade ago. Happily, the stretch of water is so large it appears quite natural.

True to the fashion of the time, the kitchen garden is a short distance from the house. Originally, it covered 1.25 hectares/3 acres: huge by today's standards but quite usual for a country house in Victorian England. For this was the hey-day of the

The fruit tunnel clothed with climbing roses, hops and clematis.

English kitchen garden when the smart thing was to impress your guests with an astonishing display of horticultural expertise. At the end of a magnificent meal in the bedecked dining room, the Victorian host liked to lead his guests on a gentle tour of the kitchen garden to see where his cornucopia of fruit, vegetables and flowers was grown.

Such display of affluence did not go uncriticized. In *The English Gardener*, William Cobbett writes, '. . . long experience and observation have convinced me that a large garden is of very little use . . .' He suggests that for an average size family a kitchen garden of about one acre is ideal and that a large garden 'is really a valid pretence for the employment of a great number of hands.'

Some years ago, doubtless to cut down on 'the great number of hands', the Hambleton kitchen garden was reduced to just over half its original size. And in the eight years since Tim and Stefa Hart arrived, they have concentrated on making the garden easier to run and yet remain highly productive. Fortunately, some of the historic features of the original garden are still in place.

The stone wall of the stable block forms the north side of the garden, and the west-facing wall of local brick runs at right angles to it. The glasshouses which were built against this wall have since disappeared. However, the surviving double-span glasshouse has been beautifully restored. The two remaining boundaries are formed by a hedge and the original cast-iron fence which separates the kitchen garden from the shrubbery along the drive.

The splendid Victorian fruit tunnel, or arcade, which used to run north to south down the middle of the south-sloping garden, has been moved and repainted. It now stretches east-west across the garden, to make a tunnel over the paved path to the tennis court. The wires linking the hoop-topped uprights have been replaced and climbing plants are beginning to cloth the metal frame. Traditionally, the pergola in a Victorian kitchen garden is planted with fruit trees trained as espaliers over the arches and along the horizontal wires.

At Hambleton, a golden hop plant is flourishing at one end of the pergola where its leaves soften the harsh outline of the metal struts. For centuries, hops have been grown in England for their flowers which were used in the brewing industry. And the shoots have been eaten as a vegetable. 'The buds and young tendrels . . . may be eaten raw; but more conveniently being boil'd, and cold like Asparagus,' says John Evelyn. While William Cobbett writes, 'The hop-top . . . is as delightful a vegetable as ever was put upon a table, not yielding, perhaps, during about the three weeks that it is in season, to the asparagus itself.'

After a certain amount of experiment Tim Hart has come to the conclusion that, 'It makes most sense for us to grow the crops that taste at their best straight from the garden plus all the produce that does not travel well or deteriorates fast, like salad vegetables, fresh herbs and the kind of soft fruits that our chef, Brian Baker, and I think taste superb but are not grown commercially.' And he points to the new fruit cage (a netted enclosure to protect fruit from birds) that is being constructed.

With David Marlow, the head gardener at Hambleton Hall, he hopes to repeat their considerable success with alpine strawberries which luxuriate in the large cold frames on the warm, south side of the glasshouse. David Marlow finds alpine strawberries, which are never cheap to buy, very easy to grow. 'Simply remove any dead leaves and give a light dressing of well-rotted compost in the spring. Don't cover with glass and leave well alone.' The results are impressive. He has been able to pick some of the small, sweet fruit everyday from May until November, with the heaviest cropping in the summer months of June, July and August.

A huge fig tree that could well have been planted during Queen Victoria's reign covers a large stretch of wall near the gardener's store. Nobody can remember a fig ripening on this tree, although there is plenty

A few feet above the trees and jutting out from the wall, a row of metal coping brackets reminds one of how Victorian gardeners used to protect blossoming wall-fruits from a damaging frost. These brackets were used to support straw mats or sheets of canvas which, in early spring, were hooked on to the brackets when the trees were in flower. The protective covers were left in place at night and were removed on sunny days when flying insects could fertilize the blooms. Later in the century, when the tax was removed from glass, some gardeners fixed a permanent glass coping to the brackets. And the really rich built glasshouses specially for growing tender fruits like peaches, nectarines, grapes and even pineapples.

'In a private establishment it is a mark of good management if the gardener can cut broccoli or cauliflower any day of the year,' asserted the widely-read gardening writer James Shirley Hibberd in 1877. The Victorian head gardener, dressed in a suit because he no longer performed physical tasks in the garden, organized the work. He was judged by his employer and the housekeeper in the big house by the quality of his produce. These extraordinarily high standards, so rarely seen today, were the norm in mid-Victorian England. But how do you produce year-round crops of so many different vegetables and fruits, with strawberries at Christmas, asparagus at Easter and the first crop of peas by King George III's birthday on the fourth of June? It was an incredible assignment which required the total commitment of the head gardener and his poorly-paid men.

In order to produce a succession of crops, Victorian gardeners employed methods many of which are still available to today's skilful gardener. The earliest crops were grown in the warmest south-facing borders, mid-season crops were planted in the central beds of the garden, and crops intended to grow more slowly were placed in the cooler, east- and north-facing borders. The gardener had recourse to a vast choice of seeds with a range of maturing times. For the nineteenth century saw more varieties of plants than at any other era in the history of horticulture. During what Lytton Strachey called this 'very seed-time of modern progress' lived scores of talented gardeners, epitomized by Sir Joseph Paxton, and hybridizers like Thomas Andrew Knight and nurserymen like Thomas Rivers. And all of us who garden or enjoy gardens continue to benefit from the work of these pioneers.

Backed by the yellow daisy flowers of the Jerusalem artichoke, the main vegetable border at Hambleton Hall contains a wide range of different lettuces – bronze oak-leaf, lime-green frilled and two Victorian favourites. 'Little Gem' and 'Continuity'. Next to them a row of salad dandelions and some endive frisée are large enough to be covered with pots

of fruit. And so I wonder whether at some time the stable block was rebuilt further inside the garden so that it now shades the fig tree in the late afternoon. Because figs do ripen in Rutland – Tim Hart eats them from another tree a few miles away.

'Plant pears for your heirs' runs the gardening proverb. Against the warm wall of the stable block, two very old beautifully-trained pears still produce a good crop. Fortunately, present-day pear-lovers do not have to wait a generation before they can pick this wonderful fruit. Today's pear trees are grafted on dwarfing rootstock, which means that the tree produces fruit within three years. What has lasted in pear culture, though, are the old varieties. All our best pears, such as 'Doyenné du Comice' and 'Williams' Bonne Chrétien', date from the nineteenth century or earlier. We are indeed the heirs to their pears.

Apricots, which were far more widely appreciated in Victorian times, grow well at Hambleton Hall. Finding the old nectarine and peach trees bore little fruit, Messrs Hart and Marlow grubbed them out and planted some fan-trained 'Moor Park' apricots. These new trees are not only a fine example of period restoration but they are proving to be highly productive, with at least 13.6 kg/30 lb of fruit from each tree in 1989.

the old fashioned vegetable Good King Henry – which the Victorian gardener William Robinson particularly recommended 'for a poor man's garden' – grows next to the relatively recent introduction to English gardens, the oriental plant, pak-choi.

Naturally, in this long-established huntin', shootin', fishin' country, Brian Baker prepares a wide variety of game dishes. And he has developed some fine subtle sauces to accompany them. In early autumn he makes a delicious dark lustrous sauce from the jet-black elderberries that festoon the east wall of the garden. 'We also pick masses of elderflower in May and June to make a sorbet and an elderflower syrup for pouring over melon. Mind you,' says Brian, 'one of the nicest things to make with elderflower is June Champagne. It's fantastic mixed with vodka or gin and plenty of ice.'

Eliza Acton, the estimable Victorian cooker writer, devoted an unusual amount of space to fruit and vegetable recipes. In *Modern Cookery for Private Families*, she wrote, 'The quality of vegetables depends both on the soil in which they are grown, and on the degree of care bestowed upon their culture.' Of course, the growing quality of the soil in a Victorian garden, and the maintenance of the essential hot-bed for forcing early crops, depended as much upon the horse as upon the gardener. When the internal combustion engine was introduced towards the end of the century, gardeners were compelled to look elsewhere for their fertilizer. And the compost heap that many of us depend upon for soil improvement was born.

A century after it was built, Hambleton Hall is still surrounded by the hunting shires and can continue to call upon a generous supply of horse manure. A considerable quantity has been incorporated into the ground in the new fruit cage where David Marlow has planted many Victorian favourites. These include the almost-forgotten dessert gooseberry and both red- and yellow-fruiting raspberries, black currants, and large, juicy blackberries. Quince trees and dessert apples have been planted in the new orchard next to the pergola, and there is talk of planting the cuttings from the Victorian fig tree along the west-facing wall to see if they will grow as well but ripen better than the parent plant.

The restoration of the kitchen garden at Hambleton is in the great Victorian tradition. 'It was a time of sure values and lack of doubt,' says Asa Briggs in *Victorian People*. And every gardener will be heartened to see how skillfully the advice *'Fay ce que voudras'*, given on the coat of arms at Hambleton Hall, has been heeded in the garden. For, as William Cobbett wrote, 'If well managed, nothing is more beautiful than the kitchen garden.'

for one to three weeks in order to blanch their leaves and make them less bitter and more palatable. This old technique was used on many vegetables in the past such as seakale, 'Witloof' chicory and scarole. Although seedsmen sell a dandelion with slightly thicker fleshy leaves, you can discover whether you like the taste of this vegetable by blanching an ordinary garden dandelion to produce some pale yellow-green leaves for adding to a salad. But remember to put a stone or piece of broken tile over the hole in the bottom of the flowerpot to exclude all light.

'You'd have to be crazy not to grow chives in a kitchen garden,' maintains Tim Hart. So they do, in short neat rows that can be cropped like a cut-and-come-again lettuce. Next to the chives are rows of flat-leaf parsley, sorrel and French tarragon. Clumps of blue-flowered hyssop and the fragrant lemon verbena (that Victorian gentlemen brushed their hats against to pick up the perfume), are used as edging herbs. In a good summer, tender herbs like chervil and basil are also grown outside. Otherwise they are grown in the warm refuge of the glasshouse. A patch of

GRILLED ESCALOPE OF FOIE GRAS WITH A CELEBRATION OF *SPRING* VEGETABLES

16 small radishes

16 asparagus tips, trimmed to 5 cm/2 in

16 baby carrots

16 baby silverskin onions, peeled

8 baby turnips

8 baby globe artichokes

115 g/4 oz extra fine French (green) beans

115 g/4 oz small mangetout (snow peas)

salt

90 ml/3 fl oz olive oil

1 tbsp sherry vinegar

350 g/12 oz foie gras, cut into 4 equal slices

1 tbsp finely chopped mixed chervil, basil and coriander (cilantro) leaves

Wash and trim all the vegetables, and peel the onions remembering to leave short green tops on the radish, carrots and turnips. Cook all the vegetables separately in lightly salted boiling water. As soon as the vegetables are tender, drain well and keep warm.

Mix the olive oil and vinegar in a large bowl, add the vegetables and toss gently until coated with the vinaigrette. Arrange the vegetables on four warm plates, leaving a space in the middle.

Cook the slices of foie gras on a hot dry griddle or heavy-based pan for 30-40 seconds on each side. Do not use oil, as the foie gras will emit its own fat. When nicely brown, place each 'escalope' in the centre of the vegetables. Spoon any foie gras juices over the vegetables. Sprinkle the chopped herbs over the vegetables and serve with sea salt. *Serves 4*

SADDLE OF FALLOW BUCK WITH AN ELDERBERRY AND PEPPERCORN SAUCE AND SPAGHETTI VEGETABLES

1 loin of fallow buck, weighing about 1.4 kg/3 lb, including the bones

sprigs of thyme, to garnish

SAUCE:

1 carrot

1 onion

1 leek

2 stalks celery

2 cloves garlic

4 juniper berries

1 vegetable or chicken stock (bouillon) cube

225 g/8 oz/1½ cups elderberries

120 ml/4 fl oz port wine

60 ml/2 fl oz brandy

30 g/1 oz/¼ cup green peppercorns

SPAGHETTI VEGETABLES:

6 large carrots

4 large potatoes

6 large courgettes (zucchini)

oil for deep-frying

Ask your butcher to bone the meat, strip off the sinew and fat, and tie into a long sausage shape.

Make the sauce first. Brown the bones, sinew and meat trimmings in a roasting pan, in the oven or on top of the stove. Dice all the vegetables to make a *mirepoix* and add to the roasting pan. Cook until brown. Transfer the contents of the pan to a stock pot, add the stock (bouillon)

cube and cover with cold water. Bring to the boil and simmer for 3-4 hours, skimming the stock at regular intervals. Add more water if required, but the stock should reduce by half.

Place half the elderberries, the port, brandy and peppercorns in a pan and cook until mushy. Strain the stock into the elderberry mixture and boil to reduce over high heat until the sauce lightly coats the back of a spoon. Pass through a fine sieve. Add the remaining elderberries and keep warm.

Roast the meat in an oven preheated to 220°C/425°F/Gas Mark 7 for about 30 minutes; allow longer if you like the meat well done. Remove from the oven and allow the meat to rest for 15 minutes.

Meanwhile, to make the spaghetti vegetables, peel the carrots and potatoes; leave the skin on the courgettes (zucchini). Shred each vegetable separately using a mandoline or a sharp knife. Do not wash the potato spaghetti. Using a fork, curl each pile of vegetables into six small rounds. Deep-fry the potatoes and drain on paper towels. Place the piles of carrot and courgettes (zucchini) on a small plate and steam just before serving.

To serve, cut the loin of meat into six pieces and place each in the middle of a warm plate. Place one pile of each vegetable around the meat and garnish with a sprig of thyme. Spoon the warm sauce over the meat and serve. *Serves 6*

COMICE PEAR GLAZED WITH A POIRE WILLIAM SABAYON AND *TOASTED* RICE PUDDING

6 large Comice pears

600 ml/1 pint/2½ cups water

350 g/12 oz/1½ cups caster (US granulated) sugar

zest (rind) and juice of 2 lemons

pinch of salt

strings of red currants and sprigs of mint, to decorate

RICE PUDDING:

90 g/3 oz/7 tbsp pudding (short-grain) rice

600 ml/1 pint/2½ cups milk

4 egg yolks

60 g/2 oz/4 tbsp vanilla-flavoured sugar (see page 55)

300 ml/½ pint/1¼ cups double (heavy) cream

vanilla essence (extract)

grated nutmeg

SABAYON:

6 egg yolks

2 tbsp Poire William eau-de-vie

small piece of butter

Peel, halve and core the pears. Measure the water into a pan wide enough to hold the pears. Add the sugar, zest and juice of the lemons and salt, and stir over medium heat until the sugar has dissolved. Bring to the boil, add the pears, lower the heat and cook gently until almost cooked. Remove from the heat and leave the fruit to cool in the liquor.

Cook the rice gently in the milk until tender. Drain the rice and reserve the excess milk. Whisk the egg yolks with the vanilla sugar and mix with the cooked rice, 4 tablespoons of the reserved rice milk, the cream and a little vanilla and freshly grated nutmeg. Pour the mixture into a shallow oven dish – the mixture should be 4-5 cm/1½-2 in deep. Bake in an oven preheated to 180°C/350°F/Gas Mark 4 for about 20 minutes or until the mixture is set like an egg custard. Cool slightly, then cut out six rounds with a pastry cutter. Place them on a baking sheet and toast under a hot grill (broiler) until the top is turning brown. Set aside and keep warm.

To make the sabayon, place the egg yolks and Poire William in the top of a ceramic double boiler or a mixing bowl over simmering water. Add 150 ml/¼ pint/⅔ cup of the poaching liquor from the pears. Whisk vigorously for about 5 minutes or until the mixture is frothy and the whisk leaves a trail over the top when lifted out. Remove from the heat and continue whisking for 3-4 minutes. Add the butter.

To assemble the dish, drain the pears and slice each half lengthways almost to the top; fan out the slices on a plate. Place a second half on each plate and fan out the slices to make a circle. Spoon some sabayon over each pear and grill (broil) lightly – note that the sabayon browns very quickly under a hot grill (broiler). Place the toasted rice pudding to one side of the plate and garnish the dish with strigs of red currants and mint leaves. Serve straight away. *Serves 6*

Plants of seakale with its frosty grey foliage.
Like brassicas and wallflowers, seakale belongs
to the family Cruciferae.

SEAKALE
Crambe maritima

THE VICTORIAN FASHION FOR FORCED VEGETABLES – MADE POSSIBLE BY A READY supply of horse manure and a full complement of kitchen gardeners – brought seakale to prominence on the dining tables of the wealthy. This maritime plant grows wild on the shores of many parts of Britain and had been eaten by local people for centuries, although it is said that the seakale was favoured by the inhabitants of Dublin Bay far earlier than elsewhere in the British Isles.

Both Gerard and Evelyn refer to the wild vegetable, and during the eighteenth century seakale moved into the kitchen garden. In 1767, Dr Lettsom of Camberwell wrote a treatise on its garden cultivation. And twenty years later William Curtis contributed his more well-known pamphlet. It reached its peak of popularity during the nineteenth century, and most Victorian gardening books devote considerable space to it. To produce a crop before Christmas the roots were forced in boxes of sandy loam placed close to the heating pipes in a glasshouse. After Christmas, seakale was forced in the slightly lower temperature of the mushroom house, or in an outhouse where the roots were submerged in decaying dead leaves. The outdoor roots of seakale produced a spring crop which was forced under large clay pots with lids (this enabled the gardener to cut the shoots without moving the pot). The temperature inside the pots was increased by covering them with straw or manure.

Although the small young leaves of seakale can be cooked and eaten, it is the creamy-white forced shoots that are prized. These are cut just below soil level, and are steamed or boiled, and eaten in the same style as asparagus. There the resemblance ends. The flavour of cooked seakale (the shoots can also be eaten raw) is closer to a globe artichoke – slightly smoky yet buttery, with a hint of crispness when not overcooked.

In 1978, Jane Grigson wrote of seakale, 'Commerce remains unmoved by the enthusiasm – the long enthusiasm – of keen gardeners and cooks.' So it is good news for non-gardeners that the largest seakale grower in the country, Michael Paske of Grantham, Lincolnshire, who has 5.6 hectares/14 acres of seakale under production, is now supplying seakale to a major supermarket chain.

The gourmet gardener, though, can quite easily grow his own seakale. The plant is perennial and deciduous. So it is a good idea to mark out an area as a permanent bed – referred to by Victorian gardeners as a seakale plantation. Buy roots, or thongs, of seakale from a reputable grower and plant 60-90 cm/2-3 ft apart, during the spring. Seakale prefers a sandy, free-draining soil similar to its natural habitat. And the best fertilizer is liquid seaweed. A few frilled leaves will appear during the first year as the root establishes itself. But it is wiser not to force the vegetable until the second year. Then, in January, cover the root with a black plastic pot, block up its drainage hole and place a house brick on top to weight it down. Six to eight weeks later, some of the blanched shoots should be long enough to cut. Remove the pot during the late spring and allow the plant to grow normally. A full-grown head of seakale looks like a blue-green loose-leaved cabbage.

LEMON VERBENA
Aloysia triphylla (syn. *Lippia citriodora*)

Culinary use: leaves in sweet sauces and syrups, sorbets, ice cream, tisanes, jams and jellies; flowers as a garnish and decoration for salads, cakes and desserts.

Cultivation: half-hardy perennial with pale pink flowers, height 30-60 cm/1-2 ft; grow in light, well-drained soil in a sheltered position in full sun.

ENDIVE, BATAVIAN ENDIVE, SCAROLE
Cichorium endivia

O VID WROTE OF ENDIVE IN 43 BC

'A garden Salad was the third supply,
Of Endive, Radishes, and Succory.'

The 'Succory' is chicory, another member of the *Cichorium* genus. The most familiar variety of endive is the frisée with its crisp, narrow-toothed leaves that grow like an unruly wig, creamy white in the centre and shading to pale green and mid-green along each leaf. This handsome plant has a delicious bitter flavour much appreciated by the ancient Egyptians who cultivated the plant over 2000 years ago.

The fringed varieties of endive, 'Moss Curled' and 'Green Curled', are grown for cropping in the late summer and autumn. Endive frisée is an easy salad vegetable to grow in a moist, humus-rich soil. Sow seed thinly, as for lettuce, from early spring onwards, covering with a cloche in cold areas. Thin to 30 cm/12 in apart, and after two to three months, cover a few plants at a time, with a flowerpot, a cardboard box or a heap of straw, excluding all light. After two to three weeks, the blanched endive will have a less bitter flavour and it can be cut for salads.

Broad-leaved endive is known as batavian endive and scarole (in France escarole). These hardier varieties are grown for winter cropping. Sow seed outside in late summer, then thin or transplant the seedlings until 30 cm/12 in apart and feed with an organic fertilizer after two months. Cut the batavian endive from November onwards and in cold areas cover some of the plants with cloches to give a succession. Batavian endive and scarole intended for salads are best blanched as for endive frisée, but if intended for cooking the vegetable can be used unblanched because the heat destroys some of its bitterness.

All varieties of endive need a salad dressing with a pronounced flavour. I favour a dressing made with Roquefort cheese blended with crème fraîche or thin cream and a generous splash of walnut oil and lemon juice. Endive leaves are braised by French and Italian cooks. Also try batavian endive and scarole tossed in warm olive oil with a dash of bitter orange or lime juice and garnished with a mixture of finely chopped anchovy fillets and crisp garlic-rich croûtons for a satisfying winter salad.

HYSSOP
Hyssopus officinalis

Culinary use: sprigs of leaves in a 'bouquet garni' for tomato sauces and casseroles of rich meats and game, to flavour fruit compotes especially of peaches; flowers as a garnish for salads and desserts.

Cultivation: hardy semi-evergreen with blue, pink or white flowers, height 30-60 cm/1-2 ft best clipped after flowering; grow in well-drained soil in full sun.

ORIENTAL VEGETABLES

A T THE MOMENT ONLY A FRACTION OF THE VAST ARRAY OF VEGETABLES THAT ARE grown in the Far East reach our shores. A walk around the food shops of Chinatown in London or San Francisco shows which vegetables and fruit are considered essential to oriental cooking and will weather the long journey from the countries where they are grown. Increasingly, some varieties of oriental vegetables are grown by local suppliers. But so far few seedsmen are offering more than a handful of varieties of oriental seeds of interest to the adventurous gardener. This is bound to change. An experimental farm near Loughborough is testing the suitability of oriental seeds for British culture, and I look forward to the day when every gourmet gardener has a wider choice of exotic vegetables.

Right: The magnificently veined leaves of the oriental vegetable, Pak Choi.

CHINESE CABBAGE
Brassica rapa Chinensis group, *B.r.* Pekinensis group

IN CHINA THE WORD FOR VEGETABLE IS THE SAME AS THE WORD FOR CABBAGE: *choi*. and Chinese cabbage was one of the first oriental vegetables to become well-known to the British gardening cook. This is an easy vegetable to grow in a fertile soil. And there are now some excellent F1 hybrids like 'China Pride' available. Sow seed in early summer in open ground and thin the plants to 30 cm/12 in apart. Cut the vegetable from August onwards. The leaves may be eaten raw in salads, but I reckon they are more delicious shredded and stir-fried in sesame oil with slivers of fresh ginger and garlic.

CHOP SUEY GREENS
Chrysanthemum coronarium

THIS IS A VERY DECORATIVE VEGETABLE WITH DEEPLY-CUT BRIGHT GREEN LEAVES and an intriguing flavour. The variety 'Shungiku' is recommended. Sow seed in early spring and then every month to provide a succession throughout the summer. Thin to 10 cm/4 in apart and cut the centre shoots to encourage fresh side shoots. Steam, braise or stir-fry the leaves and serve with soy sauce.

EDIBLE BURDOCK
Arctium lappa

AN EASILY-GROWN ROOT VEGETABLE, SOW THIS IN EARLY SPRING AND THIN to 10 cm/4 in apart. Dig the roots from July onwards. Scrub or peel the roots and cut into pencil-size pieces, then stir-fry with fresh ginger and garlic, or steam and serve with toasted sesame seeds.

PAK CHOI
Brassica rapa Chinensis group

THIS IS SPECIALLY RECOMMENDED FOR AREAS OF LIGHT RAINFALL. SOW SEED IN spring and in late summer. Thin seedlings to 20 cm/8 in apart, and cut every other plant for the kitchen to allow the remaining plants to grow on. The variety 'White Celery Mustard' is grown for its large green leaves and thick white stalks, and is slow to bolt. The small young leaves are good in salads and the larger leaves and stems are sliced and braised in the dish chow mein.

FLOWERING PURPLE PAK CHOI
Brassica rapa Chinensis group

A DECORATIVE VEGETABLE WITH PURPLE STALKS AND YELLOW BUDS AND FLOWERS. For an early summer crop, sow in spring as soon as the ground can be worked. Leave some plants to flower, and pick the petals for strewing over salads and as a garnish to soups. The purple shoots are delicious steamed and served with sesame oil and chopped coriander leaves.

CHINESE MUSTARD
Brassica rapa Chinensis group

LIKE ALL MEMBERS OF THE MUSTARD FAMILY THIS IS AN EASY CROP TO GROW. SOW from midsummer onwards and thin to 30 cm/12 in apart and it will continue to produce fresh leaves all winter. Cut the leaves from early autumn onwards, remove the stems if tough and slice the leaves. Stir-fry with garlic and ginger or braise with toasted cashew nuts and Japanese radish. Recommended variety: 'Green-in-Snow'.

JAPANESE RADISH OR MOOLI
Raphanus sativus Longipinnatus group

THE VARIETY 'MINO EARLY' SHOULD BE SOWN IN EARLY SUMMER IN MOIST, well-drained soil. Do not allow to dry out, and dig the roots from July onwards. This radish has a more delicate flavour than the European salad radish. Serve raw, in slices or shredded – a mixture of half carrot, and half Japanese radish makes a good salad, dressed with yoghurt and honey. The radish can also be cooked – add it diced to stir-fried and braised dishes.

JAPANESE ONIONS
Allium fistulosum

THESE ONIONS ARE ALSO KNOWN AS BUNCHING ONIONS AND ARE SIMILAR TO THE perpetual Welsh onion. Sow in spring and use the thinnings in the kitchen. These onions do not bolt and remain like spring onions over a long period. Cut into slivers and sprinkle over steamed fish and stir-fried vegetables.

OKRA
Abelmoschus esculentus, synonym *Hibiscus e.*

ALSO KNOWN AS LADIES' FINGERS OR BHINDI, OKRA IS AN INTRIGUING AND satisfying vegetable for growing under glass. Sow the seed in early spring at a minimum temperature of 12°C/55°F and prick out when large enough to handle. Plant in beds or pots of rich compost, as for tomatoes. Feed with liquid organic fertilizer once a month. Pick the tapering green pods from July. Okra are widely used in India and Afghanistan cuisine and Creole cooking. The pods have a pleasant flavour, and when cooked become mucilaginous, making a natural sauce. Shallow-fry okra in oil or butter and cook with chopped tomatoes and ground fenugreek. Serve with plain yoghurt and finely chopped mint.

CHICORY
Cichorium intybus

THERE ARE TWO KINDS OF GREEN-LEAF CHICORY OF INTEREST TO THE GARDENING cook. Belgian or Brussels chicory is grown for its 'chicons', the creamy-white leaves which are produced by forcing the vegetable during autumn and winter. The best varieties are 'Witloof', 'Witloof Zoom' F1 and 'Normanto'.

Sow seed of Belgian chicory in late spring and thin to 15 cm/6 in apart. During October, dig up the plants and cut off the top growth. Expose the roots to the air for twenty-four hours. Then plant them in a box of slightly moist peat, with their tops just showing. Store in total darkness in a cold place like an unheated cupboard or a cellar. The chicons start to grow after two to four weeks, depending upon the ambient temperature. Either remove just the outer leaves and allow the centre to continue growing or cut the whole chicon straight across.

A cultivated dandelion whose bitter-tasting leaves enhance the flavour of a green salad.

Belgian chicory has a satisfying slightly bitter taste and a good crunchy texture. The leaves make excellent salads; their flavour combines well with peeled sections of orange and halved walnuts dressed with walnut oil and orange juice. In France and Belgium, the chicons are braised in stock or meat juices. I like to cut the chicons in half lengthways and braise them in butter or olive oil with some chopped mushrooms and garden herbs. Or slow-cook the chicons with tomatoes and aubergine (eggplant) and serve with plain yoghurt and chopped coriander leaves.

The second kind of garden chicory resembles a cos lettuce or a Chinese cabbage. Good varieties are 'Sugar Loaf' ('Pain de Sucre'), 'Sugarhat', 'Bianca di Milano' and 'Crystal Heart'. This lettuce-type of chicory is grown unblanched as a summer salad vegetable. Sow seed in fairly rich soil in early summer and thin to 30 cm/12 in apart. Do not allow the soil to dry out and cut the heads when the heart has formed. Small leaves can be left whole; large leaves are best torn into pieces for a green salad. Alternatively, shred the leaves and dress with a green herb mayonnaise or a vinaigrette.

DANDELION
Taraxacum officinale

IN EARLIER TIMES, WHEN OUR FOREFATHERS COLLECTED WILD FOODS NOT just as a form of sustenance but also for their curative powers, the dandelion was valued. Now that, for many people, a limp lettuce is the most accessible basis for a green salad this edible weed has been forgotten. Patience Gray, in her book, *Honey from a Weed*, reminds us of this loss of folk wisdom, this respect and care for wild plants that affluence threatens. And she tells of how in the spring, the impoverished country people of Italy, Greece and Spain scour the hillsides for leaves and roots of plants that they know are beneficial to their health. She writes, 'Knowledge of these and other plants was for centuries our common European heritage. The English, once familiar with these weeds and their specific virtues, as described in early herbals, are now showing a revived interest in this heritage.'

So perhaps the time has come to re-appraise the dandelion – or *pissenlit*, its French name acknowledging its diuretic properties. French cooks have always appreciated the slightly bitter taste of the dandelion's leaves. One of their best winter salads is comprised of crisp blanched dandelion leaves with hot fried lardons (thin strips) of smoked bacon and a dressing made by swilling the cooking pan with a dash of wine or vinegar. The hot dressing is poured over the salad, the leaves are tossed and served straight away – a genuine *salad tiède*.

Although there is nothing wrong with a wild dandelion, and some of them have particularly pretty lion's teeth leaves, I recommend growing one of the cultivated strains of this vegetable. The variety, 'A Coeur Plein', has fleshier leaves and, obviously, a good heart. Sow seed in spring and thin to 20 cm/8 in apart. Grow in the same way as lettuce or endive. Cover some of the plants with a flowerpot or a dustbin to

Vegetable spaghetti is grown in the same way as the vegetable marrow of other members of the squash family. Sow seed edge side down in pots of compost from early spring under glass, or directly into the ground from early summer. Transfer to a final growing position, in full sun, once all danger of frost is over. This vegetable likes a moderately rich soil with plenty of moisture-retaining humus. Pinch out the ends of the shoots once you have five to six flowers on each plant. Do not allow the plants to dry out and water generously in dry weather.

Harvest the fruits when they are fully grown and a buttery yellow. Store in a cool, dry place until needed.

BORAGE
Borago officinalis

Culinary use: flowers in salads, wine cups, fruit compotes, crystallized for decorating cakes, custards and ice cream; small pieces of very young leaves in salads or cooked with spinach.

Cultivation: hardy annual with blue flowers that fade to pink, height 30-60 cm/1-2 ft; grow in fertile, well-drained soil in full sun.

CLAYTONIA OR WINTER PURSLANE
Montia perfoliata

Culinary use: leaves and flowers in salads and as a garnish for cold vegetable dishes.

Cultivation: half-hardy annual with white flowers, height 15-20 cm/6-8 in; grow in fertile, well-drained soil in full sun or light shade.

---

blanch the leaves for two to four weeks to make them pale and crisp. Cut the leaves and use in salads.

In the autumn, dig up some of the plants, cut off their top growth and pack the roots close together in a box of sand or peat — as for 'Witloof' chicory. Store in a cool, dark place, and cut the pale, forced leaves as they appear for adding to a green salad.

VEGETABLE SPAGHETTI
Curcubita

THIS DELICIOUS ANNUAL VEGETABLE IS ALSO KNOWN AS THE SPAGHETTI SQUASH. Unlike other members of the curcubitae family the flesh of the vegetable is in the form of narrow threads that do, indeed, resemble spaghetti. Also, the flavour is delicate and slightly like pasta. The vegetable is boiled or baked, either whole in which case puncture the skin in several places to allow the steam to escape, or halved and wrapped in buttered foil, for 20-30 minutes depending on size. Scoop the cooked threads into a hot serving dish and add plenty of unsalted butter, freshly milled black pepper and some sea salt. I like the vegetable on its own as a separate course. And like spaghetti, some freshly-grated Parmesan cheese sprinkled over the top is very good.

ELDER
Sambucus nigra

Culinary use: to obtain the lovely flavour of muscat grapes flowers added to syrups, jams and jellies, tisanes, gooseberry fool, flummery and compote; ripe berries in pies, puddings, jams, jellies and sauces for game.

Cultivation: deciduous perennial shrub or tree with flat heads of creamy-white flower, purple-black berries, height up to 5 m/15 ft; grow in moist, well-drained soil in full sun.

Far right: The formal rose garden overlooking Rutland Water at Hambleton Hall.

APRICOT
Prunus armeniaca

THE WILD APRICOT IS A NATIVE OF CHINA WHERE IT WAS ALREADY cultivated during the time of Emperor Yu over 4000 years ago. The fruit was introduced into Britain from Italy in 1542 by Henry VIII's gardener, a French priest, Jean de Loup. In 1548, Turner, in his list of plants grown in Britain, described the fruit as the 'hasty peach' because it ripened earlier than the usual peach. The popularity of the fruit – which was also known as the abrecocke, abricote and apricock – appears to have spread quickly. A few years later, apricots grew on the heated wall in the famous herb garden at Acorn Bank in Cumbria. And there is evidence that apricots were grown in Scotland: Lady Castlehill in her cookery book of 1712 gives several recipes for fresh apricots which were most likely grown on her own estate on the banks of the Clyde.

At Blenheim Palace near Oxford, the daughter of the gardener, a Miss Shipley, grew a seedling apricot which was given her name; it later became known as the Blenheim. Could it be the Blenheim that was planted against the walls of nearly every house in nearby Aynho? The trees prospered so well that the place was known as Apricot Village. When there was still a lord of the manor in Aynho, the villagers paid part of their annual rent with baskets of fresh apricots.

For all its delicious flavour, the apricot is not a widely grown fruit in Britain. In 1904, George Bunyard and Owen Thomas, the authors of *The Fruit Garden*, wrote: 'When one realises that this valuable fruit has been with us for a matter of nearly 400 years, it does seem incredible that its merits, especially as an article of commerce, have not been more fully recognised. We cannot here shelter ourselves under the plea that the climate of France is so much better suited to the growth of this fruit tree than that of England.' Yet, this sound gardening advice seems to have gone unheeded, for I'd guess that now, more than eighty years later, fewer apricots grow in the British Isles. And most of our fresh apricots are imported from France.

I do not know about commercial possibilities, but the gastronomic future of home-grown apricots is most promising.

Dr Muffet, the seventeenth-century entomologist, who was thought to be the father of the curds-and-whey Miss Muffet, said, (in an article praising the medical qualities of the fruit) 'Apricots are plums concealed beneath a peach's coat'.

In confirmation, perhaps, of Dr Muffet's theories and backed by stories of longevity from Armenia and Turkey, recent medical research has suggested that in addition to being a healthy food, apricots have a role to play in combatting degenerative diseases.

A bowl of home-grown apricots is something to celebrate; serve them freshly picked at the end of a summer meal. The smaller, less juicy fruits, and those bought from the greengrocer, are usually best poached in a vanilla syrup. Dissolve 115 g/4 oz/½ cup sugar in 500 ml/16 fl oz water, add a vanilla pod broken in two, and simmer steadily for five minutes. Add the halved and stoned apricots and poach gently for four to five minutes. Remove from the heat, cover the pan and leave for five to ten minutes to complete cooking. Remove the vanilla pod and transfer the fruit to a serving dish, then boil the syrup until it has thickened slightly and pour it over the apricots.

Recommended varieties are 'Moor Park': large, juicy orange/yellow fruit, in late August; 'Royal Orange': well-flavoured oval yellow fruit splashed with purple, in early August; 'Alfred': excellent flavour fruit of medium size, in early August, and resistant to die back disease (partial shrivelling and dying in response to an especially hard winter). All varieties of apricot are self-fertile.

Apricots like the warmest position in the garden, ideally against a south-facing wall or chimney breast. Plant in a good-sized hole just a little larger than the tree's roots in humus-rich soil. Like all stone fruits, apricots benefit from some lime in the soil. Prune the trees in winter and tie in the branches to form a good fan shape.

QUINCE
Cydonia oblonga

THE ROMAN BURIAL GROUND OF ALYCAMPS IS A SHORT WALK off the Boulevarde des Lices in Arles. There are still a few ancient sarcophagi standing among the avenues of cypresses, but most of the stone memorials to the dead have been moved to the Musée d'Art Chrétien in the centre of town. An hour or two spent here is curiously exhilarating and provides an engrossing insight into the life and values of Roman Provence. Many of the tombs carry exquisitely-carved scenes of feasts and festivals. Fruit appears in great abundance as a decorative motif, principally the vine and the quince. Such quinces – fat, shapely and decidely female. Even in stone, the fruit is voluptuous and the temptation to touch it is irresistible.

Fresh, ripe yellow quinces exert the same power and you find yourself raising the fruit to your face to inhale its sweet musky scent. The quince is the symbol of love, happiness and fruitfulness. The fruit was dedicated to Venus, and Plutarch tells us that by tradition the quince was served to the bridal pair on their wedding night. This curvaceous fruit was the golden apple given by Paris to Aphrodite, and on her island of Cyprus, the fruit appears in the third century mosaics recently uncovered at the House of Dionysos at Paphos. The Romans called the quince the Apple of Cydonia – its botanical name – after a town on the north coast of Crete where the fruit grew freely.

In his twelve-volume work on agriculture, *De Re Rustica*, Columella wrote in the first century BC that the best way to preserve ripe quinces was in a jar of clear honey. The quince-flavoured honey was called 'melomeli' and was served separately. If you find yourself with a perfect, ripe quince, wash off any down and try this preparation. The perfume of the fruit is absorbed by the honey wonderfully well, and the 'melomeli' is delectable trickled (using a 'runcible spoon', of course) on to

breakfast porridge or over ice cream. Even pieces of cooked quince added to a jar of clear, preferably Greek, honey scents it beautifully.

Since the time of the Norman conquest, the quince has held a special place in English gardens. During the sixteenth century, every book on fruit-growing mentioned the fruit. From that time until the nineteenth century when imported exotic fruit jostled it aside, the quince was used widely in English cooking. The fruit was cooked with poultry and game and also made many sweet recipes and preserves. Quidini was a thick syrup or jelly made from quinces, and *cotignac* – from the French *coing* – was the name given to the thick paste of puréed quinces which is still produced in Spain as *membrillo*.

The quince is a moisture-loving deciduous tree, and in France they are often to be found growing on a river bank. Although fairly hardy, the tree does better in a sheltered position where the velvety grey-green leaves and pale blush-pink flowers are more protected. In a deep, fertile, slightly acid soil, the tree grows 3.6-4.5 m/12-15 ft high with a round-headed shape, though the long side growths should be pruned back to six buds to make them fruit. This self-fertile tree normally bears fruit after five to six years. When the fruit are formed but still small, a dose of liquid manure should be applied. Quince trees can grow to a great age, and one is worth considering as a specimen subject in a lawn instead of the over-exposed flowering cherry.

The most common variety of quince is 'Vranja', also known by its Serbian name, 'Bereczki'; it produces lovely pink-flushed flowers and large pear-shaped fruit. The variety 'Champion' produces mild-flavoured apple-shaped quinces, and 'Meeche's Prolific' is a slow-growing variety which produces pear-shaped fruit after only three years. Ripe quinces are a bright daffodil yellow, but the fruit of the variety 'Portugal' is covered in a thick grey down and is orange-yellow when ripe. English quinces are peeled and cooked when still hard when the fruit or the jelly made from it turns a pretty amber-pink.

The spectacular turquoise-purple leaves of red cabbage enclose the tightly-packed heart.

BLACKCURRANT SOUP WITH GALUSKAS

This Hungarian soup, which is served hot in winter or chilled in summer, has an intriguing and delicious flavour.

450 g/1 lb/2 pints black currants

450 ml/3⁄4 pint/2 cups water

1 tsp plain (all-purpose) flour

2 tbsp granulated sugar

pinch of ground cinnamon

1 small wineglass of Tokaj Eger wine

salt and freshly milled black pepper

4 tbsp soured cream

GALUSKAS:

2 eggs, separated

2 tsp caster (superfine) sugar

Cook the black currants with the water over a moderate heat until softened. Push the fruit and liquid through a fine nylon sieve and discard the pips (seeds) and skins.

In the saucepan, blend the flour with a little water and stir in the black currant liquid. Cook, over moderate heat, stirring, until thickened. Stir in the sugar, cinnamon and wine and season to taste with salt. Whisk in the soured cream and simmer the soup very gently.

Put the egg yolks into a large bowl. Whisk the egg whites until stiff, add the caster (superfine) sugar and whisk again. Drop teaspoons of the egg white into the soup – these are the *galuskas* – and spoon the hot soup over them until they are set. Lift out carefully with a slotted spoon and place several in each soup plate. Pour the hot soup on to the egg yolks, whisking all the time. Ladle the soup into the soup plates, grind some black pepper on top and serve straight away. *Serves 4*

SLOW-COOKED RED CABBAGE

A wonderfully warming winter dish, excellent with spicy pork sausages or ham.

1 small red cabbage

salt

30 g/1 oz/2 tbsp butter

1 onion, chopped

1 tsp coriander seeds, crushed

2 large cooking apples, peeled, cored and chopped

3 tbsp wine vinegar

30 g/1 oz/2 tbsp sugar

Discard any damaged outer leaves from the cabbage. Quarter and remove the core, then shred the rest and soak in cold water for 30-60 minutes.

Melt the butter in a saucepan or flameproof casserole. Add the onion and cook until soft, then add the coriander and cook for 2 minutes longer. Drain the cabbage and add to the pan with the apples. Mix everything together and pour in boiling water to a depth of 1 cm/1⁄2 in. Add the vinegar and sugar. Cover tightly and bring to the boil.

Simmer gently on top of the stove or in an oven preheated to 180°C/ 350°F/Gas Mark 4 for about 45 minutes or until the cabbage is cooked. This dish can be cooled and reheated, if you prefer. *Serves 2-4*

Quinces ripening in the early autumn sun.

GUINEA FOWL WITH HONEY AND QUINCE

The fine flavour of a quince combines well with the slight gaminess of guinea fowl.

1 guinea fowl, weighing 1.4-1.8 kg/3-4 lb

30 g/1 oz/2 tbsp butter

1 large quince

2 'Cox's Orange Pippin' or other well-flavoured dessert apples

2-3 tbsp honey

150 ml/¼ pint/⅔ cup water

150 ml/¼ pint/⅔ cup dry (hard) cider

75 ml/2½ fl oz double (heavy) cream

Place the guinea fowl in a roasting pan and spread the butter over the skin.

Peel and core the quince and the apples and place the parings inside the bird. Cover the guinea fowl with a buttered paper and roast in an oven preheated to 190°C/375°F/Gas Mark 5 for 1-1¼ hours or until the juice from the leg runs clear. Halfway through the cooking, brush some honey over the skin of the bird and turn on to the breast to keep the breast meat moist. When cooked, rest the guinea fowl in a warm place until ready to serve.

Meanwhile, dice the quince and apples and mix with the remaining honey and the water in a lidded oven dish. Cook in the oven with the guinea fowl for 30-40 minutes or until tender.

Transfer the guinea fowl to a serving dish and spoon the quince mixture around it. Pour off any surplus fat from the roasting pan and deglaze with the cider over high heat. Boil to reduce the liquid by half, then stir in the cream. Spoon the sauce over the guinea fowl and serve. *Serves 4*

TO MAKE A QUIDDONY OF ALL KINDS OF PLUMS

To my mind, the seventeenth century word 'Quiddony' is evocative and bewitching. It means a fruit preserve: sometimes a purée dried slowly over a low fire until the mixture is so stiff it can be cut with knife, and on other occasions, a fruit jelly, clear as crystal and set in a small jar or pot. This recipe for a plum jelly comes from *A Queens Delight or The Art of Preserving, Conserving and Candying*, one volume of the trilogy published in 1655, and entitled *The Queens Closet Opened*. The original manuscript book was said to have belonged to Queen Henrietta Maria, widow of Charles I.

'Take your Apple-water, and boil the Plums in it till it be red as Claret wine, and when you have made it strong as the Plums, put to every pint half a pound of Sugar, and so boil it till a drop of it hang on the back of a spoon like a quaking gelly. If you will have it of an Amber colour, then boil it with a quick fire, that is all the difference of the colouring of it.'

As a cook, I appreciate the author's careful and helpful observation that the colour of a jelly is affected by how long you cook it. The recipe contains about half the amount of sugar that we put into a fruit jelly today. But provided that the fruit is not over-ripe and the apple juice, which is made by boiling apples with water and straining through a jelly bag, is rich in pectin, then the jelly sets nicely. Its slightly sharp flavour makes it an ideal accompaniment to roast game and cold ham. One final point: the colour and variety of plums that you use also affects its colour; for instance, yellow-skinned plums make a golden jelly and damsons give a rich burgundy red.

English peaches supported on horizontal lines against a white-washed wall of a glasshouse.

COMPÔTE OF PEACHES WITH LEMON VERBENA AND LAVENDER

This delightfully-scented fruit compôte is very good served chilled – with or without pouring cream.

115 g/4 oz/½ cup sugar

300 ml/½ pint/1¼ cups cold water

1 sprig of lemon verbena

3 spikes of lavender flowers

8 firm peaches

1 tsp arrowroot

1 tbsp cold water

few lemon verbena and lavender flowers

Measure the sugar and water into a pan and stir over moderate heat until dissolved. Bring to the boil and simmer for 5 minutes. Remove from the heat and add the lemon verbena and lavender. Set aside to infuse.

Meanwhile, cover the peaches, one or two at a time, with boiling water. Lift out and peel the fruit, then slice or quarter it.

Extract the herbs from the syrup, add the peaches and simmer for 3-4 minutes or until the fruit is just tender. Use a slotted spoon to transfer the peaches to a glass bowl.

Blend the arrowroot with the cold water and add to the hot syrup. Cook, stirring, until the syrup is clear. Pour over the peaches and set aside to cool, then chill.

Before serving, sprinkle the herb flowers over the compôte. *Serves 6*

SUN-DRIED TOMATOES

Home-cured tomatoes have a milder, sweeter flavour than those imported from Italy. Choose a spell of hot, sunny weather and pick ripe, firm fruit of a variety, like Italian plum tomatoes, that has a high proportion of flesh to juice.

Halve the tomatoes and squeeze out the juice and seeds – reserve the strained juice for use in soups. Arrange the tomatoes, cut side up, on a wire rack set over a wooden board. Sprinkle sea salt over the fruit and leave in an airy, sunny position for 3-5 days, depending on the season. Take the fruit indoors at night and leave in a warm room or in a very low oven to speed up the drying process.

Place the dried tomatoes in a preserving jar, add a few sprigs of thyme and cover with virgin oil. Cover tightly and store in a cold place until needed.

CHAPTER EIGHT

Asparagus, Broad *or* Fava, French *and* Runner Beans, Angelica, Clary, Cardoon, Musk Mallow, Rosemary, Celery, Celeriac, Parsnip, Potato, Rhubarb, Cape Gooseberry

A CLASSIC COUNTRY HOUSE KITCHEN GARDEN IN THE MENDIP HILLS
HUNSTRETE HOUSE

John Evelyn was twenty-six years of age when he entered in his diary for 1646, 'Old Sir Frances, he lived like a hog at Hownstret in Somerset, with a modest pittance'. He was referring to Sir Frances Popham, master of Hunstrete House, now an elegant stone building surrounded by a 40-hectare/100 acre estate, eight miles south-west of Bath. It is difficult to tell from Evelyn's brief reference whether Sir Frances lived in some style, 'high on the hog', or quite simply in a piggish fashion, only contemplating the next meal.

What is certain is that if, by some trick of time,

Festoons of summer roses with a low lavender hedge in the formal garden in front of Hunstrete House.

John Evelyn could visit the present garden at Hunstrete, he would faint with pleasure. Only a handful of gardens in England so well represent the classical early seventeenth-century tradition of growing fruit and vegetables with flowers and herbs in such magnificent abundance.

It was a namesake of Evelyn's, John Dupays, who bought Hunstrete House in 1978. Until then the house had been the home of the Chancellor family and although, when John and Thea Dupays moved in, the garden was unavoidably neglected, he is generous in his praise of how well Lady Chancellor had maintained the garden.

163

Walking past a border of peonies planted at the foot of the wall, you draw level with the second gateway into the garden, and on turning right there is an entrancing vista of blue and white blossom stretching almost halfway down the length of the kitchen garden. The white 'Pax' roses are trained along catenary ropes (suspended and curving ropes) that dip and rise above a sea of blue cranesbill, geranium *Macrorrhizum* 'Ingwerson' and the grey-leaved soft saxe blue catmint, *Nepeta* × *faassenii*. Somewhere in the middle of this tunnel of blooms there is a grassed path that leads to the large central area of the kitchen garden, where most of the annual vegetables are grown.

The vegetables grow in rows, each bearing a label stating the variety of seed and the date of sowing. This information is an invaluable record of the garden which enables a comparison of results in different years and seasons.

In June the summer vegetables are reaching perfection: lettuces, radishes, finger carrots, courgettes (zucchini), golden beetroot as well as the familiar crimson root, white and red-stemmed Swiss chard, broad (fava) beans, endive, spring onions, and baby leeks – sown thickly and thinned for the kitchen until well spaced for growing through the autumn. John Evelyn would have been delighted. In his garden at Sayes Court he endeavoured to produce salad vegetables for every day of the year.

There are a good few rows of potatoes, for John Dupays is an aficionado of the potato, with childhood memories of growing the famous 'Jersey Royals' on the family farm. 'But, my goodness, the price of 'Jersey Royals' in Bath this morning – ridiculous. Now, here is the best roasting and baking potato in the world,' he declares, and begins to dig up a root of the potato, 'Golden Wonder'. 'They take longer to cook but, by Jove, it's worth it. We used to grow the aptly named 'Concorde' – it is quick – but we now prefer 'Sharpe's Express'. We also grow 'Kirsty', 'Cara', 'Pink Fir Apple' and an old French variety which is similar, 'Ratte'. As a result we're pretty well self-sufficient in potatoes.'

With the exception of exotic fruit, the garden provides almost all the vegetables, fruit and herbs for Hunstrete's talented chef, Robert Elsmore, and his sous-chef, Michael Ashcroft. Their cooking depends on this pristine produce and they are to be seen in the garden several times a day choosing the most perfect crops for the kitchen. This close connection between the garden and the kitchen reflects the best cookery of the seventeenth and eighteenth centuries, as seen in the dishes of Robert May and Hannah Glasse. The delightful volume entitled *Adam's Luxury and Eve's Cookery* is one of the finest examples of a book that moves easily between growing and cooking and back again.

John Dupays would have fitted admirably into the seventeenth century. It was a time of enormous interest in gardening. Both volumes of *The New Orchard and Garden* and *The Country Housewife's Garden*, published in 1618 by William Lawson, appeared in many editions until 1683. The titles reflect the curious division of labour of the earlier century, with the orchard considered a male preserve and the cultivation of vegetables, fruit and flowers the responsibility of women. These books were followed in 1629 by John Parkinson's influential, *Paradisi in Sole Paradisus Terrestris*, which includes in its subtitle, 'A choice garden of all sorts of rarest flowers . . . useful for physic or admired for beauty. To which is annexed a kitchen-garden furnished with all manner of herbs, roots and fruits, for meat or sauce used with us.'

According to John Tucker, the head gardener at Hunstrete, 'June is when the garden is really at its best.' And, in midsummer, the garden is indeed bountiful. The mixed border in front of the long stone wall overlooking the large lawn is a rich blend of roses and delphiniums, with a stone seat and an Italian cherub nestling amongst them. Two gateways in the wall lead into another world, an enclosed kitchen garden of neat straight paths and rectangular borders burgeoning with luxuriance.

*Serried rows of 'Lollo' and 'Salad Bowl' lettuces
planted with military precision.*

*Serried rows of 'Lollo' and 'Salad Bowl' lettuces
planted with military precision.*

Next to the potatoes the sugar peas, 'Oregon', climb up plastic sheep netting stretched between posts. At Hunstrete they find that although 'Oregon' is a short variety – it grows 90-120 cm/3-4 ft high – timing is important when giving the vines some support. Either install the netting when sowing the seed or before the plants are 15 cm/6 in tall. Otherwise, you can spend a lot of time trying to coax the tendrils to cling to the supports.

Six years after making his diary entry about Hunstrete, John Evelyn took over Sayes Court in Deptford from his father-in-law and began to develop the garden. He also travelled widely in France, Italy and Holland (he was a Royalist and spent some years in exile), bringing back seeds and plants. John Evelyn was an accomplished man, interested in painting, science and the planting of trees. He was highly educated about food and enterprising in his approach to gardening. He designed a glasshouse and compiled, for his gardener, a calendar of vegetables which was published in 1664 and appeared in ten editions. His most famous work, *Acetaria: A Discourse of Sallets*, was published in 1699, and still makes inspiring reading.

For the leisured classes at this time, visiting friends in the country to admire their new gardens adorned with exciting and recently-introduced plants became a popular pastime. In a letter that has survived from 1615, John Chamberlain wrote of a visit to Sir Henry Fanshawe in Hertfordshire: 'We have had a long, dry summer, and the best and fairest melons and grapes that I ever knew in England.'

A few months earlier Giacomo Castelvetro, an Italian staying with Sir Adam Newton at Eltham, wrote a treatise for private publication on *The Fruit, Herbs and Vegetables of Italy*, which lists eighty-four edible plants in an endearing attempt to encourage the English to be more adventurous in their kitchen gardening and in their cooking. Evidently some people – at least in Hertfordshire – were already converts.

The Hunstrete gardeners are assuredly in this tradition. 'When we arrived, half the kitchen garden was a donkey paddock', says John Dupays. 'There were masses of raspberries, some rather clapped-out strawberries and rhubarb everywhere.' The rhubarb has been coralled into a neat corner of the kitchen garden annexe beyond the laurel walk. The raspberries have been replaced, and now Hunstrete is growing some sumptuous new fruit.

The fruit cage is separated into two halves by a long narrow border of oriental poppies in day-glo colours. Although compared with the average-size garden there is plenty of space here for hangers-on, every fruit and vegetable is rigorously assessed. Nothing survives if it fails to satisfy the exacting palates of the Dupays and Robert Elsmore and his team.

'Gooseberries, for example, were found to be simply not popular,' bemoans John Dupays. I also am disappointed, for in my view, a cool, jade-green gooseberry fool scented with elderflower is one of the glories of English summer cooking. 'So we grubbed them up,' he continued, 'and planted a tayberry, a boysenberry and three kiwi fruits. We like the raspberry, 'Autumn Bliss,' and are very keen on loganberries. We also grow a lot of red currants and black currants.' In the polytunnel (plastic tunnel supported by hoops) where the tomatoes are grown, towering plants of physalis produce the sharp-sweet fruit known as the Cape gooseberry. And sweet cherry trees reach an amazing size in the garden. Plenty of well-rotted compost is applied to enrich the soil.

Inspecting the fine, quick-draining soil prompts me to look for an asparagus bed. And I remembered how Mrs John Evelyn was given some particularly fine spears of asparagus, each weighing 115 g/4 oz, by their friend, John Hatton. Evelyn commented on the superior flavour compared with the usual imported Dutch asparagus which was always grown on beds of manure. This English asparagus, he wrote, had been grown on the 'more natural, sweet' soil of Battersea.

At Hunstrete, they no longer grow asparagus – the king of vegetables. The queen of vegetables, the globe artichoke, is grown

165

Runner beans, parsnips and leeks are cultivated in the additional kitchen garden at Hunstrete House.

instead. Seed sown in early spring produces a crop of small heads by September. Then the plants are earthed up and protected through the winter with a blanket of straw. In the spring they get away to a good start and make a considerable number of fair-sized heads by June and July. The variety that does well in their light soil is 'Green Globe'.

Close by the bed of globe artichokes, its Mediterranean relative, the cardoon, towers over the roses and the runner beans. The flower heads and stems are removed in July, and the base of the large fleshy stalks is loosely wrapped in sacking to blanch them for cutting in December.

To produce tender herbs like dill and sorrel, coriander and chervil early in the season, they are grown in cold frames whose covers have fallen apart. The protection of the sides alone is sufficient to bring on the plants.

Hardy herbs such as sage, salad burnet, hyssop, thyme and lovage grow in full sun amongst the rock roses, cornflowers and mallows. Hunstrete has one most attractive mallow with a variegated leaf recently grown from seed by John Tucker. Three centuries ago, mallow leaves were dipped in batter and fried. John Evelyn describes them as 'curl'd, emollient and friendly to the Ventricle, and so rather Medicinal; yet may the Tops, well boil'd be admitted'. Mallow flowers were eaten raw in salads and as a decoration for sweet dishes.

In a square border between the restored glasshouses and the hospital beds, where ailing plants are nursed back to health, a splash of pink, blue and purple clary, *Salvia virides* (*S. horminum*), attracts attention. 'When tender not to be rejected, and in omlets, made up with Cream, fried in sweet Butter, and eaten with Sugar, Juice of Orange, or Limon', according to John Evelyn in *Acetaria*. He concludes his book with a passage that might have been written about the garden at Hunstrete: 'And thus have we presented you a Taste of our English Garden Housewifry in the matter of Sallets: And though some of them may be vulgar, (as are most of the best things;) Yet she was willing to impart them, to shew the Plenty, Riches and Variety of the Sallet-Garden: And to justify what has been asserted of the Possibility of living (not unhapily) on Herbs and Plants, according to Original and Divine Institution, improved by Time and long Experience.'

Surrounded by these many old and new plants in this quintessentially English garden, I am reminded of Geoffrey Grigson's description of plants as 'vehicles of life', capable of continuing beyond our stewardship. John Dupays has since retired from his garden of Hunstrete, but thankfully his head gardener, John Tucker, has remained to tend this magnificent and joyful garden for Clipper Hotels Limited, the new owners of Hunstrete House.

WHOLE 'GALIA' MELON FILLED WITH BLACK CURRANT SORBET

1 medium-size ripe 'Galia' melon

sprigs of black currants and black currant leaves, to decorate

SORBET:

350 g/12 oz/1½ pints black currants

225 g/8 oz/1 cup sugar

450 ml/¾ pint/2 cups water

1 lemon

2 tbsp Crème de cassis

1 egg white

Left: Broad beans, carrots, leeks, lettuces and potatoes thrive within the sheltered kitchen garden.

Purée the black currants and push through a fine sieve. Dissolve the sugar in the water, add a strip of lemon zest (rind) and bring to the boil. Simmer the syrup steadily for 10 minutes, then remove from the heat. Discard the zest of lemon and cool the syrup.

Mix the blackcurrant purée, cassis and the strained juice of the lemon into the sugar syrup. Whisk the egg white until stiff and fold into the mixture. Freeze in a sorbetière (ice cream maker). Or freeze in a lidded plastic box in the freezer until firm. Mix in a food processor until smooth, then return to the freezer.

Wash and dry the melon. Use a sharp pointed knife to remove the top of the melon by making four curved petal-like cuts into the melon about one-third from the top. Scoop out the seeds, replace the lid and chill the melon until ready to serve.

Fill the melon with scoopfuls of sorbet and place 4-5 scoopfuls on top. Replace the lid if you wish and garnish with sprigs of black currants. Arrange a layer of black currant leaves on a serving plate. Place the melon on top and serve straight away. *Serves 3-4*

PARMA HAM SALAD
(PROSCIUTTO SALAD)

450 g/1 lb baby vegetables: carrots, turnips, radishes, sweetcorn, leeks, mangetout (snow peas), spring onions (scallions), cherry tomatoes

a wide selection of young salad leaves: red radicchio, endive frisée (curly endive) lamb's lettuce (corn salad), feuilles de chêne lettuce, etc.

8 slices of Parma (Prosciutto) ham

DRESSING:

120 ml/4 fl oz red wine

2 tbsp red wine vinegar

90-115 g/3-4 oz/¹⁄₂-²⁄₃ cup shallots, chopped

60 ml/2 fl oz olive oil

60 ml/2 fl oz walnut oil

1 tbsp clear honey

sea salt

freshly milled green peppercorns

Wash, peel and trim the baby vegetables. Cook each kind separately in salted boiling water or steam them until tender. Keep warm.

Measure the wine and wine vinegar into a pan and add the shallots. Bring to the boil and simmer until reduced by half. Remove from the heat, whisk in the oils and honey and season to taste with salt and pepper. Keep warm.

If necessary, wash and dry the salad leaves. Toss lightly with a little of the dressing and divide between four plates, arranging the leaves in a heap. Carefully place the slices of Parma ham around the salad leaves, almost enclosing them. Toss the vegetables in the remaining dressing and divide between the plates, arranging some on top of the leaves and some outside the ham. Spoon the remaining dressing over the dish and serve straight away. *Serves 4*

FEUILLETTÉ OF ASPARAGUS WITH A LEMON BUTTER SAUCE

115 g/4 oz weight puff pastry

beaten egg

24 spears fresh green asparagus

salt

sugar

lemon juice

LEMON HOLLANDAISE SAUCE:

2 shallots, chopped

6 white peppercorns

1 sprig of thyme

3 parsley stalks

½ bay leaf

6 tbsp dry white wine

4 tbsp white wine vinegar

2 egg yolks

juice of 2 lemons

200 g/7 oz/scant 1 cup warm clarified butter

Roll out the pastry large enough to cut four rounds, 7.5 cm/3 in across. Mark the top of the pastry rounds by dragging the prongs of a fork across it and place on a wetted baking sheet. Brush the top of the pastry with beaten egg. Bake in an oven preheated to 220°C/425°F/Gas Mark 7 for 8-10 minutes or until well puffed up and golden brown. Transfer to a wire rack and keep warm.

Trim the cut ends of the asparagus to make each spear 15-18 cm/6-7 in long. Make a bundle of the asparagus. Cook in an asparagus pan, or stand the cut ends in lightly salted boiling water containing ½ tsp of sugar and a squeeze of lemon juice and cover the spears with a hood of foil so that they steam. The asparagus is cooked when a pointed knife goes easily into the cut ends of the spears. Drain well and wrap in a clean tea (dish) towel to keep warm.

In a small pan, simmer the shallots with the peppercorns, thyme, parsley stalks, bay leaf, white wine and vinegar until the liquid has reduced to 2 tablespoons. Strain and set aside.

In the top of a porcelain double boiler (or a bowl over simmering water), whisk the egg yolks with the strained lemon juice. Gradually beat in the clarified butter until the sauce thickens and 'mounts'. Whisk in the wine reduction and season to taste with salt.

To serve, have ready four warm plates. Slice each puff pastry case across, and place the bases on the plates. Arrange six spears of asparagus on top and spoon over some of the hollandaise sauce. Cover with the lid of puff pastry and spoon a little more sauce around the pastry. If you wish, slip the dish under a very hot grill (broiler) to very lightly toast the sauce and give it a golden top. Serve straight away. *Serves 4*

SALAD OF LOBSTER WITH *SUMMER* VEGETABLES AND SALAD LEAVES

2 live lobsters

450 g/1 lb mixed summer vegetables: cherry tomatoes, baby carrots, baby turnips, mangetout (snow peas), French beans (fine green beans)

1 small ripe 'Galia' melon

150 ml/¼ pint/⅔ cup olive oil

1 tbsp lemon juice

young leaves of endive frisée (curly endive), 'Lollo Rosso' lettuce and 'Oak Leaf' lettuce

sprigs of basil, flat-leaf parsley, chervil and dill, to garnish

COURT-BOUILLON:

3.6 litres/6 pints/3½ quarts water

1.2 litres/2 pints/5 cups dry white wine

300 ml/½ pint/1¼ cups white wine vinegar

1 onion

white part of 1 leek

2 carrots

2 stalks celery

juice of 1 lemon

4 parsley stalks

2 sprigs of rosemary

1 bay leaf

12 white peppercorns

salt

Prepare the court-bouillon by measuring the water, wine and vinegar into a pan large enough to contain the lobsters. Wash or peel and roughly chop the onion, leek, carrots and celery. Add the lemon juice, parsley stalks, rosemary, bay leaf and peppercorns to the pan with some salt and bring almost to the boil.

Add the lobsters and bring to the boil. Simmer for 6-8 minutes, then remove the pan from the heat and set aside until cool.

Wash the baby vegetables and peel if necessary, leaving a short stalk on the root vegetables. Cook the vegetables separately in salted boiling water. Drain and place in a large bowl. Halve the melon, deseed and use a Parisienne spoon (melon ball cutter) to cut out balls of melon flesh. Add to the vegetables. Mix the olive oil with the lemon juice and pour over the vegetables and melon balls. Toss gently until evenly coated.

Remove the lobsters from the court-bouillon and cut them in half lengthways. Remove the meat from the tails and claws leaving body meat in the shell.

Spoon some of the vinaigrette from the vegetables over the salad leaves and arrange them with the baby vegetables and melon balls on four plates. Arrange a half lobster shell and body meat with the tail and claw meat in the middle and garnish each dish with the sprigs and leaves of basil, parsley, chervil and dill. Serve straight away. *Serves 4*

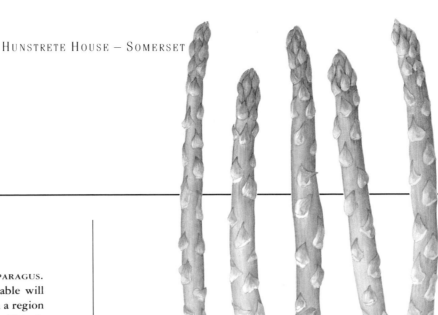

ASPARAGUS
Asparagus officinalis

FEW VEGETABLES ARE AS SHROUDED IN MYSTIQUE AS ASPARAGUS. It is often described as hard to grow, yet the vegetable will flourish in most soils provided that it is well-drained. In a region with heavy soil, an asparagus bed is usually 'raised'. This is simply done by digging a trench around the outside of the bed with the soil from it thrown into the centre to make it higher. Professional asparagus-growers in the Vale of Evesham and Norfolk grow the vegetable on long quick-draining ridges which warm up quickly in the spring.

The spring is the best time to plant an asparagus bed. There is a choice of plants – seedling asparagus grown in peat blocks, and often sold as modules, or asparagus crowns. The latter – usually one- or two-years-old – are spider-like plants of fleshy rhizomes which need to be kept damp while they are out of the ground; their chief advantage is that you have less time to wait for your asparagus crop. Both seedlings and crowns come in named varieties. Plant the seedling modules so that the top of the peat block is just below soil level. Plant asparagus crowns about 7.5 cm/3 in below the surface of the soil, taking care to fan out the roots evenly. If you are unable to plant your asparagus as soon as it arrives from the nursery, keep it in a cool place covered by a damp sack so that the roots don't dry out. After planting, apply a top dressing of fertilizer high in nitrogen and potash but low in phosphates, and repeat the application each spring.

Cut the spears when 15-17.5 cm/6-7 in tall; depending on the weather, they usually take one to three days to grow to this height. Rinse the cut ends under a cold tap to remove any trace of soil and tie the spears in a bundle with cotton tape. The simplest way to cook the vegetable is to place the cut ends in 7.5-10 cm/3-4 in of lightly salted boiling water in a deep pan. Make a loose hood of foil and place it over the asparagus tips, tucking the ends down into the pan. This way the fat stalks cook in the water and the rest of the stems are steamed. Depending on the size of the spears, the asparagus is cooked in five to eight minutes or when a pointed knife goes easily into the thickest part of the stalk. Drain the asparagus well and serve immediately with melted butter.

For this simple yet luxurious way of serving asparagus, just pick up the fat end of each spear and gradually eat it from the tip, finally licking the butter from your fingers. Fingerbowls are useful for the fastidious. This is wonderfully sensual food which helps to account for another myth about asparagus: that it is an aphrodisiac.

If only on grounds of sympathetic magic, asparagus looks like an aphrodisiac. The spears 'manifestly provoketh Venus' according to an Elizabethan writer. Of course, virtually any food – or drink for that matter – can be aphrodisiac if you are so inclined. Poor Madame de Pompadour nearly faded away by restricting her diet to asparagus tips with egg yolks, in addition to celery leaves, truffles and vanilla – all to no avail – not realizing that although love begins in the mind, passion requires a healthy body.

When you start to harvest your asparagus you'll be perfectly happy to serve it plain with butter. Later, when the crop develops you'll enjoy it with its classic accompaniment, Hollandaise sauce, or a light vinaigrette flavoured with tarragon. Next you'll make a pale jade green asparagus soup which tastes wonderful served hot or chilled. Or you will cook the spears in an omelette or a soufflé or roll them in thin brown bread and butter for sandwiches at afternoon tea. Finally, the gourmet gardener reaches that unusual state of satisfaction – you will have eaten sufficient asparagus. Until next year.

Recommended varieties of asparagus include 'Cito', 'Connover's Colossal', 'Franklin', 'Jersey Giant', 'Martha Washington', and the highly productive all-male Limbras varieties which can be raised from seed quite easily.

Small, delicious pods of tender broad beans.

Sutton', 'Imperial Green Longpod' and 'Express' are best sown in deep, fertile ground during early spring. Because I live in an area of high rainfall, I prefer to sow all beans in wooden boxes and large pots in the greenhouse during March. When the plants are 10-15 cm/4-6 in high and the weather is warmer, I transplant the seedlings 15-20 cm/6-8 in apart. One of my gardening friends claims that the beans prefer to be transplanted. Certainly they do not seem to suffer a set-back provided that you harden them off first. I usually make successive sowings straight into the ground, and that earliest row can be cut down to 20 cm/8 in after cropping to produce a second growth.

I prefer to grow 'The Sutton' because it is a highly productive short bean that needs no staking. Taller varieties usually benefit from having their tops pinched out. This has a double advantage: it is said to discourage blackfly and the tops also make a delicious green vegetable, when cooked like spinach. Broad beans need no extra feeding and, even better, fix nitrogen in the soil through the nodules on their roots. If you wish, you can pick some of the first pods when very small and cook them whole, but I prefer to wait until the beans are larger. That first dish of baby broad beans is utterly delectable. They are cooked in salted boiling water in just one to two minutes. Drain and serve with butter and a sprinkling of zest of lemon or finely chopped flat-leaf parsley. Reserve the summer savory and béchamel sauce for the more mature broad bean later in the season.

FRENCH BEANS
Phaseolus vulgaris

THE FRENCH BEAN, ALSO KNOWN AS THE KIDNEY BEAN DUE TO THE SHAPE OF the seed, was brought to Europe by Columbus. Although French by adoption, the bean has clearly become their own since the country's gardeners have developed an enormous number of varieties; each one is grown for a different dish or style of cooking. There are, of course, the dwarf fine green beans, or *haricot vert*, popular with every gardening cook. There is now a climbing variety, like 'Blue Lake', which I prefer since it has a long cropping season. There are also flat-style green French beans like 'Chevrier Vert' developed from the French bean intended for drying. The dried French bean has two forms: those picked semi-sec (half dry) in July and August and known as *haricots flageolets*, and those that are dried for keeping – the familiar green or white *haricot sec* (navy) beans that are sold in packets.

All these beans are easy to grow in a warm climate. Sow from mid-spring outdoors or under glass – an early crop can be raised very easily in a greenhouse. French beans should be planted 20-30 cm/8-12 in apart in deep, fertile soil. Make sure the ground does not dry out and give a fine overhead spray in dry weather. Pick the beans small – not only because they taste best but also to encourage further crops. Recommended varieties: dwarf French bean – 'Sprite', 'Tendergreen', 'Triomph de Farcy', the purple-skinned 'Royalty' (when cooked they turn green) and the very fine

BEANS

THE ANCIENT WORLD SURVIVED ON BEANS – BROAD (FAVA) BEANS MAINLY, AND chick peas. And with the growth of vegetarianism in the affluent west, I sometimes wonder if we are slowly returning to a more interesting and tasty version of the diet of the ancient Greeks. For the bean is, indeed, a wonder-plant in the garden and the kitchen.

BROAD (FAVA) BEAN
Vicia faba

THE BROAD OR FAVA BEAN IS OUR OLDEST BEAN – IT DATES FROM THE BRONZE, age and the Romans must have introduced us to new varieties. The broad bean has long been grown in Egypt where it still plays an important role in their cooking. In its dried state, the broad bean is a staple Egyptian food. Because this bean is the hardiest of the legume family, the variety 'Aquadulce Claudia' can be sown outdoors during November, to produce an early crop during the late spring. Other varieties like 'The

A picking of runner beans, one of Britain's most popular vegetables.

Sow seed in pots during spring for transplanting later. Or sow directly into the ground when all danger of frost is over. Runner beans produce considerable top-growth and therefore need a deep, rich soil. In light soils it is a good idea to dig out a trench and line it with upturned turves (turfs) or wet newspapers before filling in with well-rotted compost or manure-enriched loam. Provide netting or canes for the plants to climb up. Nip out the growing shoot once they reach the top of their supports. Like all legumes, the roots fix the nitrogen in the soil so leave the plants in position for as long as possible. There is no need to fertilize, but give a good drenching of water in dry weather and spray overhead now and again. Runner bean varieties seem much the same to me. I usually grow 'Prizewinner' or 'Scarlet Emperor' but mainly because my parents did. There is a dwarf runner bean called 'Pickwick' which trails over the ground and needs no support, which a friend with a very exposed garden recommends. Good US varieties include 'Garrafal de Encarnada' and 'Zefa Fino'.

To my mind, the most important aspect of growing runner beans is to pick the beans YOUNG. Steam or cook in salted boiling water and serve plain with a herb butter or with diced crisp bacon and chopped chives.

ANGELICA
Angelica archangelica

Culinary use: whole and chopped leaves cooked with tart-tasting fruits like rhubarb to reduce acidity; pieces of young leaves added to salads; stem crystallized in sugar syrup for flavouring for cakes, tarts and custards.

Cultivation: hardy, herbaceous biennial will grow for three to four years if the lime-green flowers are removed as soon as they form, height 1-2 m/3-6 ft; grow in fertile, moist soil in full sun.

CLARY
Salvia sclarea

Culinary use: whole leaves or bracts in salads, in omelettes, as garnishes, crystallized for decorating cakes; chopped leaves in butter for pasta.

Cultivation: hardy annual with coloured leaves or bracts in pink, purple, blue and white marked with fine green or white veins, height 45 cm/18 in; grow in fertile soil in full sun.

yellow-podded 'Mont d'Or'; climbing French bean – 'Blue Lake' and 'Purple Podded'; French beans for drying – 'Chevrier Vert' and 'Blue Lake'.

French beans taste superb, simply steamed or cooked in salted boiling water and tossed in butter. Later, older beans are very good in a tomato sauce or cooked, cooled and added to salads.

RUNNER BEAN
Phaseolus coccineus

THE SCARLET RUNNER BEAN WAS SLOW TO BE REGARDED AS A FOOD. FROM ITS introduction in 1633, the plant was grown mainly for its flowers. Early Victorian gardeners trained the variety 'Painted Lady', with its pink and white flowers, over archways and trellises in their kitchen gardens. But as the century progressed, the bean itself began to be appreciated. The flavour of a runner bean is more pronounced and coarser than a French bean. But picked young and cooked whole or in short pieces, the bean has a pleasing earthy flavour which is inseparable from English summer food. Gone are the days, thank heavens, of preserving bushels of these beans in brine for winter eating. The English runner bean is a late summer vegetable, best cooked straight from the garden.

175

CARDOON
Cynara cardunculus

DRIVING NORTH UP THE RHÔNE VALLEY IN LATE AUTUMN IS A VISUAL TREAT. The morning mist hangs low over the river. And the vineyards of Burgundy are ablaze with leaves of gold and russet-orange, burnt amber and vermilion. But suddenly you see a field of metre-high black plastic sacks, sprouting with grey-green leaves. These are cardoon plants, being blanched for cutting at Christmas. For cardoons are an important part of the traditional Provençal meal, *Le Gros Souper*, served on Christmas Eve.

In Britain, this relative of the globe artichoke is little known. I grow the stately plant beside my globe artichokes, and its spectacular toothed, silver-green leaves are always a pleasure to contemplate. In the summer the 'edible thistle' atop the 1.8-2.4 m/6-8 ft high stalk can be cooked and eaten just like the globe artichoke. However, the cardoon is intended as a winter vegetable. During the autumn, the leaves are cut down to 90 cm/3 ft, and the broad fleshy stalks at the base of the plant are blanched by wrapping them in straw, cardboard or black plastic. I find that dustbin (or garbage can) liners, with the base trimmed off to make a tube, work well.

The cardoon is a perennial that grows best in a deep, rich soil in full sun. Sow seed in pots during the spring and transplant in early autumn. You can grow cardoons in a trench, like celery – it makes blanching the leaves easier, I suppose, although they would need careful washing before cooking. Fork well-rotted manure or compost into the soil during the spring and harvest the globes when still small. In Britain, one can cut the blanched leaves from December onwards. Suffolk Herbs sell seed of the Italian variety, 'Gigante di Romagna'; otherwise it's worth bringing back a packet of seed from France.

The edible stalk's resemblance to celery has meant that English cooks have prepared the cardoon in similar ways – trimmed, then braised or boiled and served with a sauce. In Mediterranean countries, where the carbon is a valued vegetable, they do things rather differently: the trimmed stalks are boiled and served with a sauce of anchovies or dusted with finely grated Parmesan cheese and browned under the grill. As a footnote to his two pages on the globe artichoke, John Evelyn wrote, 'That the Spanish Cardon, a wild and smaller Artichoak, with sharp pointed Leaves, and lesser head; the Stalks being Blanch'd and tender, are serv'd-up à la Poiverade (that is with Oyl, Pepper, &c) as the French term is.'

MUSK MALLOW
Malva moschata

Culinary use: young leaves dipped in batter and deep fried; petals and flowers in salads and garnishes; petals candied for decorating ice cream, cakes and desserts.

Cultivation: hardy herbaceous perennial with pink, white or mauve flowers, height 1 m/3 ft; grow in fertile, well-drained soil in full sun.

ROSEMARY
Rosmarinus officinalis

Culinary use: leaves and sprigs in sauces, stocks and fish, lamb and vegetable dishes; branches as skewers for grilled vegetables and fruit, for burning over charcoal under grilled fish, poultry, lamb and game; chopped leaves for flavouring sugars and syrups, sorbets, ice creams, cakes and biscuits; flowers in salads, cakes, and as garnishes, and for candying.

Cultivation: hardy evergreen with blue, white or pink flowers, height 1-2 m/3-6 ft; grow in well-drained soil in a sheltered position in full sun.

CELERY
Apium graveolens var. *dulce*

ALTHOUGH ESSENTIAL IN THE KITCHEN, CELERY CAN BE DIFFICULT TO GROW IN the garden. But even if you are unable to achieve large heads of celery similar to those on sale at the greengrocers, it is worth growing a few plants of this vegetable for its valuable leaves and stalks. The bundles of pot herbs sold in every French market for soups and stews includes either a stick of celery or some leaves of celeriac. For celery is a vegetable that transforms and rounds out the taste of other ingredients. And I find that a short piece of celery is vital to a court bouillon (homemade stock) for fish. For serving with roast game, nothing beats celery hearts slowly braised in butter.

Raw celery is equally delicious. John Evelyn wrote: 'Sellery, Apium Italicum, was formerly a stranger with us (nor very long since in Italy) is an hot and more generous sort of Macedonian Persley, or Smallage. The tender Leaves of the Blanch't Stalk do well in our Sallet, as likewise the slices of the whiten'd Stems, which being crimp and short, first peel'd and slit longwise, are eaten with Oyl, Vinegar, Salt, and Peper, and for its high and grateful Taste, is ever plac'd in the middle of the Grand Sallet.' Just so, its appetizing crunchiness brings life to an otherwise indifferent green salad. Celery is also good when mixed with crisp diced apple and walnuts, as it is in a Waldorf salad.

A purple-flowered mallow with variegated leaves and climbing roses against the Mendip stone wall.

Nowadays, self-blanching varieties of celery with pale green stalks reduce the work in growing this vegetable. In the past, the gardener grew celery in a trench with plenty of black soot from the chimney heaped around the stalks to blanch them. Mind you, those pearly-white sticks of celery tasted magnificent. Sometimes you are lucky enough to come across a head of celery grown in the old-fashioned way. Snap it up – it's sure to be excellent.

Celery seed is sown on the surface (the seed needs light to germinate) of a pan of compost in late winter in a temperature of 18°C/65°F. Prick out and harden off the seedlings before planting out in early summer. Or buy seedling plants of celery from a quality stockist. Self-blanching celery is grown on flat ground; blanching celery is grown in trenches. Plant 23-30 cm/9-12 in apart in well-manured and fertile soil, applying an organic fertilizer in midsummer. Self-blanching celery should be harvested before the first frost. A light frost is reckoned to improve the flavour of blanched celery. Certainly, those Christmas heads of celery with a powdering of snow on their leaves taste superb.

CELERIAC
Apium graveolens var. *rapaceum*

RON BUTLER, TECHNICAL DIRECTOR OF SUTTONS SEEDS, SAYS THAT IF YOU CAN grow celeriac in your garden, you can grow anything. I can grow celeriac, but the roots refuse to grow any larger than a tennis ball. Celeriac needs a highly fertile, humus-rich soil, and I think that my free-draining sandy loam fails to sustain the plant adequately. Still, I'm happy with my diminutive celeriac and find it a satisfying vegetable to grow.

One of my Victorian gardening books describes celeriac as turnip-rooted or knob celery. This bulbous, slightly fibrous root has the fine flavour of celery and the attributes of most root vegetables. Though it was introduced into Britain from Egypt during the early eighteenth century, the vegetable is still little known. In France celeriac, or *céleri-rave*, is the basis of one of the most ubiquitous cold salads – the blanched root is grated and mixed with mayonnaise – served as an hors d'oeuvre and available at every *charcuterie*.

Cooked celeriac is even more delicious. Try celeriac 'chips' (fries) deep-fried or oven-roasted. And it makes an excellent vegetable dish when mashed with an equal amount of boiled potato and some butter, black pepper and a grating of nutmeg. Reheat in a hot oven and serve with roasted or grilled meat. It is also good simmered in soup, or braised in a brown sauce to mellow its flavour.

Sow celeriac seed in a pan of seed compost at room temperature during spring. Prick out when large enough to handle, and plant out, 25 cm/10 in apart, in fertile ground when all danger of frost is over. Most of the root grows above the soil, so keep weed-free, do not allow to dry out and water if necessary.

PARSNIP
Pastinaca sativa

MY EARLIEST MEMORY OF PARSNIPS IS OF GROWING THE TOPS OF THE ROOTS IN A saucer of water on my bedroom windowsill. This usually involved some kind of rivalry with my brother, and I can remember blowing warm air on the pretty feathery leaves to encourage them to grow faster and higher than those of my sibling. Since then, over the years, my own children have grown countless parsnip and carrot tops on every available surface, but I remain enthusiastic about this sweet-tasting and versatile root vegetable.

The cultivated parsnip has been grown in Britain since the arrival of the Romans. Pliny so valued the vegetable – which he liked cooked and served with a honey wine sauce – that he insisted on having his own personal supply sent from the Rhine valley. The English fondness for sweet things kept the parsnip popular long after the introduction of both the potato and the sweet potato. In the eighteenth century, parsnips were peeled and dried in the oven then beaten to a powder as in this recipe from *Adam's Luxury and Eve's Cookery*; 'Mix them then with an equal Quantity of Flower, and make them up with cream and Spices powder'd; then mould them into Cakes and bake them in a gentle Oven. Note: The Sweetness of the Parsnip Powder answers the want of Sugar.'

Pink-skinned 'Fir Apple' potatoes with their unusual long narrow tubers and fine flavour.

In the nineteenth century, parsnip leaves were fed to cattle because it was thought that they enriched the milk. The vegetable's hardiness – in fact, the flavour is reckoned to be improved by a touch of frost – has made it popular in the north of England where the parsnip was turned into pies, deep-fried puffs and cakes. Yet one of the most delicious ways of cooking this vegetable is the simplest: peel, blanch and roast whole small parsnips around a joint of meat until tender and lightly browned. Similarly, parsnips can be cut into fingers, blanched, tossed in flour and deep-fried like French fries. Or try round slices of peeled, cooked parsnip layered in an oven dish with thin slices of Gruyère cheese and fresh bay leaves. Pour over some cream mixed with a dash of Fino sherry and bake until bubbling hot. This is a splendid light meal in itself.

Parsnips are easy to grow provided that the soil is deeply-dug and free of stones. A too-rich or stony soil can make the long tapering roots fork and bend which makes them less useful in the kitchen. Parsnip seed germinates most readily in a soil temperature above 12°C/45°F. Sow seed thinly in rows, or broadcast, and thin to 10 cm/4 in apart. Dig every other root when small and leave the rest to grow on. In mild areas, parsnips can be left in the ground during the winter; otherwise dig the roots, trim off the leaves and store in dry sand. I have grown the variety 'Tender and True' for as long as I've gardened and am still perfectly happy with it. For clay soils, the shorter-rooted 'White Gem' is recommended.

POTATO
Solanum tuberosum

THE POTATO IS NO 'MERE VEGETABLE, BUT RATHER AN INSTRUMENT OF DESTINY', in the view of Edward Bunyard. Indeed, this unprepossessing-looking tuber, which was fertilized with human blood by the Incas, and was the cause of the nineteenth-century Irish famines, provided the only form of sustinence for thousands of prisoners and civilians in both World Wars. This South American plant took some time to find favour in Britain, but today, most of us eat 110 kg/242 lb of potatoes a year, and in a sample of 2244 people 74 per cent felt that you need potatoes to make a proper meal.

Fortunately, given its huge popularity, the potato is good for us: rich in Vitamin C, minerals and – if you eat the skins – fibre. To my mind, there are few foods that match the satisfying comfort on a baked jacket potato, straight from the oven, slit in half and covered in slivers of butter with a grinding of black pepper. In the winter, baked potatoes are my favourite and unchanging lunch when working on a book.

It's extraordinary how we never tire of potatoes, and it's been good to see how during the last decade the quality potato has made a come-back. Gone are the days when they were blamed for obesity – it's the butter on baked potatoes or the fat on chips that makes potatoes fattening – but only if you eat too many. (And, anyway, when did you last see a fat gardener?) Nowadays, we have the marketing man's notion of a 'gourmet spud'. Of course, any fruit or vegetable is gourmet food if you know how to treat it properly.

Our gardening grandfathers would smile to see that the latest swing of potato fashion has re-introduced two varieties of potatoes grown in Queen Victoria's day: 'Pink Fir Apple' and 'Ratte'. Both these long, tapering potatoes have a yellow, waxy flesh and fine flavour that makes them excellent for salads or for shallow-frying in butter or oil. Scrub the potatoes and boil in their skins, then peel if you wish – it's not essential – and slice.

Although you can, of course, use a waxy potato for baking and roasting, most people prefer the soft, fluffy result of a floury potato like the varieties 'Golden Wonder', 'King Edward', 'Epicure', 'White Cobbler' (US) and 'Maris Piper'. On the whole I prefer the flavour of red-skinned potatoes, and an excellent all-rounder for baking, roasting, mashing, salad and frying is 'Desiree'. It is, I suppose, the new potato that is most mouth-watering. For me, 'Sutton's Foremost' is quite the best. It is a fabulous early potato that keeps that new-potato taste even if left in the ground some time. 'Yukon Gold' is a very good US variety.

Once upon a time I grew, every year, all the potatoes our family could eat. Now I'm older, the children live elsewhere, and our potato needs have reduced. So I concentrate on growing smaller quantities of the foods I care a lot about. I plant a few 'Foremost', 'Pink Fir Apple' and 'Ratte' and buy main crop 'Desiree' potatoes from a neighbouring farmer.

The small seed potatoes arrive by post early in the New Year, and I spread them out on egg trays in a cold light place for four to six weeks until they have chitted, that is produced short shoots. Potatoes like an acid soil that is deeply dug the previous autumn, with plenty of well-rotted compost incorporated. In Devon, we try to 'plant out tatties' on Good Friday. But any dry day in early spring is fine. Plant each sprouted potato, 15 cm/6 in deep and 30 cm/12 in apart in rows 60 cm/24 in apart. As soon as the shoots appear above the soil, earth up to cover them with soil. Earth up again one month later. Dig the first delicious potatoes when the plants have come into flower.

Simply wash – and scrape them if you wish – and cook the potatoes in salted water until tender. Serve with melted butter and some finely chopped mint or parsley. And why not serve them as a separate course – they deserve it.

RHUBARB
Rheum × cultorum

MOST PLANTS, LIKE ASPARAGUS AND SEAKALE, WITH EDIBLE LEAF STALKS ARE classified as vegetables. Rhubarb is an exception. The long pink or red sticks of rhubarb with their yellow or green crinkled leaves are a delicious and under-rated fruit. Sadly its reputation as a fine food has been tarnished by ruinous cooking of the sort that, at times, has given British cooking a bad name.

One thing must be said about cooking rhubarb for dessert. Never let it touch water. Wine or fruit juice, yes, even butter or cream but NO WATER.

For the most delectable dish of cooked rhubarb, select slim, stiff, pink stalks of forced rhubarb. Cut off the leaves (which contain considerable oxalic acid and are poisonous) and the base of the stalk and discard. Use a sharp knife to cut the rhubarb, diagonally across the stalks, into 2.5 cm/1 in lengths. Toss the rhubarb in caster (superfine granulated) sugar mixed with the finely grated zest (rind) and juice of 2-3 tangerines, or mix clear honey with some sweet white wine and pour over the fruit in a pan or a baking dish. Cook the fruit very gently over moderate heat, or, covered, in a moderate oven until almost tender. Remove from the heat and leave, covered, until cool. The heat of the cooking vessel should be sufficient to complete the cooking. If not, then place over the heat for a little longer. Serve the cool rhubarb plain or with lightly sweetened cream flavoured with a little rosewater.

Plant historians consider that garden rhubarb has been developed from a wild Bulgarian species. For thousands of years the powdered root of the plant has been used medicinally. The fruit itself became highly popular during the reign of Queen Victoria when it was regarded as an easy-to-grow and health-promoting fruit. And so a large bed, in a cool corner of every cottage garden, was devoted to it. The names of some of the older varieties, for instance, 'Prince Albert' (which is also known as 'Early Albert' and 'Royal Albert') and 'Victoria', clearly date from the heyday of rhubarb.

The Ministry of Agriculture Research Station at Stockbridge House in Yorkshire has recently developed some improved virus-free varieties of rhubarb which are well worth growing. This new generation of rhubarb includes the varieties 'Cawood Castle', 'Cawood Delight', 'Stockbridge Arrow' and 'Stockbridge Harbinger'. Established varieties which are still good are 'Timperley Early', 'Reed's Early Super', 'The Sutton', 'MacDonald', 'Valentine' and 'Fenton Special'.

Rhubarb prefers a moist, fertile soil. A good dressing of well-rotted farmyard manure or compost forked into the soil around the plants in the autumn pays dividends in the better crop. Since forced rhubarb is more delicious than open-ground rhubarb, it is worth covering some of the larger robust clumps with an upturned dustbin, bucket or, best of all, a chimney pot, in December or January (or early spring in the US). In cold districts, surround the rhubarb crown with clean straw before covering. Keep out the light, and after four to six weeks you should be rewarded with slender sticks of rhubarb ready to cook straight away.

An alternative way to force rhubarb – which I have found excellent when my garden or allotment (community garden) was some distance from home – is to carefully dig up a large crown with some of the soil still clinging to the fleshy rhizomes. Place the root in a black plastic dustbin bag and gather the top of the bag together but don't seal it. Store the bag in a dark place – a cool cupboard, dry cellar or garage is ideal. Again you should have plenty of sticks of rhubarb to pull after just a few weeks. Replant the crown in the ground after cropping and rest it without forcing the following year.

CAPE GOOSEBERRY
Physalis peruviana

As its name indicates, this perennial plant, which is a member of the potato family is native to Peru. By the beginning of the last century the physalis had become such an important cultivated fruit in the Cape of Good Hope that it became known as the Cape gooseberry. The juicy, cherry-size fruit is also known as the golden berry. The leaf of the physalis resembles the potato in colour and shape, but the main growth above ground can reach 2.4 m/8 ft high. The yellow flower appears in July and August and ripens into a husk-covered fruit during the autumn.

The pale brown husk or calyx, which resembles a Chinese paper lantern in shape and texture, is particularly attractive. When fully ripe, the calyx can be peeled back to reveal the yellowy-orange fruit. These are either eaten as they are, or they are particularly delicious dipped in glacé icing and served as a petit fours. Mix 100 g/4 oz/⅔ cup sieved icing sugar with strong black coffee to make a thick pouring consistency. Fold back the papery husks on each goose-berry and dip in the icing. Leave in a warm place until set.

Sow seed of physalis under glass in March or April. When two true leaves appear, prick out into 10 cm/4 in pots. Plant into a humus-rich soil in an open bed or in a 25 cm/10 in pot and grow under glass or in a warm protected position outdoors rather as you would tomatoes. Water generously and give an occasional foliar feed.

The ripe fruit can be left on the plant for three to four weeks before picking, and the picked fruit, still in their decorative giftpack-like husks, can be stored in a cool, dry place for up to six weeks without deterioration.

AROMATIC OILS

*Golden-leaved oregano jostles for space with
clumps of flowering chives.*

*When you grow your own herbs it is extremely simple to prepare
a range of individual and unusually-flavoured oils for making
vinaigrettes and dressings for salads.
Before you start it is worth thinking about the style of aromatic
oil you want to produce. A big, bold-tasting garlic-flavoured oil
is best made with freshly-peeled cloves of young garlic and a
robust fruity olive oil. On the other hand, a herb with a delicate
flavour like chervil is often at its best combined with mild-
tasting oil like safflower or grapeseed.
You can also make oils with a blend of flavours – say, thyme and
rosemary with chilli and coriander. Once you've started to
experiment you will find the possibilities are endless.*

Slide 2-3 short stems of your chosen herb into a 600 ml/1 pint/2½ cup bottle of oil and replace the lid or cork on the bottle. Place the bottle in a warm place and leave for 2-4 days for the oil to absorb the herb flavours. Strain the oil into a fresh bottle and taste the oil; if you would prefer a bolder flavour, simply repeat the process. Woody herbs like rosemary and wild thyme can be left in contact with the oil for the few weeks while you use the oil, but fleshy herbs like basil and tarragon need to be extracted before storing the oil. Store the strained oil in a cool place.

TOMATO CHILLI SAUCE

*Fresh chilli peppers give tomato sauce a bit of a zip. This sauce
goes well with pasta, gnocchi or cold chicken.*

700 g/1½ lb ripe tomatoes

3 tbsp olive oil

2 shallots, chopped

1 large clove garlic, chopped

1 tsp sugar

1 tbsp chopped oregano or marjoram

*3 or 4 green chilli peppers, seeded
and chopped*

salt

Cover the tomatoes with boiling water for a few minutes, then replace with cold water. Nick the skins with a knife, then peel completely. Chop the tomatoes.

Heat the oil and cook the shallots and garlic for 3-4 minutes until golden. Add the tomatoes, sugar, oregano and chillies and bring to the boil. Lower the heat and simmer for 20-30 minutes or until thick.

Season with salt and spoon into a bowl or jug. Serve hot or cold.

Below: Maincrop potatoes of the varieties 'King Edward' and red-skinned 'Desirée'. Left: Seedling leeks grow in well-spaced roots.

HERB AND POTATO GNOCCHI

450 g/1 lb old potatoes

2-3 tbsp chopped herbs: chives, marjoram, thyme etc.

90 g/3 oz/10 tbsp plain (all-purpose) flour

salt and freshly milled pepper

90 g/3 oz/6 tbsp butter, melted, or olive oil

freshly grated Parmesan cheese

Scrub the potatoes and cook in salted boiling water. Drain and peel the potatoes. Sieve or push through a vegetable mill on its finest setting into a bowl.

Mix in the herbs and work in almost all the flour with some salt and pepper, to make a smooth dough. Divide the dough into three.

On a floured surface, roll out each portion to make a sausage as thick as your thumb. Cut the potato sausage into 2 cm/¾ in lengths and shape each piece by pressing them against the prongs of a fork, making a dent with your fingers. Set the gnocchi aside on a floured plate until ready to cook.

Have ready a very large pan of simmering salted water. Cook ten gnocchi at a time. Drop them into the water. Once they rise to the surface, let them cook for 10 seconds. Remove with a slotted spoon and drain on a clean cloth. Keep the gnocchi hot in a gratin dish while you cook the rest. Then pour over the melted butter or olive oil and sprinkle with Parmesan cheese. Serve straight away. *Serves 4*

GRILLED ASPARAGUS

This is a highly delicious way of cooking freshly picked asparagus. It works especially well with the newer green varieties of asparagus now widely grown in Britain and the US.

1 kg/2 lb asparagus spears

115 g/4 oz/1 stick unsalted butter

squeeze of lemon juice

1 tablespoon finely chopped parsley

4 sprigs of flat-leaf parsley

sea salt

lemon wedges

If necessary, trim away the drier cut end of each spear of asparagus until the whole spear is tender enough to be eaten raw. (Fresh garden asparagus is usually this tender anyway).

Melt three-quarers of the butter in a wide shallow pan with a flameproof handle (if necessary, cook the asparagus in batches). When it starts to bubble, but before it browns, add the asparagus. Spoon the butter over the spears until well coated with butter, then place the pan under a very hot grill (broiler) and cook, turning the asparagus over now and again, until tender and the green spears are starting to turn golden in places.

Transfer the asparagus to a hot serving plate. Add the remaining butter to the pan, stir in the chopped parsley and a good squeeze of lemon juice and spoon over the asparagus. Garnish with the parsley leaves and serve straight away, with sea salt and wedges of lemon. *Serves 4*

The dark, celery-like leaves of the root crop, celeriac.

TO MAKE A SALLET OF ALL KINDE OF HEARBS

A delightful seventeenth-century salad of garden herbs and flowers.

'Take your Hearbs and pick them very fine in faire water, and pick your Flowers by themselves, and wash them clean, then swing them in a strayner, and when you put them into a dish mingle them with Cucumbers or Lemmons pared and sliced, also scrape sugar, and put in Vinegar and Oyle, then spread the Flowers on the top of the sallet, and with every sort of the aforesaid things garnish the dish about, then take Eggs boyled hard, and lay them about the dish and upon the Sallet.'

BRAISED PHEASANTS WITH RAISINS AND A PURÉE OF CELERIAC

The pheasant is a fine game bird whose meat is more succulent and well flavoured when braised rather than roasted.

a brace of pheasants (1 hen and 1 cock)

60 g/2 oz/4 tbsp butter

1 shallot, chopped

1 bay leaf

few sprigs of thyme

salt and freshly milled black pepper

4 tbsp pale dry sherry

2 tbsp water

60 g/2 oz/⅓ cup California raisins

1 good-size root of celeriac

2 medium-size potatoes

4 tbsp double (heavy) cream

pinch of ground cinnamon

1 tbsp chopped chives

Melt half the butter in a flameproof casserole and brown the pheasants all over. Add the shallot, bay leaf, thyme and a little salt and pepper. Add half the sherry with the water. Cover the casserole and cook in an oven preheated to 170°C/325°F/Gas Mark 3 for 45 minutes.

Meanwhile, mix the raisins with the remaining sherry and leave in a warm place until the fruit has absorbed the liquid. Then add to the casserole and cook for a further 15 minutes. Remove the herbs, but keep the birds in the casserole in a warm place until ready to serve.

Peel the celeriac and potatoes and cut into pieces. Cook together in salted boiling water for 15-20 minutes or until tender. Drain well, then purée in a food processor. Beat in the remaining butter and the cream. Season with ground cinnamon and stir in the chives.

Transfer the pheasants to a hot serving dish. Spoon the raisins and cooking juices over the birds and serve with the celeriac purée. *Serves 4*

COMPÔTE OF *ROSE-SCENTED* RHUBARB

Leaves of rose-scented geranium give this dish of pink forced rhubarb a delightful flavour.

8 leaves of rose geranium

450 g/1 lb slim sticks of rhubarb, trimmed

90-115 g/3-4 oz/1/3-1/2 cup caster (superfine) sugar

4 tbsp Muscat de Beaumes de Venise

150 ml/1/4 pint/2/3 cup single (light) cream

1 tbsp rose-scented sugar (see page 141)

rose water to taste

Place a geranium leaf in four small oven dishes. Cut the rhubarb diagonally into 2.5 cm/1 in pieces. Toss in a bowl with the sugar and place in the dishes. Put a spoonful of wine into each dish and place the remaining geranium leaves on top. Cover each dish with buttered paper.

Place the dishes on a baking sheet and cook in an oven preheated to 180°C/350°F/Gas Mark 4 for 20-25 minutes until the rhubarb is cooked.

Serve the compôte hot or cold, with the cream mixed with rose-scented sugar and rose water. *Serves 4*

PETITS COEURS À LA CRÈME WITH *ROSE-FROSTED SUMMER* FRUITS

This is an exquisitely pretty summer dessert decorated with crystallized rose petals and fruit frosted with rose-scented sugar.

300 ml/1/2 pint/1 1/4 cups crème fraîche

4 egg whites

2 handfuls of scented pink or red rose petals

60-90 g/2-3 oz/1/4-1/3 cup caster (superfine) sugar

350 g/12 oz/about 1 1/2 pints mixed summer fruits: sprigs of red and black currants, raspberries, strawberries, wineberries, dessert gooseberries, etc.

Scoop the cream into a bowl and stir until smooth. Whisk 2 egg whites until stiff and fold into the cream.

Line four heart-shaped pierced china moulds with damp muslin or cheesecloth, smoothing out the creases. Divide the cream mixture between the moulds. Place the moulds on saucers and leave to drain overnight in the refrigerator.

Reserve 24 of the most attractive rose petals. Place the remaining petals in a glass jar and add two-thirds of the sugar. Shake gently to distribute the petals, cover the jar tightly and leave in a warm place overnight.

Lightly whisk one egg white. Brush both sides of a rose petal with egg white and dust with sugar. Place the petal on a wire rack in a warm place to dry. Repeat with each petal.

Just before serving, prepare the fruit. Sieve the rose-scented sugar into a wide soup plate and discard the petals. Lightly whisk the remaining egg white and brush each fruit with the mixture. Dip the fruit in the sugar and set aside to dry.

Unmould each coeur à la crème on to a small plate and surround with some of the frosted fruit. Decorate each plate with crystallized rose petals and serve. *Serves 4*

Roses and delphiniums in full bloom in the Hunstrete House kitchen garden.

ACKNOWLEDGEMENTS

WHEN, TWO YEARS AGO, COLIN WEBB OF PAVILION BOOKS INVITED me to write this book, for which I thank him, I was immediately attracted to the idea. Today, as I record my gratitude to everyone who made the book possible, I feel even more enthusiastic about cooks' gardens. My thanks go to Hugh Palmer for his photographs which owe much to his skill, patience and sense of fun; and to Fiona Bell Currie for our enjoyable horticultural conversations and her sensitive illustrations.

This book could not have happened without the co-operation, encouragement and generosity of the gardeners, chefs and cooks involved. I should like to record my gratitude to Michael Ashcroft, Brian Baker, Raymond Blanc, Antonio Carluccio, Della Connelly and her gardeners at Peper Harrow, Francis Coulson, Nick Cross, Lindsay Davison, Alex Dufort, John and Thea Dupays, Robert Elsmore, Alan Ford, Helen Greenwood, Tim and Stefa Hart, Paul and Kay Henderson, Peter and Sue Herbert, Shaun Hill, Stanley and Aileen Maguire, Keith Mansfield, David Marlow, Mark Raffan, Albert Ring, Brian Sack, John Tucker, and Ruth and David Watson. For valuable discussion and advice about the book I am grateful to Pamela Todd, Vivien Bowler, Jane Grigson, Alan Davidson, Helen Sudell, Tony Lord, Norma MacMillan and the book's designer, David Fordham.

All my gardening life I have consulted two RHS publications, *The Vegetable Garden Displayed* and *The Fruit Garden Displayed*, I recommend them in addition to *Successful Organic Gardening* by Geoff Hamilton (Dorling Kindersley), *The New Kitchen Garden* by Andrew Bicknell (Viking), *Growing Tree Fruits* by Bonham Bazeley (Collins), *The Plant Finder* edited by Richard Bird (fourth edition) which now includes fruit and Joy Larkham's books. Membership of the Royal Horticultural Society and the Soil Association is invaluable.

STOCKISTS

UK Sources

Seeds:
Samuel Dobie & Son Ltd., Broomhill Way, Torquay, Devon TQ2 7QW
Mr Fothergill's Seeds Ltd., Kentford, Newmarket, Suffolk CB8 7BR
Heritage Seeds, National Centre for Organic Gardening, Rhyton-on-Dunsmore, Coventry CV8 3LG
Johnson's Seeds, London Road, Boston, Lincolnshire PE21 8AD
S. E. Marshall & Co Ltd., Wisbech, Cambridgeshire PE13 2RF
Suffolk Herbs, Sawyers Farm, Little Cornard, Sudbury, Suffolk CO10 0NY
Suttons Seeds, Hele Road, Torquay, Devon TQ2 7QJ
Thompson and Morgan, London Road, Ipswich, Suffolk IP2 0BA

Fruit Trees and Vegetable Plants:
Chris Bowers & Sons, Whispering Trees Nursery, Wimbotsham, Norfolk PE34 8QB
Deacons Nursery, Godshill, Isle of Wight PO38 3HW
Highfield Nurseries, Whitminster, Gloucester GL2 7PL
A. R. Paske & Co Ltd., The South Lodge, Gazeley Road, Kentford, Newmarket, Suffolk CB8 7QA
Scotts Nurseries, Merriott, Somerset TA16 5PJ
The Royal Horticultural Society, Vincent Square, London SW1P 2PE

Herb Nurseries:
Hollington Nurseries Ltd., Woolton Hill, Newbury, Berkshire RG15 9XT
Iden Croft Herb Farm, Frittenden Road, Staplehurst, Kent TN12 9DH
The Seed Bank, Cowcombe Farm, Gipsy Lane, Gloucestershire GL6 8LP

US Sources

For Fruiting shrubs and berries:
Raintree Nursery and Northwood Nursery, 391 Butts Road, Morton Washington 98356, (206) 496-5410
Edible Landscaping, P.O. Box 77, Afton, Virginia 22920, (804) 361-9134

For fruiting trees:
Henry Leuthardt Nurseries, Montauk Highway, Box 666, East Moriches, New York 11940
New York State Fruit Testing Co-op, Geneva, New York 14456
St Lawrence Nurseries, Potsdam, New York 13676

For Vegetable seeds, etc.:
Vermont Bean Seed Company, Garden Lane, Fair Haven, Vermont 05743
Shepherd's Garden Seeds, 6116 Highway 9, Felton, California 95018, (203) 482-3638 and (408) 335-5311
Johnny's Selected Seeds, 310 Foss Hill Road, Albion, Maine 04910, (207) 437-9394
The Cook's Garden, P.O. Box 65, Londonderry, Vermont 05148, (082) 824-3400
Piedmont Plant Co., (*seeds*), P.O. Box 424, Albany, Georgia 31703, (912) 883-7029
Pinetree Garden Seeds, Route 100, New Gloucester, Maine 04260, (207) 926-3400

For many vegetables and flowers
Thompson and Morgan, Inc., P.O. Box 1308, Jackson, New Jersey 08527, (201) 343-2225
(*This is a British seed company with an American outlet/catalogue. They carry Galia melon, for example.*)